The Speed of Green, Grade 8

What if you could challenge your eighth graders to design a racing
environmental impact, while exploring the role of renewable and non-renewable energy sources?
With this volume in the *STEM Road Map Curriculum Series*, you can!

The Speed of Green outlines a journey that will steer your students toward authentic problem
solving while grounding them in integrated STEM disciplines. Like the other volumes in the series,
this book is designed to meet the growing need to infuse real-world learning into K–12 classrooms.

This interdisciplinary, eight-lesson module uses project- and problem-based learning to help
students explore the potential role of renewable and non-renewable energy sources in transportation,
with an emphasis on the auto industry. Using their understanding of the engineering design
process (EDP), scientific concepts, and environmental conservation considerations, student teams
will develop a plan for a competitive automobile racing team to fuel its vehicle with minimal
environmental impact. To support this goal, students will do the following:

- Identify finite energy resources and distinguish between these and renewable energy
  sources, and identify implications of the use of those fuel sources on the environment;

- Conduct life cycle analyses (LCAs) of various fuel sources and apply the results to make
  decisions about the effects of various fuel sources;

- Identify several ways that carbon-based fuels have impacted the U.S. economy and foreign
  relations;

- Identify the effects of human activities on the biosphere with an emphasis on the effects of
  the widespread use of carbon-based fuels;

- Apply the engineering design process (EDP) to solve a problem, and design and build a
  small-scale electric vehicle;

- Synthesize their learning and working collaboratively by creating and presenting a plan for a
  race team that minimizes its environmental impact;

- Create an engaging presentation incorporating oral presentations and visual displays to
  present projects to an audience of peers, teachers, and industry professionals.

The *STEM Road Map Curriculum Series* is anchored in the Next Generation Science Standards,
the Common Core State Standards, and the Framework for 21st Century Learning. In-depth and
flexible, *The Speed of Green* can be used as a whole unit or in part to meet the needs of districts,
schools, and teachers who are charting a course toward an integrated STEM approach.

Carla C. Johnson is a Professor of Science Education and Office of Research and Innovation Faculty
Research Fellow at North Carolina State University, North Carolina, USA.

Janet B. Walton is a Senior Research Scholar at North Carolina State's College of Education in
Raleigh, North Carolina, USA.

Erin E. Peters-Burton is the Donna R. and David E. Sterling Endowed Professor in Science Education
at George Mason University in Fairfax, Virginia, USA.

THE STEM ROAD MAP CURRICULUM SERIES

Series editors: Carla C. Johnson, Janet B. Walton, and Erin E. Peters-Burton

Map out a journey that will steer your students toward authentic problem solving as you ground them in integrated STEM disciplines.

Co-published by Routledge and NSTA Press, in partnership with the National Science Teaching Association, this K–12 curriculum series is anchored in the Next Generation Science Standards, the Common Core State Standards, and the Framework for 21st Century Learning. It was developed to meet the growing need to infuse real-world STEM learning into classrooms.

Each book is an in-depth module that uses project- and problem-based learning. First, your students are presented with a challenge. Then, they apply what they learn using science, social studies, English language arts, and mathematics. Engaging and flexible, each volume can be used as a whole unit or in part to meet the needs of districts, schools, and teachers who are charting a course toward an integrated STEM approach.

Modules are available from NSTA Press and Routledge, and organized under the following themes. For an update listing of the volumes in the series, please visit https://www.routledge.com/STEM-Road-Map-Curriculum-Series/book-series/SRM (for titles co-published by Routledge and NSTA Press), or www.nsta.org/book-series/stem-road-map-curriculum (for titles published by NSTA Press).

Co-published by Routledge and NSTA Press:

Optimizing the Human Experience:

- *Our Changing Environment, Grade K: STEM Road Map for Elementary School*
- *Genetically Modified Organisms, Grade 7: STEM Road Map for Middle School*
- *Rebuilding the Natural Environment, Grade 10: STEM Road Map for High School*
- *Mineral Resources, Grade 11: STEM Road Map for High School*

Cause and Effect:

- *Formation of the Earth, Grade 9: STEM Road Map for High School*

Published by NSTA Press:

Innovation and Progress:

- *Amusement Park of the Future, Grade 6: STEM Road Map for Elementary School*
- *Transportation in the Future, Grade 3: STEM Road Map for Elementary School*
- *Harnessing Solar Energy, Grade 4: STEM Road Map for Elementary School*
- *Wind Energy, Grade 5: STEM Road Map for Elementary School*
- *Construction Materials, Grade 11: STEM Road Map for High School*

The Represented World:

- *Patterns and the Plant World, Grade 1: STEM Road Map for Elementary School*

- *Investigating Environmental Changes, Grade 2: STEM Road Map for Elementary School*
- *Swing Set Makeover, Grade 3: STEM Road Map for Elementary School*
- *Rainwater Analysis, Grade 5: STEM Road Map for Elementary School*
- *Packaging Design, Grade 6: STEM Road Map for Middle School*
- *Improving Bridge Design, Grade 8: STEM Road Map for Middle School*
- *Radioactivity, Grade 11: STEM Road Map for High School*
- *Car Crashes, Grade 12: STEM Road Map for High School*

Cause and Effect:

- *Physics in Motion, Grade K: STEM Road Map for Elementary School*
- *Influence of Waves, Grade 1: STEM Road Map for Elementary School*
- *Natural Hazards, Grade 2: STEM Road Map for Elementary School*
- *Human Impacts on Our Climate, Grade 6: STEM Road Map for Middle School*
- *The Changing Earth, Grade 8: STEM Road Map for Middle School*
- *Healthy Living, Grade 10: STEM Road Map for High School*

The Speed of Green

Grade 8

STEM Road Map for Middle School

Edited by Carla C. Johnson, Janet B. Walton, and Erin E. Peters-Burton

Routledge
Taylor & Francis Group

NEW YORK AND LONDON

nsta Press
NATIONAL SCIENCE TEACHING ASSOCIATION

Designed cover image: © Getty Images and © Shutterstock

First published 2023
by Routledge
605 Third Avenue, New York, NY 10158

and by Routledge
4 Park Square, Milton Park, Abingdon, Oxon, OX14 4RN

Routledge is an imprint of the Taylor & Francis Group, an informa business

A co-publication with NSTA Press

Library of Congress Cataloging-in-Publication Data
Names: Johnson, Carla C., 1969– editor. | Walton, Janet B., 1968– editor. |
    Peters-Burton, Erin E., editor.
Title: The speed of green, grade 8 : STEM road map for middle school /
    edited by Carla C. Johnson, Janet B. Walton, Erin E. Peters-Burton.
Other titles: Speed of green, grade eight
Description: New York, NY : Routledge, 2023. | Series: STEM road map curriculum series |
    Includes bibliographical references and index.
Identifiers: LCCN 2022042364 (print) | LCCN 2022042365 (ebook) | ISBN 9781032423401 (hardback) |
    ISBN 9781032423388 (paperback) | ISBN 9781003362357 (ebook)
Subjects: LCSH: Power resources—Study and teaching (Middle school)—Textbooks. |
    Renewable energy sources—Study and teaching (Middle school)—Textbooks. |
    Sustainable engineering—Study and teaching (Middle school)—Textbooks. |
    Alternative fuel vehicles—Design and construction—Programmed instruction. |
    Project method in teaching. | Problem-based learning.
Classification: LCC TJ163.23 .S697 2023 (print) | LCC TJ163.23 (ebook) |
    DDC 621.042071/2—dc23/eng/20221214
LC record available at https://lccn.loc.gov/2022042364
LC ebook record available at https://lccn.loc.gov/2022042365

ISBN: 978-1-032-42340-1 (hbk)
ISBN: 978-1-032-42338-8 (pbk)
ISBN: 978-1-003-36235-7 (ebk)

DOI: 10.4324/9781003362357

Typeset in Palatino LT Std
by Apex CoVantage, LLC

CONTENTS

Part 1: The STEM Road Map: Background, Theory, and Practice

Part 2: The Speed of Green: STEM Road Map Module

CONTENTS

4 The Speed of Green Lesson Plans 47

Janet B. Walton, James M. Caruthers, and Carla C. Johnson

CONTENTS

ABOUT THE EDITORS AND AUTHORS

Dr. Carla C. Johnson is a Professor of Science Education and Office of Research and Innovation Faculty Research Fellow at NC State University. Dr. Johnson has served (2015–2021) as the director of research and evaluation for the Department of Defense–funded Army Educational Outreach Program (AEOP), a global portfolio of STEM education programs, competitions, and apprenticeships. She has been a leader in STEM education for the past decade, serving as the director of STEM Centers, editor of the *School Science and Mathematics* journal, and lead researcher for the evaluation of Tennessee's Race to the Top–funded STEM portfolio. Dr. Johnson has published over 200 articles, books, book chapters, and curriculum books focused on STEM education.

She is a former science and social studies teacher and was the recipient of the 2013 Outstanding Science Teacher Educator of the Year award from the Association for Science Teacher Education (ASTE), the 2012 Award for Excellence in Integrating Science and Mathematics from the School Science and Mathematics Association (SSMA), the 2014 award for best paper on Implications of Research for Educational Practice from ASTE, and the 2006 Outstanding Early Career Scholar Award from SSMA. Her research focuses on STEM education policy implementation, effective science teaching, and integrated STEM approaches.

Dr. Janet B. Walton is a senior research scholar at NC State's College of Education in Raleigh, North Carolina. Formerly the STEM workforce program manager for Virginia's Region 2000 and founding director of the Future Focus Foundation, a nonprofit organization dedicated to enhancing the quality of STEM education in the region, she merges her economic development and education backgrounds to develop K–12 curricular materials that integrate real-life issues with sound cross-curricular content. Her research focus includes collaboration between schools and community stakeholders for STEM education, problem- and project-based learning pedagogies, online learning, and mixed methods research methodologies. She leverages this background to bring contextual STEM experiences into the classroom and provide students and educators with innovative resources and curricular materials. She is the former assistant director of evaluation of research and evaluation for the Department of Defense–funded Army Educational Outreach Program (AEOP), a global portfolio of STEM education programs, competitions, and apprenticeships and specializes in evaluation of STEM programs.

Dr. Erin E. Peters-Burton is the Donna R. and David E. Sterling endowed professor in science education at George Mason University in Fairfax, Virginia. She uses her experiences from 15 years as an engineer and secondary science, engineering, and mathematics teacher to develop research projects that directly inform classroom practice in science and engineering. Her research agenda is based on the idea that all students should build self-awareness of how they learn science and engineering. She works to help students see themselves as "science-minded" and help teachers create classrooms that support student skills to develop scientific knowledge. To accomplish this, she pursues research projects that investigate ways that students and teachers can use self-regulated learning theory in science and engineering, as well as how inclusive STEM schools can help students succeed. She received the Outstanding Science Teacher Educator of the Year award from ASTE in 2016 and a Teacher of Distinction Award and a Scholarly Achievement Award from George Mason University in 2012, and in 2010 she was named University Science Educator of the Year by the Virginia Association of Science Teachers.

Dr. James M. Caruthers is the Gerald and Sarah Skidmore Professor of Chemical Engineering at Purdue University's Davidson School of Chemical Engineering.

Dr. Toni A. May is an associate professor of assessment, research, and statistics in the School of Education at Drexel University in Philadelphia. Dr. May's research concentrates on assessment and evaluation in education, with a focus on K–12 STEM.

Dr. Tamara J. Moore is an associate professor of engineering education in the College of Engineering at Purdue University. Dr. Moore's research focuses on defining STEM integration through the use of engineering as the connection and investigating its power for student learning.

ACKNOWLEDGMENTS

This module was developed by Purdue University's MSTEM^3 education outreach initiative (James M. Caruthers, PI) in collaboration with the STEM Road Map project (Carla C. Johnson, PI). Funding for this project was provided by: Purdue University's MSTEM^3 initiative, the Purdue University College of Education, The Haas Foundation, General Motors, and the Wabash Valley Education Center.

See *www.routledge.com/9781138804234* for more information about *STEM Road Map: A Framework for Integrated STEM Education.*

PART 1

THE STEM ROAD MAP

BACKGROUND, THEORY, AND PRACTICE

OVERVIEW OF THE *STEM ROAD MAP CURRICULUM SERIES*

Carla C. Johnson, Erin E. Peters-Burton, and Tamara J. Moore

The *STEM Road Map Curriculum Series* was conceptualized and developed by a team of STEM educators from across the United States in response to a growing need to infuse real-world learning contexts, delivered through authentic problem-solving pedagogy, into K–12 classrooms. The curriculum series is grounded in integrated STEM, which focuses on the integration of the STEM disciplines – science, technology, engineering, and mathematics – delivered across content areas, incorporating the Framework for 21st Century Learning along with grade-level-appropriate academic standards. The curriculum series begins in kindergarten, with a five-week instructional sequence that introduces students to the STEM themes and gives them grade-level-appropriate topics and real-world challenges or problems to solve. The series uses project-based and problem-based learning, presenting students with the problem or challenge during the first lesson, and then teaching them science, social studies, English language arts, mathematics, and other content, as they apply what they learn to the challenge or problem at hand.

Authentic assessment and differentiation are embedded throughout the modules. Each *STEM Road Map Curriculum Series* module has a lead discipline, which may be science, social studies, English language arts, or mathematics. All disciplines are integrated into each module, along with ties to engineering. Another key component is the use of STEM Research Notebooks to allow students to track their own learning progress. The modules are designed with a scaffolded approach, with increasingly complex concepts and skills introduced as students progress through grade levels.

The developers of this work view the curriculum as a resource that is intended to be used either as a whole or in part to meet the needs of districts, schools, and teachers who are implementing an integrated STEM approach. A variety of implementation formats are possible, from using one stand-alone module at a given grade level to using

DOI: 10.4324/9781003362357-2

all five modules to provide 25 weeks of instruction. Also, within each grade band (K–2, 3–5, 6–8, 9–12), the modules can be sequenced in various ways to suit specific needs.

STANDARDS-BASED APPROACH

The *STEM Road Map Curriculum Series* is anchored in the *Next Generation Science Standards* (*NGSS*), the *Common Core State Standards for Mathematics* (*CCSS Mathematics*), the *Common Core State Standards for English Language Arts* (*CCSS ELA*), and the Framework for 21st Century Learning. Each module includes a detailed curriculum map that incorporates the associated standards from the particular area correlated to lesson plans. The STEM Road Map has very clear and strong connections to these academic standards, and each of the grade-level topics was derived from the mapping of the standards to ensure alignment among topics, challenges or problems, and the required academic standards for students. Therefore, the curriculum series takes a standards-based approach and is designed to provide authentic contexts for application of required knowledge and skills.

THEMES IN THE *STEM ROAD MAP CURRICULUM SERIES*

The K–12 STEM Road Map is organized around five real-world STEM themes that were generated through an examination of the big ideas and challenges for society included in STEM standards and those that are persistent dilemmas for current and future generations:

- Cause and Effect

- Innovation and Progress

- The Represented World

- Sustainable Systems

- Optimizing the Human Experience

These themes are designed as springboards for launching students into an exploration of real-world learning situated within big ideas. Most important, the five STEM Road Map themes serve as a framework for scaffolding STEM learning across the K–12 continuum.

The themes are distributed across the STEM disciplines so that they represent the big ideas in science (Cause and Effect; Sustainable Systems), technology (Innovation and Progress; Optimizing the Human Experience), engineering (Innovation and Progress; Sustainable Systems; Optimizing the Human Experience), and mathematics (The Represented World), as well as concepts and challenges in social studies and 21st century skills that are also excellent contexts for learning in English language arts. The process of developing themes began with the clustering of the *NGSS* performance expectations

and the National Academy of Engineering's grand challenges for engineering, which led to the development of the challenge in each module and connections of the module activities to the *CCSS Mathematics* and *CCSS ELA* standards. We performed these mapping processes with large teams of experts and found that these five themes provided breadth, depth, and coherence to frame a high-quality STEM learning experience from kindergarten through 12th grade.

Cause and Effect

The concept of cause and effect is a powerful and pervasive notion in the STEM fields. It is the foundation of understanding how and why things happen as they do. Humans spend considerable effort and resources trying to understand the causes and effects of natural and designed phenomena to gain better control over events and the environment and to be prepared to react appropriately. Equipped with the knowledge of a specific cause-and-effect relationship, we can lead better lives or contribute to the community by altering the cause, leading to a different effect. For example, if a person recognizes that irresponsible energy consumption leads to global climate change, that person can act to remedy his or her contribution to the situation. Although cause and effect is a core idea in the STEM fields, it can actually be difficult to determine. Students should be capable of understanding not only when evidence points to cause and effect but also when evidence points to relationships but not direct causality. The major goal of education is to foster students to be empowered, analytic thinkers, capable of thinking through complex processes to make important decisions. Understanding causality, as well as when it cannot be determined, will help students become better consumers, global citizens, and community members.

Innovation and Progress

One of the most important factors in determining whether humans will have a positive future is innovation. Innovation is the driving force behind progress, which helps create possibilities that did not exist before. Innovation and progress are creative entities, but in the STEM fields, they are anchored by evidence and logic, and they use established concepts to move the STEM fields forward. In creating something new, students must consider what is already known in the STEM fields and apply this knowledge appropriately. When we innovate, we create value that was not there previously and create new conditions and possibilities for even more innovations. Students should consider how their innovations might affect progress and use their STEM thinking to change current human burdens to benefits. For example, if we develop more efficient cars that use by-products from another manufacturing industry, such as food processing, then we have used waste productively and reduced the need for the waste to be hauled away, an indirect benefit of the innovation.

The Represented World

When we communicate about the world we live in, how the world works, and how we can meet the needs of humans, sometimes we can use the actual phenomena to explain a concept. Sometimes, however, the concept is too big, too slow, too small, too fast, or too complex for us to explain using the actual phenomena, and we must use a representation or a model to help communicate the important features. We need representations and models such as graphs, tables, mathematical expressions, and diagrams because it makes our thinking visible. For example, when examining geologic time, we cannot actually observe the passage of such large chunks of time, so we create a timeline or a model that uses a proportional scale to visually illustrate how much time has passed for different eras. Another example may be something too complex for students at a particular grade level, such as explaining the *p* subshell orbitals of electrons to fifth graders. Instead, we use the Bohr model, which more closely represents the orbiting of planets and is accessible to fifth graders.

When we create models, they are helpful because they point out the most important features of a phenomenon. We also create representations of the world with mathematical functions, which help us change parameters to suit the situation. Creating representations of a phenomenon engages students because they are able to identify the important features of that phenomenon and communicate them directly. But because models are estimates of a phenomenon, they leave out some of the details, so it is important for students to evaluate their usefulness as well as their shortcomings.

Sustainable Systems

From an engineering perspective, the term *system* refers to the use of "concepts of component need, component interaction, systems interaction, and feedback. The interaction of subcomponents to produce a functional system is a common lens used by all engineering disciplines for understanding, analysis, and design" (Koehler et al., 2013, p. 8). Systems can be either open (e.g., an ecosystem) or closed (e.g., a car battery). Ideally, a system should be sustainable, able to maintain equilibrium without much energy from outside the structure. Looking at a garden, we see flowers blooming, weeds sprouting, insects buzzing, and various forms of life living within its boundaries. This is an example of an ecosystem, a collection of living organisms that survive together, functioning as a system. The interaction of the organisms within the system and the influences of the environment (e.g., water, sunlight) can maintain the system for a period of time, thus demonstrating its ability to endure. Sustainability is a desirable feature of a system because it allows for existence of the entity in the long term.

In the STEM Road Map project, we identified different standards that we consider to be oriented toward systems that students should know and understand in the K–12 setting. These include ecosystems, the rock cycle, Earth processes (such as erosion, tectonics, ocean currents, weather phenomena), Earth-Sun-Moon cycles, heat transfer, and the interaction among the geosphere, biosphere, hydrosphere, and atmosphere. Students and teachers should understand that we live in a world of systems that are not independent of each other, but rather are intrinsically linked such that a disruption in one part of a system will have reverberating effects on other parts of the system.

Optimizing the Human Experience

Science, technology, engineering, and mathematics as disciplines have the capacity to continuously improve the ways humans live, interact, and find meaning in the world, thus working to optimize the human experience. This idea has two components: being more suited to our environment and being more fully human. For example, the progression of STEM ideas can help humans create solutions to complex problems, such as improving ways to access water sources, designing energy sources with minimal impact on our environment, developing new ways of communication and expression, and building efficient shelters. STEM ideas can also provide access to the secrets and wonders of nature. Learning in STEM requires students to think logically and systematically, which is a way of knowing the world that is markedly different from knowing the world as an artist. When students can employ various ways of knowing and understand when it is appropriate to use a different way of knowing or integrate ways of knowing, they are fully experiencing the best of what it is to be human. The problem-based learning scenarios provided in the STEM Road Map help students develop ways of thinking like STEM professionals as they ask questions and design solutions. They learn to optimize the human experience by innovating improvements in the designed world in which they live.

THE NEED FOR AN INTEGRATED STEM APPROACH

At a basic level, STEM stands for science, technology, engineering, and mathematics. Over the past decade, however, STEM has evolved to have a much broader scope and implications. Now, educators and policy makers refer to STEM as not only a concentrated area for investing in the future of the United States and other nations but also as a domain and mechanism for educational reform.

The good intentions of the recent decade-plus of focus on accountability and increased testing has resulted in significant decreases not only in instructional time for teaching science and social studies but also in the flexibility of teachers to promote authentic, problem-solving–focused classroom environments. The shift has had a detrimental impact on student acquisition of vitally important skills, which many refer to as 21st century skills, and often the ability of students to "think." Further, schooling has become increasingly siloed into compartments of mathematics, science, English

language arts, and social studies, lacking any of the connections that are overwhelmingly present in the real world around children. Students have experienced school as content provided in boxes that must be memorized, devoid of any real-world context, and often have little understanding of why they are learning these things.

STEM-focused projects, curriculum, activities, and schools have emerged as a means to address these challenges. However, most of these efforts have continued to focus on the individual STEM disciplines (predominantly science and engineering) through more STEM classes and after-school programs in a "STEM-enhanced" approach (Breiner et al., 2012). But in traditional and STEM-enhanced approaches, there is little to no focus on other disciplines that are integral to the context of STEM in the real world. Integrated STEM education, on the other hand, infuses the learning of important STEM content and concepts with a much-needed emphasis on 21st century skills and a problem- and project-based pedagogy that more closely mirrors the real-world setting for society's challenges. It incorporates social studies, English language arts, and the arts as pivotal and necessary (Johnson, 2013; Rennie et al., 2012; Roehrig et al., 2012).

FRAMEWORK FOR STEM INTEGRATION IN THE CLASSROOM

The *STEM Road Map Curriculum Series* is grounded in the Framework for STEM Integration in the Classroom as conceptualized by Moore, Guzey, and Brown (2014) and Moore et al. (2014). The framework has six elements, described in the context of how they are used in the *STEM Road Map Curriculum Series* as follows:

1. The STEM Road Map contexts are meaningful to students and provide motivation to engage with the content. Together, these allow students to have different ways to enter into the challenge.

2. The STEM Road Map modules include engineering design that allows students to design technologies (i.e., products that are part of the designed world) for a compelling purpose.

3. The STEM Road Map modules provide students with the opportunities to learn from failure and redesign based on the lessons learned.

4. The STEM Road Map modules include standards-based disciplinary content as the learning objectives.

5. The STEM Road Map modules include student-centered pedagogies that allow students to grapple with the content, tie their ideas to the context, and learn to think for themselves as they deepen their conceptual knowledge.

6. The STEM Road Map modules emphasize 21st century skills and, in particular, highlight communication and teamwork.

All of the STEM Road Map modules incorporate these six elements; however, the level of emphasis on each of these elements varies based on the challenge or problem in each module.

THE NEED FOR THE *STEM ROAD MAP CURRICULUM SERIES*

As focus is increasing on integrated STEM, and additional schools and programs decide to move their curriculum and instruction in this direction, there is a need for high-quality, research-based curriculum designed with integrated STEM at the core. Several good resources are available to help teachers infuse engineering or more STEM-enhanced approaches, but no curriculum exists that spans K–12 with an integrated STEM focus. The next chapter provides detailed information about the specific pedagogy, instructional strategies, and learning theory on which the *STEM Road Map Curriculum Series* is grounded.

REFERENCES

Breiner, J., Harkness, M., Johnson, C. C., & Koehler, C. (2012). What is STEM? A discussion about conceptions of STEM in education and partnerships. *School Science and Mathematics, 112*(1), 3–11.

Johnson, C. C. (2013). Conceptualizing integrated STEM education: Editorial. *School Science and Mathematics, 113*(8), 367–368.

Koehler, C. M., Bloom, M. A., & Binns, I. C. (2013). Lights, camera, action: Developing a methodology to document mainstream films' portrayal of nature of science and scientific inquiry. *Electronic Journal of Science Education, 17*(2).

Moore, T. J., Guzey, S. S., & Brown, A. (2014). Greenhouse design to increase habitable land: An engineering unit. *Science Scope, 37*(7), 51–57.

Moore, T. J., Stohlmann, M. S., Wang, H.-H., Tank, K. M., Glancy, A. W., & Roehrig, G. H. (2014). Implementation and integration of engineering in K–12 STEM education. In S. Purzer, J. Strobel, & M. Cardella (Eds.), *Engineering in pre-college settings: Synthesizing research, policy, and practices* (pp. 35–60). Purdue Press.

Rennie, L., Venville, G., & Wallace, J. (2012). *Integrating science, technology, engineering, and mathematics: Issues, reflections, and ways forward*. Routledge.

Roehrig, G. H., Moore, T. J., Wang, H. H., & Park, M. S. (2012). Is adding the E enough? Investigating the impact of K–12 engineering standards on the implementation of STEM integration. *School Science and Mathematics, 112*(1), 31–44.

STRATEGIES USED IN THE *STEM ROAD MAP CURRICULUM SERIES*

Erin E. Peters-Burton, Carla C. Johnson, Toni A. May, and Tamara J. Moore

The *STEM Road Map Curriculum Series* uses what has been identified through research as best-practice pedagogy, including embedded formative assessment strategies throughout each module. This chapter briefly describes the key strategies that are employed in the series.

PROJECT- AND PROBLEM-BASED LEARNING

Each module in the *STEM Road Map Curriculum Series* uses either project-based learning or problem-based learning to drive the instruction. Project-based learning begins with a driving question to guide student teams in addressing a contextualized local or community problem or issue. The outcome of project-based instruction is a product that is conceptualized, designed, and tested through a series of scaffolded learning experiences (Blumenfeld et al., 1991; Krajcik & Blumenfeld, 2006). Problem-based learning is often grounded in a fictitious scenario, challenge, or problem (Barell, 2006; Lambros, 2004). On the first day of instruction within the unit, student teams are provided with the context of the problem. Teams work through a series of activities and use open-ended research to develop their potential solution to the problem or challenge, which need not be a tangible product (Johnson, 2003).

ENGINEERING DESIGN PROCESS

The *STEM Road Map Curriculum Series* uses engineering design as a way to facilitate integrated STEM within the modules. The engineering design process (EDP) is depicted in Figure 2.1 (p. X). It highlights two major aspects of engineering design – problem scoping and solution generation – and six specific components of working

DOI: 10.4324/9781003362357-3

Figure 2.1. Engineering Design Process

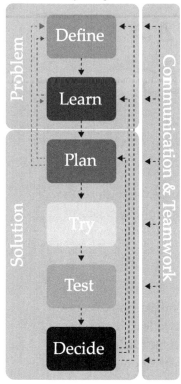

Copyright © 2015 PictureSTEM, Purdue University Research Foundation

toward a design: define the problem, learn about the problem, plan a solution, try the solution, test the solution, decide whether the solution is good enough. It also shows that communication and teamwork are involved throughout the entire process. As the arrows in the figure indicate, the order in which the components of engineering design are addressed depends on what becomes needed as designers progress through the EDP. Designers must communicate and work in teams throughout the process. The EDP is iterative, meaning that components of the process can be repeated as needed until the design is good enough to present to the client as a potential solution to the problem.

Problem scoping is the process of gathering and analyzing information to deeply understand the engineering design problem. It includes defining the problem and learning about the problem. Defining the problem includes identifying the problem, the client, and the end user of the design. The client is the person (or people) who hired the designers to do the work, and the end user is the person (or people) who will use the final design. The designers must also identify the criteria and the constraints of the problem. The criteria are the things the client wants from the solution, and the constraints are the things that limit the possible solutions. The designers must spend significant time learning about the problem, which can include activities such as the following:

- Reading informational texts and researching about relevant concepts or contexts

- Identifying and learning about needed mathematical and scientific skills, knowledge, and tools

- Learning about things done previously to solve similar problems

- Experimenting with possible materials that could be used in the design

Problem scoping also allows designers to consider how to measure the success of the design in addressing specific criteria and staying within the constraints over multiple iterations of solution generation.

Solution generation includes planning a solution, trying the solution, testing the solution, and deciding whether the solution is good enough. Planning the solution includes generating many design ideas that both address the criteria and meet the constraints. Here the designers must consider what was learned about the problem during problem scoping. Design plans include clear communication of design ideas through media such as notebooks, blueprints, schematics, or storyboards. They also include details about the design, such as measurements, materials, colors, costs of materials, instructions for how things fit together, and sets of directions. Making the decision about which design idea to move forward involves considering the trade-offs of each design idea.

Once a clear design plan is in place, the designers must try the solution. Trying the solution includes developing a prototype (a testable model) based on the plan generated. The prototype might be something physical or a process to accomplish a goal. This component of design requires that the designers consider the risk involved in implementing the design. The prototype developed must be tested. Testing the solution includes conducting fair tests that verify whether the plan is a solution that is good enough to meet the client and end user needs and wants. Data need to be collected about the results of the tests of the prototype, and these data should be used to make evidence-based decisions regarding the design choices made in the plan. Here, the designers must again consider the criteria and constraints for the problem.

Using the data gathered from the testing, the designers must decide whether the solution is good enough to meet the client and end user needs and wants by assessment based on the criteria and constraints. Here, the designers must justify or reject design decisions based on the background research gathered while learning about the problem and on the evidence gathered during the testing of the solution. The designers must now decide whether to present the current solution to the client as a possibility or to do more iterations of design on the solution. If they decide that improvements need to be made to the solution, the designers must decide if there is more that needs to be understood about the problem, client, or end user; if another design idea should be tried; or if more planning needs to be conducted on the same design. One way or another, more work needs to be done.

Throughout the process of designing a solution to meet a client's needs and wants, designers work in teams and must communicate to each other, the client, and likely the end user. Teamwork is important in engineering design because multiple perspectives and differing skills and knowledge are valuable when working to solve problems. Communication is key to the success of the designed solution. Designers must communicate their ideas clearly using many different representations, such as text in an engineering notebook, diagrams, flowcharts, technical briefs, or memos to the client.

LEARNING CYCLE

The same format for the learning cycle is used in all grade levels throughout the STEM Road Map, so that students engage in a variety of activities to learn about phenomena in the modules thoroughly and have consistent experiences in the problem- and

project- based learning modules. Expectations for learning by younger students are not as high as for older students, but the format of the progression of learning is the same. Students who have learned with curriculum from the STEM Road Map in early grades know what to expect in later grades. The learning cycle consists of five parts – Introductory Activity/Engagement, Activity/Exploration, Explanation, Elaboration/Application of Knowledge, and Evaluation/Assessment – and is based on the empirically tested 5E model from BSCS (Bybee et al., 2006).

In the Introductory Activity/Engagement phase, teachers introduce the module challenge and use a unique approach designed to pique students' curiosity. This phase gets students to start thinking about what they already know about the topic and begin wondering about key ideas. The Introductory Activity/Engagement phase positions students to be confident about what they are about to learn, because they have prior knowledge, and clues them into what they don't yet know.

In the Activity/Exploration phase, the teacher sets up activities in which students experience a deeper look at the topics that were introduced earlier. Students engage in the activities and generate new questions or consider possibilities using preliminary investigations. Students work independently, in small groups, and in whole-group settings to conduct investigations, resulting in common experiences about the topic and skills involved in the real-world activities. Teachers can assess students' development of concepts and skills based on the common experiences during this phase.

During the Explanation phase, teachers direct students' attention to concepts they need to understand and skills they need to possess to accomplish the challenge. Students participate in activities to demonstrate their knowledge and skills to this point, and teachers can pinpoint gaps in student knowledge during this phase.

In the Elaboration/Application of Knowledge phase, teachers present students with activities that engage in higher-order thinking to create depth and breadth of student knowledge, while connecting ideas across topics within and across STEM. Students apply what they have learned thus far in the module to a new context or elaborate on what they have learned about the topic to a deeper level of detail.

In the last phase, Evaluation/Assessment, teachers give students summative feedback on their knowledge and skills as demonstrated through the challenge. This is not the only point of assessment (as discussed in the section on Embedded Formative Assessments), but it is an assessment of the culmination of the knowledge and skills for the module. Students demonstrate their cognitive growth at this point and reflect on how far they have come since the beginning of the module. The challenges are designed to be multidimensional in the ways students must collaborate and communicate their new knowledge.

STEM RESEARCH NOTEBOOK

One of the main components of the *STEM Road Map Curriculum Series* is the STEM Research Notebook, a place for students to capture their ideas, questions, observations, reflections, evidence of progress, and other items associated with their daily work. At the beginning of each module, the teacher walks students through the setup of the STEM Research Notebook, which could be a three-ring binder, composition book, or spiral notebook. You may wish to have students create divided sections so that they can easily access work from various disciplines during the module. Electronic notebooks kept on student devices are also acceptable and encouraged. Students will develop their own table of contents and create chapters in the notebook for each module.

Each lesson in the *STEM Road Map Curriculum Series* includes one or more prompts that are designed for inclusion in the STEM Research Notebook and appear as questions or statements that the teacher assigns to students. These prompts require students to apply what they have learned across the lesson to solve the big problem or challenge for that module. Each lesson is designed to meaningfully refer students to the larger problem or challenge they have been assigned to solve with their teams. The STEM Research Notebook is designed to be a key formative assessment tool, as students' daily entries provide evidence of what they are learning. The notebook can be used as a mechanism for dialogue between the teacher and students, as well as for peer and self-evaluation.

The use of the STEM Research Notebook is designed to scaffold student notebooking skills across the grade bands in the *STEM Road Map Curriculum Series*. In the early grades, children learn how to organize their daily work in the notebook as a way to collect their products for future reference. In elementary school, students structure their notebooks to integrate background research along with their daily work and lesson prompts. In the upper grades (middle and high school), students expand their use of research and data gathering through team discussions to more closely mirror the work of STEM experts in the real world.

THE ROLE OF ASSESSMENT IN THE *STEM ROAD MAP CURRICULUM SERIES*

Starting in the middle years and continuing into secondary education, the word *assessment* typically brings grades to mind. These grades may take the form of a letter or a percentage, but they typically are used as a representation of a student's content mastery. If well thought out and implemented, however, classroom assessment can offer teachers, parents, and students valuable information about student learning and misconceptions that does not necessarily come in the form of a grade (Popham, 2013).

The *STEM Road Map Curriculum Series* provides a set of assessments for each module. Teachers are encouraged to use assessment information for more than just assigning grades to students. Instead, assessments of activities requiring students to actively engage in their learning, such as student journaling in STEM Research Notebooks, collaborative presentations, and constructing graphic organizers, should be used to move student learning forward. Whereas other curriculum with assessments may include

objective-type (multiple-choice or matching) tests, quizzes, or worksheets, we have intentionally avoided these forms of assessments to better align assessment strategies with teacher instruction and student learning techniques. Since the focus of this book is on project- or problem-based STEM curriculum and instruction that focuses on higher-level thinking skills, appropriate and authentic performance assessments were developed to elicit the most reliable and valid indication of growth in student abilities (Brookhart & Nitko, 2008).

Comprehensive Assessment System

Assessment throughout all STEM Road Map curriculum modules acts as a comprehensive system in which formative and summative assessments work together to provide teachers with high-quality information on student learning. Formative assessment occurs when the teacher finds out formally or informally what a student knows about a smaller, defined concept or skill and provides timely feedback to the student about his or her level of proficiency. Summative assessments occur when students have performed all activities in the module and are given a cumulative performance evaluation in which they demonstrate their growth in learning.

A comprehensive assessment system can be thought of as akin to a sporting event. Formative assessments are the practices: It is important to accomplish them consistently, they provide feedback to help students improve their learning, and making mistakes can be worthwhile if students are given an opportunity to learn from them. Summative assessments are the competitions: Students need to be prepared to perform at the best of their ability. Without multiple opportunities to practice skills along the way through formative assessments, students will not have the best chance of demonstrating growth in abilities through summative assessments (Black & Wiliam, 1998).

Embedded Formative Assessments

Formative assessments in this module serve two main purposes: to provide feedback to students about their learning and to provide important information for the teacher to inform immediate instructional needs. Providing feedback to students is particularly important when conducting problem- or project-based learning because students take on much of the responsibility for learning, and teachers must facilitate student learning in an informed way. For example, if students are required to conduct research for the Activity/Exploration phase but are not familiar with what constitutes a reliable resource, they may develop misconceptions based on poor information. When a teacher monitors this learning through formative assessments and provides specific feedback related to the instructional goals, students are less likely to develop incomplete or incorrect conceptions in their independent investigations. By using formative assessment to detect problems in student learning and then acting on this information, teachers help move student learning forward through these teachable moments.

Formative assessments come in a variety of formats. They can be informal, such as asking students probing questions related to student knowledge or tasks or simply observing students engaged in an activity to gather information about student skills. Formative assessments can also be formal, such as a written quiz or a laboratory practical. Regardless of the type, three key steps must be completed when using formative assessments (Sondergeld et al., 2010). First, the assessment is delivered to students so that teachers can collect data. Next, teachers analyze the data (student responses) to determine student strengths and areas that need additional support. Finally, teachers use the results from information collected to modify lessons and create learning environments that reinforce weak points in student learning. If student learning information is not used to modify instruction, the assessment cannot be considered formative in nature. Formative assessments can be about content, science process skills, or even learning skills. When a formative assessment focuses on content, it assesses student knowledge about the disciplinary core ideas from the *Next Generation Science Standards* (*NGSS*) or content objectives from *Common Core State Standards for Mathematics* (*CCSS Mathematics*) or *Common Core State Standards for English Language Arts* (*CCSS ELA*). Content-focused formative assessments ask students questions about declarative knowledge regarding the concepts they have been learning. Process skills formative assessments examine the extent to which a student can perform science and engineering practices from the *NGSS* or process objectives from *CCSS Mathematics* or *CCSS ELA*, such as constructing an argument. Learning skills can also be assessed formatively by asking students to reflect on the ways they learn best during a module and identify ways they could have learned more.

Assessment Maps

Assessment maps or blueprints can be used to ensure alignment between classroom instruction and assessment. If what students are learning in the classroom is not the same as the content on which they are assessed, the resultant judgment made on student learning will be invalid (Brookhart & Nitko, 2008). Therefore, the issue of instruction and assessment alignment is critical. The assessment map for this book (found in Chapter 3) indicates by lesson whether the assessment should be completed as a group or on an individual basis, identifies the assessment as formative or summative in nature, and aligns the assessment with its corresponding learning objectives.

Note that the module includes far more formative assessments than summative assessments. This is done intentionally to provide students with multiple opportunities to practice their learning of new skills before completing a summative assessment. Note also that formative assessments are used to collect information on only one or two learning objectives at a time so that potential relearning or instructional modifications can focus on smaller and more manageable chunks of information. Conversely, summative assessments in the module cover many more learning objectives,

as they are traditionally used as final markers of student learning. This is not to say that information collected from summative assessments cannot or should not be used formatively. If teachers find that gaps in student learning persist after a summative assessment is completed, it is important to revisit these existing misconceptions or areas of weakness before moving on (Black et al. 2003).

SELF-REGULATED LEARNING THEORY IN THE STEM ROAD MAP MODULES

Many learning theories are compatible with the STEM Road Map modules, such as constructivism, situated cognition, and meaningful learning. However, we feel that the self-regulated learning theory (SRL) aligns most appropriately (Zimmerman, 2000). SRL requires students to understand that thinking needs to be motivated and managed (Ritchhart et al., 2011). The STEM Road Map modules are student centered and are designed to provide students with choices, concrete hands-on experiences, and opportunities to see and make connections, especially across subjects (Eliason & Jenkins, 2012; NAEYC, 2016). Additionally, SRL is compatible with the modules because it fosters a learning environment that supports students' motivation, enables students to become aware of their own learning strategies, and requires reflection on learning while experiencing the module (Peters & Kitsantas, 2010).

Figure 2.2. SRL Theory

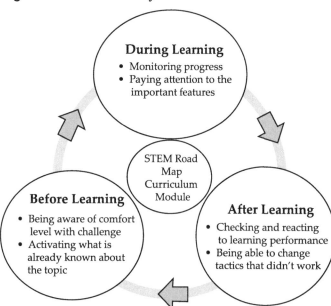

Source: Adapted from Zimmerman (2000).

The theory behind SRL (see Figure 2.2) explains the different processes that students engage in before, during, and after a learning task. Because SRL is a cyclical learning process, the accomplishment of one cycle develops strategies for the next learning cycle. This cyclic way of learning aligns with the various sections in the STEM Road Map lesson plans on Introductory Activity/Engagement, Activity/ Exploration, Explanation, Elaboration/Application of Knowledge, and Evaluation/Assessment. Since the students engaged in a module take on much of the responsibility for learning, this theory also provides guidance for teachers to keep students on the right track.

The remainder of this section explains how SRL theory is embedded within the five sections of each module and points out ways to support students in becoming independent learners of STEM while productively functioning in collaborative teams.

Before Learning: Setting the Stage

Before attempting a learning task such as the STEM Road Map modules, teachers should develop an understanding of their students' level of comfort with the process of accomplishing the learning and determine what they already know about the topic. When students are comfortable with attempting a learning task, they tend to take more risks in learning and as a result achieve deeper learning (Bandura, 1986).

The STEM Road Map curriculum modules are designed to foster excitement from the very beginning. Each module has an Introductory Activity/Engagement section that introduces the overall topic from a unique and exciting perspective, engaging the students to learn more so that they can accomplish the challenge. The Introductory Activity also has a design component that helps teachers assess what students already know about the topic of the module. In addition to the deliberate designs in the lesson plans to support SRL, teachers can support a high level of student comfort with the learning challenge by finding out if students have ever accomplished the same kind of task and, if so, asking them to share what worked well for them.

During Learning: Staying the Course

Some students fear inquiry learning because they aren't sure what to do to be successful (Peters, 2010). However, the STEM Road Map curriculum modules are embedded with tools to help students pay attention to knowledge and skills that are important for the learning task and to check student understanding along the way. One of the most important processes for learning is the ability for learners to monitor their own progress while performing a learning task (Peters, 2012). The modules allow students to monitor their progress with tools such as the STEM Research Notebooks, in which they record what they know and can check whether they have acquired a complete set of knowledge and skills. The STEM Road Map modules support inquiry strategies that include previewing, questioning, predicting, clarifying, observing, discussing, and journaling (Morrison & Milner, 2014). Through the use of technology throughout the modules, inquiry is supported by providing students access to resources and data while enabling them to process information, report the findings, collaborate, and develop 21st century skills.

It is important for teachers to encourage students to have an open mind about alternative solutions and procedures (Milner & Sondergeld, 2015) when working through the STEM Road Map curriculum modules. Novice learners can have difficulty knowing what to pay attention to and tend to treat each possible avenue for information as

equal (Benner, 1984). Teachers are the mentors in a classroom and can point out ways for students to approach learning during the Activity/Exploration, Explanation, and Elaboration/Application of Knowledge portions of the lesson plans to ensure that students pay attention to the important concepts and skills throughout the module. For example, if a student is to demonstrate conceptual awareness of motion when working on roller coaster research, but the student has misconceptions about motion, the teacher can step in and redirect student learning.

After Learning: Knowing What Works

The classroom is a busy place, and it may often seem that there is no time for self-reflection on learning. Although skipping this reflective process may save time in the short term, it reduces the ability to take into account things that worked well and things that didn't so that teaching the module may be improved next time. In the long run, SRL skills are critical for students to become independent learners who can adapt to new situations. By investing the time it takes to teach students SRL skills, teachers can save time later, because students will be able to apply methods and approaches for learning that they have found effective to new situations. In the Evaluation/Assessment portion of the STEM Road Map curriculum modules, as well as in the formative assessments throughout the modules, two processes in the after-learning phase are supported: evaluating one's own performance and accounting for ways to adapt tactics that didn't work well. Students have many opportunities to self-assess in formative assessments, both in groups and individually, using the rubrics provided in the modules.

The designs of the *NGSS* and *CCSS* allow for students to learn in diverse ways, and the STEM Road Map curriculum modules emphasize that students can use a variety of tactics to complete the learning process. For example, students can use STEM Research Notebooks to record what they have learned during the various research activities. Notebook entries might include putting objectives in students' own words, compiling their prior learning on the topic, documenting new learning, providing proof of what they learned, and reflecting on what they felt successful doing and what they felt they still needed to work on. Perhaps students didn't realize that they were supposed to connect what they already knew with what they learned. They could record this and would be prepared in the next learning task to begin connecting prior learning with new learning.

SAFETY IN STEM

Student safety is a primary consideration in all subjects but is an area of particular concern in science, where students may interact with unfamiliar tools and materials that may pose additional safety risks. It is important to implement safety practices within the context of STEM investigations, whether in a classroom laboratory or in the field. When you keep safety in mind as a teacher, you avoid many potential issues with the lesson while also protecting your students.

STEM safety practices encompass things considered in the typical science classroom. Ensure that students are familiar with basic safety considerations, such as wearing protective equipment (e.g., safety glasses or goggles and latex-free gloves) and taking care with sharp objects, and know emergency exit procedures. Teachers should learn beforehand the locations of the safety eyewash, fume hood, fire extinguishers, and emergency shut-off switch in the classroom and how to use them. Also be aware of any school or district safety policies that are in place and apply those that align with the work being conducted in the lesson. It is important to review all safety procedures annually.

STEM investigations should always be supervised. Each lesson in the modules includes teacher guidelines for applicable safety procedures that should be followed. Before each investigation, teachers should go over these safety procedures with the student teams. Some STEM focus areas such as engineering require that students can demonstrate how to properly use equipment in the maker space before the teacher allows them to proceed with the lesson.

Information about classroom science safety, including a safety checklist for science classrooms, general lab safety recommendations, and links to other science safety resources, is available at the Council of State Science Supervisors (CSSS) website at www.cosss.org/Safety-Resources. The National Science Teachers Association (NSTA) provides a list of science rules and regulations, including standard operating procedures for lab safety, and a safety acknowledgement form for students and parents or guardians to sign. You can access these resources at http://static.nsta.org/pdfs/SafetyInTheScienceClassroom.pdf. In addition, NSTA's Safety in the Science Classroom web page (www.nsta.org/safety) has numerous links to safety resources, including papers written by the NSTA Safety Advisory Board.

Disclaimer: The safety precautions for each activity are based on use of the recommended materials and instructions, legal safety standards, and better professional practices. Using alternative materials or procedures for these activities may jeopardize the level of safety and therefore is at the user's own risk.

REFERENCES

Bandura, A. (1986). *Social foundations of thought and action: A social cognitive theory.* Prentice-Hall.

Barell, J. (2006). *Problem-based learning: An inquiry approach.* Corwin Press.

Benner, P. (1984). *From novice to expert: Excellence and power in clinical nursing practice.* Addison-Wesley Publishing Company.

Black, P., Harrison, C., Lee, C., Marshall, B., & Wiliam, D. (2003). *Assessment for learning: Putting it into practice*. Open University Press.

Black, P., & Wiliam, D. (1998). Inside the black box: Raising standards through classroom assessment. *Phi Delta Kappan, 80*(2), 139–148.

Blumenfeld, P., Soloway, E., Marx, R., Krajcik, J., Guzdial, M., & Palincsar, A. (1991). Motivating project-based learning: Sustaining the doing, supporting learning. *Educational Psychologist, 26*(3), 369–398.

Brookhart, S. M., & Nitko, A. J. (2008). *Assessment and grading in classrooms*. Pearson.

Bybee, R., Taylor, J., Gardner, A., Scotter, P., Carlson, J., Westbrook, A., & Landes, N. (2006). *The BSCS 5E instructional model: Origins and effectiveness*.

Eliason, C. F., & Jenkins, L. T. (2012). *A practical guide to early childhood curriculum* (9th ed.). Merrill.

Johnson, C. (2003). Bioterrorism is real-world science: Inquiry-based simulation mirrors real life. *Science Scope, 27*(3), 19–23.

Krajcik, J., & Blumenfeld, P. (2006). Project-based learning. In R. K. Sawyer (Ed.), *The Cambridge handbook of the learning sciences* (pp. 317 334). Cambridge University Press.

Lambros, A. (2004). *Problem-based learning in middle and high school classrooms: A teacher's guide to implementation*. Corwin Press.

Milner, A. R., & Sondergeld, T. (2015). Gifted urban middle school students: The inquiry continuum and the nature of science. *National Journal of Urban Education and Practice, 8*(3), 442–461.

Morrison, V., & Milner, A. R. (2014). Literacy in support of science: A closer look at cross-curricular instructional practice. *Michigan Reading Journal, 46*(2), 42–56.

National Association for the Education of Young Children (NAEYC). (2016). Developmentally appropriate practice position statements. www.naeyc.org/positionstatements/dap.

Peters, E. E. (2010). Shifting to a student-centered science classroom: An exploration of teacher and student changes in perceptions and practices. *Journal of Science Teacher Education, 21*(3), 329–349.

Peters, E. E. (2012). Developing content knowledge in students through explicit teaching of the nature of science: Influences of goal setting and self-monitoring. *Science and Education, 21*(6), 881–898.

Peters, E. E., & Kitsantas, A. (2010). The effect of nature of science metacognitive prompts on science students' content and nature of science knowledge, metacognition, and self-regulatory efficacy. *School Science and Mathematics, 110*(8), 382–396.

Popham, W. J. (2013). *Classroom assessment: What teachers need to know* (7th ed.). Pearson.

Ritchhart, R., Church, M., & Morrison, K. (2011). *Making thinking visible: How to promote engagement, understanding, and independence for all learners*. Jossey-Bass.

Sondergeld, T. A., Bell, C. A., & Leusner, D. M. (2010). Understanding how teachers engage in formative assessment. *Teaching and Learning*, 24(2), 72–86.

Zimmerman, B. J. (2000). Attaining self-regulation: A social-cognitive perspective. In M. Boekaerts, P. Pintrich, & M. Zeidner (Eds.), *Handbook of self-regulation* (pp. 13–39). Academic Press.

PART 2

THE SPEED OF GREEN

STEM ROAD MAP MODULE

THE SPEED OF GREEN MODULE OVERVIEW

Janet B. Walton, James M. Caruthers, and Carla C. Johnson

THEME: Sustainable Systems

LEAD DISCIPLINES: Science and Social Studies

MODULE SUMMARY

In this module, students will consider the potential role of various renewable and non-renewable energy sources in transportation, with an emphasis on the auto industry. Using their understanding of the engineering design process (EDP), scientific concepts, and environmental conservation considerations, student teams will each develop a plan for a competitive automobile racing team to power its vehicle with minimal environmental impact. As students move through the module, they will investigate the chemical reactions involved in combustion and in producing plant-based fuels, the effects of the use of carbon-based and other fuels on the biosphere, and will learn to recognize the difference between finite and renewable resources. Students will investigate current efforts to reduce the impact of human activities on the environment in the context of auto industry innovations for fuel efficiency and conservation. Students will investigate the role of materials in these efforts with an emphasis on the properties of natural and engineered materials. Students will also investigate the life cycle costs of various energy sources and develop an understanding of the histories of various energy sources for automobiles in the United States and the costs and benefits associated with using various types of energy to power automobiles. The module culminates with a challenge in which student teams create plans for their own "race teams" that minimize the environmental impact of powering their car. Students will design and build a prototype or model of one design innovation that will support this goal and will create a persuasive video presentation presenting their plans and prototypes or models (adapted from Johnson et al., 2015).

DOI: 10.4324/9781003362357-5

ESTABLISHED GOALS AND OBJECTIVES

At the conclusion of this module, students will be able to do the following:

- Identify finite energy resources and distinguish between these and renewable energy sources

- Identify implications of the use of various fuel sources on the environment

- Conduct life cycle analyses (LCAs) of various fuel sources and apply the results to make decisions about the effects of various fuel sources

- Explain the importance of transportation in the history of the United States

- Identify several ways that carbon-based fuels have impacted the U.S. economy and foreign relations

- Describe how atoms and molecules interact in combustion reactions

- Identify several effects of human activities on the biosphere with an emphasis on the effects of the widespread use of carbon-based fuels

- Apply the EDP to solve a problem

- Design and build a small-scale electric vehicle (EV)

- Synthesize their learning by creating and presenting a plan for a race team that minimizes its environmental impact

- Design and create a prototype or model of an energy or vehicle innovation

- Work collaboratively to create a solution to the team challenge

- Create an engaging presentation incorporating oral presentations and visual displays to present projects to an audience of peers, teachers, and industry professionals

CHALLENGE OR PROBLEM FOR STUDENTS TO SOLVE: THE SPEED OF GREEN CHALLENGE

Students will answer the following question in the module's culminating challenge: How can a motorsports race team minimize the environmental impact of powering its car in an efficient, cost-effective manner?

Student teams will be challenged to create a plan for a competitive automobile racing team designed to use a fuel source that minimizes environmental impact. Students will provide a justification for their plan including a detailed life cycle analysis of the fuel source(s) they choose and a prototype design or model of one innovation associated with their plan. Students will create a video presentation highlighting their plan.

CONTENT STANDARDS ADDRESSED IN THIS STEM ROAD MAP MODULE

A full listing with descriptions of the standards this module addresses can be found in Appendix B. Listings of the particular standards addressed within lessons are provided in a table for each lesson in Chapter 4.

STEM RESEARCH NOTEBOOK

Each student should maintain a STEM Research Notebook, which will serve as a place for students to organize their work throughout this module (see p. 12 for more general discussion on setup and use of the notebook). All written work in the module should be included in the notebook, including records of students' thoughts and ideas, fictional accounts based on the concepts in the module, and records of student progress through the EDP. The notebooks may be maintained across subject areas, giving students the opportunity to see that although their classes may be separated during the school day, the knowledge they gain is connected. You may also wish to have students include the STEM Research Notebook Guidelines student handout on page 28 in their notebooks.

Emphasize to students the importance of organizing all information in a Research Notebook. Explain to them that scientists and other researchers maintain detailed Research Notebooks in their work. These notebooks, which are crucial to researchers' work because they contain critical information and track the researchers' progress, are often considered legal documents for scientists who are pursuing patents or wish to provide proof of their discovery process.

STUDENT HANDOUT

STEM RESEARCH NOTEBOOK GUIDELINES

STEM professionals record their ideas, inventions, experiments, questions, observations, and other work details in notebooks so that they can use these notebooks to help them think about their projects and the problems they are trying to solve. You will each keep a STEM Research Notebook during this module that is like the notebooks that STEM professionals use. In this notebook, you will include all your work and notes about ideas you have. The notebook will help you connect your daily work with the big problem or challenge you are working to solve.

It is important that you organize your notebook entries under the following headings:

1. **Chapter Topic or Title of Problem or Challenge:** You will start a new chapter in your STEM Research Notebook for each new module. This heading is the topic or title of the big problem or challenge that your team is working to solve in this module.

2. **Date and Topic of Lesson Activity for the Day:** Each day, you will begin your daily entry by writing the date and the day's lesson topic at the top of a new page. Write the page number both on the page and in the table of contents.

3. **Information Gathered from Research:** This is information you find from outside resources such as websites or books.

4. **Information Gained from Class or Discussions with Team Members:** This information includes any notes you take in class and notes about things your team discusses. You can include drawings of your ideas here, too.

5. **New Data Collected from Investigations:** This includes data gathered from experiments, investigations, and activities in class.

6. **Documents:** These are handouts and other resources you may receive in class that will help you solve your big problem or challenge. Paste or staple these documents in your STEM Research Notebook for safekeeping and easy access later.

7. **Personal Reflections:** Here, you record your own thoughts and ideas on what you are learning.

8. **Lesson Prompts:** These are questions or statements that your teacher assigns you within each lesson to help you solve your big problem or challenge. You will respond to the prompts in your notebook.

9. **Other Items:** This section includes any other items your teacher gives you or other ideas or questions you may have.

MODULE LAUNCH

The opening activity will introduce students to auto racing and the idea that renewable energy can be used in motorsports. First, you will introduce students to Leilani Münter, and her goal to use renewable energy sources in motorsports. Then, students will view and discuss a video about Münter's team's use of solar power such as an introduction to the world of "green" auto racing.

PREREQUISITE SKILLS FOR THE MODULE

Students enter this module with a wide range of preexisting skills, information, and knowledge. Table 3.1 provides an overview of prerequisite skills and knowledge that students are expected to apply in this module, along with examples of how they apply this knowledge throughout the module. Differentiation strategies are also provided for students who may need additional support in acquiring or applying this knowledge.

Table 3.1 Prerequisite Key Knowledge and Examples of Applications and Differentiation Strategies

Prerequisite Key Knowledge	Application of Knowledge	Differentiation for Students Needing Knowledge
Science: • Conceptual understanding of atoms and subatomic particles as the basic building blocks of matter.	Students will use basic principles of atoms and chemical reactions in investigating fuel-related chemical reactions.	Review atomic structure and basics of chemical reactions with students. Provide individual and group opportunities to apply this understanding to identifying examples of chemical reactions and the basic chemical changes that occur.
Mathematics: • Understanding of measurement and basic units of measurement. • Understanding of arithmetic operations and simple algebraic expressions.	Students will measure distance, time, speed, and mass as part of their investigations in this module.	Review metric system and English-metric system conversions. Provide opportunities for students to practice measurements and conversions in the class. Use Just in Time Teaching (JiTT) techniques to review and prepare for activities (see http://cft.vanderbilt.edu/guides-sub-pages/just-in-time-teaching-jitt for more information).
	Students will perform various calculations including finding sums, calculating means, and calculating speeds.	Use JiTT techniques to prepare students for activities.
Technology: • Basic technology skills (keyboarding, internet search).	Students will conduct internet searches and use technology tools throughout the module.	Hold a session with a media specialist to review internet search strategies and use of technology tools incorporated in the module.

POTENTIAL STEM MISCONCEPTIONS

Students enter the classroom with a wide variety of prior knowledge and ideas, so it is important to be alert to misconceptions or inappropriate understandings of foundational knowledge. These misconceptions can be classified as one of several types: " preconceived notions," opinions based on popular beliefs or understandings; "nonscientific beliefs," knowledge students have gained about science from sources outside the scientific community; "conceptual misunderstandings," incorrect conceptual models based on incomplete understanding of concepts; "vernacular misconceptions," misunderstandings of words based on their common use versus their scientific use; and "factual misconceptions," incorrect or imprecise knowledge learned in early life that remains unchallenged (NRC, 1997, p. 28). Misconceptions must be addressed and dismantled in order for students to reconstruct their knowledge, and therefore teachers should be prepared to take the following steps:

- Identify students' misconceptions.

- Provide a forum for students to confront their misconceptions.

- Help students reconstruct and internalize their knowledge, based on scientific models. (NRC, 1997, p. 29)

Keeley and Harrington (2010) recommend using diagnostic tools such as probes and formative assessment to identify and confront student misconceptions and begin the process of reconstructing student knowledge. Keeley's *Uncovering Student Ideas in Science* series contains probes targeted toward uncovering student misconceptions in a variety of areas and may be useful resources for addressing student misconceptions in this module.

Some commonly held misconceptions specific to lesson content are provided with each lesson so that you can be alert for student misunderstanding of the science concepts presented and used during this module.

SELF-REGULATED LEARNING (SRL) PROCESS COMPONENTS

Table 3.2 illustrates some of the activities in The Speed of Green module and how they align to the SRL processes before, during, and after learning.

Table 3.2 SRL Learning Process Components

Learning Process Components	Example from The Speed of Green	Lesson Number and Learning Component
Before Learning		
Motivates students	Students watch a video of a race car driver dedicated to carbon-free living. Her work with her race team reflects students' final challenge.	Lesson 1, Introductory Activity/ Engagement
Evokes prior learning	Students collect data on energy use in the We've Bean Using Energy activity.	Lesson 1, Activity/Exploration
During Learning		
Focuses on important features	Students create a list of chemical reactions that will be used to make a Hero's engine before they construct the engine.	Lesson 2, Activity/Exploration
Helps students monitor their progress	Students create a list of pros and cons of using natural gas as a fuel in a small group so that they can compare their thoughts with other students.	Lesson 3, Activity/Exploration
After Learning		
Evaluates learning	Teams build an electric vehicle using specific design considerations and are assessed with a rubric on vehicle design and performance.	Lesson 7, Activity/Exploration
Takes account of what worked and what did not work	Students self-assess their process of building an electric vehicle with the Engineer It! handout.	Lesson 7, Activity/Exploration

INTEGRATING INSTRUCTION ACROSS SUBJECTS IN THE MIDDLE SCHOOL SETTING

The modules of the STEM Road Map take into account that logistics of middle school instruction, such as scheduling and departmentalization, can make teaching integrated subject matter difficult in middle schools. It is not uncommon for the same

grade level science and mathematics teachers to have completely different students, which makes integrating science content with content from other subjects difficult. However, we recognize that some schools allow for teachers from different content areas to team teach. The modules of the *STEM Road Map Series* are written to accommodate both situations – the singular teacher and the teachers who are able to team teach or integrate instruction across subjects in other ways. A teacher who is teaching the module by themselves may choose to follow only the lead subject, offering enrichment activities in the other connecting subjects. Teachers who are teaching the modules in a single subject course may also want to collaborate with their peers in the other disciplinary areas to get ideas for ways to incorporate the supporting connections seamlessly. Teachers who are able to teach an integrated curriculum can use the module as written for each of the four subjects in the Learning Components sections of the module.

STRATEGIES FOR DIFFERENTIATING INSTRUCTION WITHIN THIS MODULE

For the purposes of this curriculum module, differentiated instruction is conceptualized as a way to tailor instruction – including process, content, and product – to various student needs in your class. A number of differentiation strategies are integrated into lessons across the module. The problem- and project-based learning approach used in the lessons are designed to address students' multiple intelligences by providing a variety of entry points and methods to investigate the key concepts in the module (for example, investigating fuel sources using scientific inquiry, fiction and nonfiction literature, journaling, and collaborative design). Differentiation strategies for students needing support in prerequisite knowledge can be found in Table 3.1 (p. 29). You are encouraged to use information gained about student prior knowledge during introductory activities and discussions to inform your instructional differentiation. Strategies incorporated into this lesson include flexible grouping, varied environmental learning contexts, assessments, compacting, and tiered assignments and scaffolding.

> *Flexible Grouping:* Students work collaboratively in a variety of activities throughout this module. Grouping strategies you may choose to employ include student-led grouping, placing students in groups according to ability level, grouping students randomly, grouping them so that students in each group have complementary strengths (for instance, one student might be strong in mathematics, another in art, and another in writing), or grouping students according to common interests.

> *Varied Environmental Learning Contexts:* Students have the opportunity to learn in various contexts throughout the module, including alone, in groups, in quiet

reading and research-oriented activities, and in active learning in inquiry and design activities. In addition, students learn in a variety of ways through doing inquiry activities, journaling, reading a variety of texts, watching videos, class discussion, and conducting web-based research.

Assessments: Students are assessed in a variety of ways throughout the module, including individual and collaborative formative and summative assessments. Students have the opportunity to produce work via written text, oral and media presentations, and modeling. You may choose to provide students with additional choices of media for their products (for example, PowerPoint presentations, posters, or student-created websites or blogs).

Compacting: Based on student prior knowledge, you may wish to adjust instructional activities for students who exhibit prior mastery of a learning objective. Because student work in science is largely collaborative throughout the module, this strategy may be most appropriate for mathematics, ELA, or social studies activities. You may wish to compile a classroom database of research resources and supplementary readings for a variety of reading levels and on a variety of topics related to the module's topic to provide opportunities for students to undertake independent reading.

Tiered Assignments and Scaffolding: Based on your awareness of student ability, understanding of concepts, and mastery of skills, you may wish to provide students with variations on activities by adding complexity to assignments or providing more or fewer learning supports for activities throughout the module. For instance, some students may need additional support in identifying key search words and phrases for web-based research or may benefit from cloze sentence handouts to enhance vocabulary understanding. Other students may benefit from expanded reading selections and additional reflective writing or from working with manipulatives and other visual representations of mathematical concepts. You may also work with your school librarian to compile a set of topical resources at a variety of reading levels.

STRATEGIES FOR ENGLISH LANGUAGE LEARNERS

Students who are developing proficiency in English language skills require additional supports to simultaneously learn academic content and the specialized language associated with specific content areas. WIDA has created a framework for providing support to these students and makes available rubrics and guidance on differentiating instructional materials for English language learners (ELLs) (see www.wida.us). In particular, ELL students may benefit from additional sensory supports such as images, physical modeling, and graphic representations of module content, as well as interactive support through collaborative work. This module incorporates a variety of sensory supports and offers ongoing opportunities for ELL students to work collaboratively.

The focus on automobile racing and alternative energy sources provides an opportunity for ELL students to share culturally diverse experiences with these topics.

Teachers differentiating instruction for ELL students should carefully consider the needs of these students as they introduce and use academic language in various language domains (listening, speaking, reading, and writing) throughout this module. To adequately differentiate instruction for ELL students, teachers should have an understanding of the proficiency level of each student. The following five overarching grades 6–8 WIDA learning standards are relevant to this module:

- Standard 1: Social and Instructional Language. Focus on assignments/research, resources & supplies, social interaction, use of information, and use of multiple resources.

- Standard 2: The language of Language Arts. Focus on editorials, historical documents, technical texts, biographies, and multimedia.

- Standard 3: The language of Mathematics. Focus on algebraic equations, data interpretation & statistics, estimation, measures of central tendency, and percent.

- Standard 4: The language of Science. Focus on atoms & molecules, chemical building blocks, elements & compounds, forms of energy, motion & force, processes, scientific inventions or discoveries, and scientific tools or instruments.

- Standard 5: The language of Social Studies. Focus on economic trends, human resources, and maps.

SAFETY CONSIDERATIONS FOR THE ACTIVITIES IN THIS MODULE

All laboratory occupants must wear safety glasses or goggles during all phases of inquiry activities (setup, hands-on investigation, and takedown). For more general safety guidelines, see the section on Safety in STEM in Chapter 2 (p. 18) and for lesson-specific safety information, see the Safety Notes section of each lesson in Chapter 4.

DESIRED OUTCOMES AND MONITORING SUCCESS

The desired outcomes for this module are outlined in Table 3.3, along with suggested ways to gather evidence to monitor student success. For more specific details on desired outcomes, see the Established Goals and Objectives sections for the module and individual lessons.

Table 3.3 Desired Outcomes and Evidence of Success in Achieving Identified Outcomes

Desired Outcome	Evidence of Success in Achieving Identified Outcome	
	Performance Tasks	Other Measures
Students understand that chemical reactions result in products with new arrangements of atoms and molecules with different properties than the reactants.	Completion of inquiry activities and associated handouts.	• Energy Source STEM Research Notebook entries will be assessed using a rubric. • Student collaboration will be evaluated using self-assessment reflections, peer feedback, and a collaboration rubric.
Students understand the life cycle of various energy sources.	• Life Cycle Analysis handouts • Energy Source STEM Research Notebook entries	
Students understand the environmental impact of various energy sources in transportation.	• Life Cycle Analysis handouts • Energy Source STEM Research Notebook entries	
Students are able to use the engineering design process (EDP) to design and build a solution to a problem.	• Completion of design challenges throughout unit • Evidence of EDP use in culminating project	

ASSESSMENT PLAN OVERVIEW AND MAP

Table 3.4 provides an overview of the major group and individual *products* and *deliverables*, or things that comprise the assessment for this module. See Table 3.5 for a full assessment map of formative and summative assessments in this module.

Table 3.4 Major Products/Deliverables in Lead Disciplines for Groups and Individuals

Lesson	Major Group Products/Deliverables	Major Individual Products/Deliverables
1	• Blown Away Challenge product and presentation	• We've Bean Using Energy handout and graph • Engineer It! handout for Blown Away challenge • STEM Research Notebook prompt
2	• Be a Hero! Design Challenge • Fossils to Fuels Timeline	• Making Hydrocarbons handout • Heat-Free Hero's Engine handout • Engineer It! – Be a Hero Design Challenge • STEM Research Notebook prompt • Fossils to Fuels timeline handout • Energy Source STEM Research Notebook Entry – gasoline
3	• Life Cycle Analysis – Natural Gas • Gas-Powered Cars presentation	• Gas It Up! handout • Energy Source STEM Research Notebook Entry – natural gas
4	• Life Cycle Analysis – Biofuels • Life Cycle Analysis – Biodiesel (optional)	• Fermentable Fuels handout • Fermentable Fuels graph • Energy Source STEM Research Notebook Entry –biofuels • Energy Source STEM Research Notebook Entry –biodiesel (optional)
5	• A Job in the Sun presentation • Life Cycle Analysis – Solar Energy	• Energy Careers handout • Solar Circuits data sheet • Engineer It! – Solar Circuits • Lemon Power data sheet • Energy Source STEM Research Notebook entry
6	• Capturing the Wind pinwheel • Life Cycle Analysis – Wind	• Where's the Wind? handout • Capturing the Wind data sheet • Engineer It! – Capturing the Wind • Energy Source STEM Research Notebook Entry – wind
7	• EV Mini Prix vehicle design and performance	• Engineer It! – EV Mini Prix
8	• Speed of Green prototype/model • Speed of Green team presentation	• Speed of Green portfolio (Speed of Green student packet)

Table 3.5 Assessment Map for The Speed of Green Module

Lesson	Assessment	Group/ Individual	Formative/ Summative	Lesson Objective Assessed
1	We've Bean Using Energy *handout*	Individual	Formative	• Identify differences between finite (non-renewable) and renewable energy resources. • Explain the phenomenon of resource scarcity and how this phenomenon impacts the use of finite and renewable energy resources.
1	Engineer It! Blown Away Design Challenge *handout*	Individual	Formative	• Understand and describe the EDP and track their progress in using the process to solve a problem. • Understand that engineers work within design constraints, and that they must consider multiple objectives when designing products. • Apply the EDP to a group design challenge.
1	Blown Away Design Challenge *presentation rubric*	Group	Formative	• Understand and describe the EDP and track their progress in using the process to solve a problem. • Apply the EDP to a group design challenge.
1	STEM Research Notebook *prompt*	Individual	Formative	• Understand and describe the EDP and track their progress in using the process to solve a problem. • Understand that engineers work within design constraints, and that they must consider multiple objectives when designing products.
2	Fuel Figures *handout*	Individual	Formative	• Identify several uses of simple straight-chain hydrocarbons. • Identify environmental impacts associated with producing and transporting gasoline. • Identify benefits, disadvantages, and costs of using gasoline as a fuel source for automobiles.

Continued

Table 3.5 (*continued*)

Lesson	Assessment	Group/ Individual	Formative/ Summative	Lesson Objective Assessed
2	Making Hydrocarbons *handout*	Individual	Formative	• Identify carbon as an element critical for life forms and as a key element of fossil fuels. • Create models of straight-chain hydrocarbons.
2	Heat-Free Hero's Engine *handout*	Group	Formative	• Identify the difference between an endothermic and an exothermic reaction.
2	Be a Hero! Design Challenge *performance task*	Group	Formative	• Identify the difference between an endothermic and an exothermic reaction. • Apply their understanding of chemical reactions to create and power a Hero's engine type device.
2	Engineer It! – Be a Hero! *handout*	Individual	Formative	• Apply their understanding of chemical reactions to create and power a Hero's engine type device.
2	STEM Research Notebook *prompt*	Individual	Formative	• Identify causes of the 1970s energy crisis in the U.S.
2	Fossils to Fuels Timeline *performance task*	Group	Formative	• Explain the processes by which oil is created in the earth. • Identify energy costs associated with producing and transporting gasoline. • Identify environmental impacts associated with producing and transporting gasoline. • Identify benefits, disadvantages, and costs of using gasoline as a fuel source for automobiles.
2	Energy Source STEM Research Notebook Entry *rubric*	Individual	Summative	• Identify energy costs associated with producing and transporting gasoline. • Identify environmental impacts associated with producing and transporting gasoline. • Identify benefits, disadvantages, and costs of using gasoline as a fuel source for automobiles.
3	Life Cycle Analysis – Natural Gas *performance task*	Group	Formative	• Identify natural gas as a fossil fuel. • Explain how natural gas is formed. • Explain how natural gas can be used to power vehicles.

Lesson	Assessment	Group/Individual	Formative/Summative	Lesson Objective Assessed
3	Greenpeople Effect *performance task*	Group	Formative	• Demonstrate a conceptual understanding of the greenhouse effect.
3	Gas It Up! *handout*	Individual	Formative	• Simulate the creation of natural gas.
3	Energy Source STEM Research Notebook Entry *rubric*	Individual	Summative	• Identify natural gas as a fossil fuel. • Explain how natural gas is formed. • Explain how natural gas can be used to power vehicles. • Analyze the implications of using natural gas as a power source for vehicles.
3	Gas-Powered Cars presentation *rubric*	Group	Formative	• Explain how natural gas can be used to power vehicles. • Analyze the implications of using natural gas as a power source for vehicles.
4	Fermentable Fuels *handout*	Individual	Formative	• Explain the chemistry of fermentation reactions and apply this understanding to creating ethanol.
4	Fermentable Fuels *graph*	Individual	Formative	• Create a line graph using findings from an investigation.
4	Life Cycle Analysis – Biofuels *performance task*	Group	Formative	• Explain how biofuel is formed. • Analyze the implications of using biofuels as a power source for vehicles.
4	Energy Source STEM Research Notebook Entry *rubric*	Individual	Summative	• Analyze the implications of using biofuels as a power source for vehicles. • Identify and discuss the environmental and food production implications of using corn as an ethanol source.
5	PV Cell Simulation challenge *performance task*	Group	Formative	• Demonstrate a conceptual understanding of how photovoltaic cells capture solar energy.
5	Engineer It! –PV Cell challenge *handout*	Individual	Formative	• Demonstrate a conceptual understanding of how photovoltaic cells capture solar energy.
5	Energy Careers *handout*	Individual	Formative	• Identify and describe several careers associated with solar energy.

Continued

Table 3.5 (*continued*)

Lesson	Assessment	Group/ Individual	Formative/ Summative	Lesson Objective Assessed
5	A Job in the Sun *presentation*	Group	Formative	• Identify and describe various careers associated with solar energy.
5	Solar Circuits *handout*	Individual	Formative	• Demonstrate a conceptual understanding of how photovoltaic cells capture solar energy. • Apply a basic understanding of electrical circuits to create a circuit that powers a battery using solar energy. • Understand the flow of electrons within a battery.
5	Engineer It! – Solar Circuits *handout*	Individual	Formative	• Apply the EDP to solve a problem.
5	Lemon Power *handout* (optional)	Individual	Formative	• Apply their understanding of electron flows within a battery and their understanding of simple circuits to create a battery.
5	Energy Source STEM Research Notebook entry *rubric*	Individual	Summative	• Analyze the implications of using solar energy as a power source for vehicles.
6	Where's the Wind? *handout*	Individual	Formative	• Identify geographical areas that utilize wind as an energy resource.
6	Life Cycle Analysis – Wind *performance task*	Group	Formative	• Describe the basic function of a wind turbine. • Explain that wind energy is most practical as an energy source for vehicles when it is used as the energy source to charge a battery for an EV.
6	Capturing the Wind *handout*	Individual	Formative	• Apply a basic understanding of how a wind turbine works to create a wind turbine. • Demonstrate their understanding that the structure of turbine blades has implications for a wind turbine's performance.
6	Engineer It! –Capturing the Wind *handout*	Individual	Formative	• Apply the EDP to solve a problem.

Lesson	Assessment	Group/ Individual	Formative/ Summative	Lesson Objective Assessed
6	Energy Source STEM Research Notebook Entry *rubric*	Individual	Summative	• Explain that wind energy is most practical as an energy source for vehicles when it is used as the energy source to charge a battery for an EV. • Analyze the implications of using wind energy as a power source for vehicles.
7	EV Mini Prix vehicle prototype/model *rubric*	Group	Summative	• Demonstrate a conceptual understanding of friction. • Demonstrate a conceptual understanding of aerodynamic drag as a special type of friction. • Understand that weight of materials affects car performance. • Use their understanding of friction, aerodynamics, materials, and batteries to create their own EV.
7	Engineer It! – EV Mini Prix *handouts*	Individual	Formative	• Use the EDP to solve a problem.
8	Speed of Green prototype/model *rubric*	Group	Summative	• Apply their understanding of various non-renewable and renewable energy sources to identify an energy source that they believe has minimal environmental impact. • Justify their choice of energy source. • Demonstrate their understanding of technologies or products associated with their energy source by creating a prototype or model.
8	Student portfolio (Speed of Green student packet) *handout*	Individual	Summative	• Demonstrate their understanding of the EDP and use it to create a solution to the module challenge. • Apply their understanding of various non-renewable and renewable energy sources to identify an energy source that they believe has minimal environmental impact. • Justify their choice of energy source. • Demonstrate their understanding of technologies or products associated with their energy source by creating a prototype or model.

Continued

Table 3.5 (*continued*)

Lesson	Assessment	Group/ Individual	Formative/ Summative	Lesson Objective Assessed
8	Speed of Green presentation *rubric*	Group	Summative	• Apply their understanding of various non-renewable and renewable energy sources to identify an energy source that they believe has minimal environmental impact. • Justify their choice of energy source. • Demonstrate their understanding of technologies or products associated with their energy source by creating a prototype or model. • Use persuasive language in a presentation that demonstrates their learning during the module.

MODULE TIMELINE

Tables 3.6–3.10 (pp. 43–45) provide lesson timelines for the lead disciplines for each week of the module. The timelines are provided for general guidance only and are based on class times of approximately 45 minutes.

Table 3.6. STEM Road Map Module Schedule Week One

Day 1	Day 2	Day 3	Day 4	Day 5
Lesson 1	*Lesson 1*	*Lesson 1*	*Lesson 2*	*Lesson 2*
Ready, Set, Go Green!	*Ready, Set, Go Green!*	*Ready, Set, Go Green!*	*From Fossils to Fuels*	*From Fossils to Fuels*
Launch the module – Introduce Leilani Münter and the idea of carbon-free auto racing.	We've Bean Using Energy activity.	Blown Away Design Challenge.	Introduce engine function with video.	Discuss carbon as a key component of fossil fuels.
Introduce the module challenge.	Graph results of We've Bean Using Energy.	Students compile a database of careers associated with energy production.	Fuel Figures activity.	Making Hydrocarbons activity.
Review and discuss energy sources.	Discuss sources of oil.		Show video about "green" auto racing.	Introduce combustion reactions and Heat-Free Hero's Engine activity.
	Introduce/review engineering design process (EDP).		Students investigate the 1970s oil crisis.	

Table 3.7 STEM Road Map Module Schedule Week Two

Day 6	Day 7	Day 8	Day 9	Day 10
Lesson 2 *From Fossils to Fuels* Fossils to Fuels Timeline activity. Introduce Be a Hero! Design Challenge. Students create narrative essay about oil crisis.	*Lesson 2* *From Fossils to Fuels* Complete Be a Hero! Design Challenge. Discuss oil prices. STEM Research Notebook prompt.	*Lesson 3* *Gas, Naturally* Introduce natural gas-powered vehicles with video and discussion. Discuss hydraulic fracturing. Life Cycle Analysis – Natural Gas.	*Lesson 3* *Gas, Naturally* Greenpeople Effect activity. Gas It Up activity. Gas-Powered Cars activity.	*Lesson 3* *Gas, Naturally* Gas-Powered Cars presentations. Discuss environmental implications of hydraulic fracturing. Energy Source STEM Research Notebook Entry – natural gas.

Table 3.8 STEM Road Map Module Schedule Week Three

Day 11	Day 12	Day 13	Day 14	Day 15
Lesson 4 *From Photosynthesis to Fuel: Biofuels* Introduce ethanol as a gasoline additive. Life Cycle Analysis – Ethanol	*Lesson 4* *From Photosynthesis to Fuel: Biofuels* Fermentable Fuels activity. Energy Source STEM Research Notebook Entry – ethanol.	*Lesson 5* *Speed from the Sun* Introduce solar-powered cars with video. PV Cell Simulation Challenge.	*Lesson 5* *Speed from the Sun* Solar Circuits Activity.	*Lesson 5* *Speed from the Sun* Life Cycle Analysis – Solar Energy. A Job in the Sun activity and presentations.

Table 3.9 STEM Road Map Module Schedule Week Four

Day 16	Day 17	Day 18	Day 19	Day 20
Lesson 5 *Speed from the Sun* Energy Source STEM Research Notebook entry – solar energy. Lemon Power activity (optional).	*Lesson 6* *Capturing the Wind* Introduce wind-powered cars with video and introduce wind turbines. Where's the Wind? activity.	*Lesson 6* *Capturing the Wind* Capturing the Wind activity. Calculate tip-speed ratio of blades in Capturing the Wind activity.	*Lesson 7* *EV Mini Prix* Introduce the use of electric vehicles (EVs) in motorsports with videos. Read about and discuss Ralph Nader's consumer advocacy for vehicle safety. Introduce the EV Mini Prix and discuss friction and other considerations for vehicle performance.	*Lesson 7* *EV Mini Prix* Students complete EV Mini Prix challenge. Students research Ralph Nader.

Table 3.10 STEM Road Map Module Schedule Week Five

Day 21	Day 22	Day 23	Day 24	Day 25
Lesson 7 *EV Mini Prix* Students participate in time trials with their EVs. Team presentations about Ralph Nader and auto safety innovations.	*Lesson 8* *The Speed of Green Challenge* Introduce Speed of Green Challenge requirements. Students begin work on Speed of Green Challenge: decisions about fuel source, create life cycle analysis for presentation, and identify design innovations.	*Lesson 8* *The Speed of Green Challenge* Students continue work on Speed of Green Challenge: students create model of design innovation, begin work on presentation.	*Lesson 8* *The Speed of Green Challenge* Students continue work on Speed of Green Challenge: complete and video record presentations.	*Lesson 8* *The Speed of Green Challenge* Presentations to fictional investors.

RESOURCES

The media specialist can help teachers locate resources for students to view and read about energy sources, fuels, environmental sustainability, and related content. Special educators and reading specialists can help find supplemental sources for students needing extra support in reading and writing. Additional resources may be found online. Community resources for this module may include industry professionals from the energy industry and motorsports.

REFERENCES

Johnson, C. C., Moore, T. J., Utley, J., Breiner, J., Burton, S. R., Peter-Burton, E. E., Walton, J., & Parton, C. L. (2015). The STEM road map for grades 6–8. In C. C. Johnson, E. E. Peters-Burton, & T. J. Moore (Eds.), *STEM road map: A framework for integrated STEM education* (pp. 96–123). Routledge.

Keeley, P., & Harrington, R. (2010). *Uncovering student ideas in physical science* (Vol. 1). NSTA Press.

WIDA. (2012). *Amplification of the English language development standards: Kindergarten grade 12.* www.wida.us/standards/eld.aspx

THE SPEED OF GREEN LESSON PLANS

Janet B. Walton, James M. Caruthers, and Carla C. Johnson

Lesson Plan 1:
Ready, Set, Go Green!

In this lesson, students are introduced to the module challenge and the concept of renewable and non-renewable energy sources. Students will consider how product design and engineering affects consumers' choices of energy sources. The elements of the engineering design process (EDP) will be reviewed, and students will use the EDP in a mini design challenge.

ESSENTIAL QUESTIONS

- What are finite and renewable energy resources?

- What careers are associated with the renewable energy industry?

- What is resource scarcity?

- How can we use the EDP to solve a problem?

ESTABLISHED GOALS AND OBJECTIVES

At the conclusion of this lesson, students will be able to do the following:

- Identify differences between finite (non-renewable) and renewable energy resources

- Explain the phenomenon of resource scarcity and how this phenomenon impacts the use of finite and renewable energy resources

- Categorize energy resources as either finite or renewable and justify their categorizations

DOI: 10.4324/9781003362357-6

- Describe the EDP and track their progress in using the process to solve a problem

- Explain that engineers work within design constraints, and that they must consider multiple objectives when designing products

- Apply the EDP to a group design challenge

TIME REQUIRED

3 days (approximately 45 minutes each day; see Table 3.6, p. 43).

MATERIALS

Required Materials for Lesson 1

- STEM Research Notebooks (one per student; see p. 28 for STEM Research Notebook student handout)

- internet access for research

- handouts (attached at the end of this lesson)

- paper or white board for each team of three to four students

Additional Materials for We've Bean Using Energy (for each group of students unless otherwise indicated; team size will vary depending on your class size; you should plan to divide students into six groups)

- white beans (number per group will vary – 600 total)

- brown beans (number per group will vary – 150 total)

- 1 lunch-sized paper bag

- We've Bean Using Energy handout (1 per student)

- We've Bean Using Energy datasheet (1 per student)

Additional Materials for Blown Away Design Challenge (for each group of 3–4 students unless otherwise indicated)

- 5 drinking straws

- 3 index cards (4″ × 6″)

- 4 lifesaver mints

- 15 paper clips
- 4 small paper cups
- 1 plastic sandwich bag
- 4 rubber bands
- ruler
- scissors
- 1 sheet of paper
- 3 feet of string
- 1 roll of masking tape
- Blown Away Design Challenge handouts (1 per student)

SAFETY NOTES

1 Caution students not to eat beans used in the We've Bean Using Energy activity.

2 Students should use caution when handling scissors, as the sharp points and blades can cut or puncture skin.

3 Tell students to take care handling and bending paper clips to avoid puncturing skin.

4 Have students wash hands with soap and water after activities are completed.

5 Have students wear safety goggles during the Blown Away design challenge.

CONTENT STANDARDS AND KEY VOCABULARY

Table 4.1 lists the content standards from the *Next Generation Science Standards* (*NGSS*), *Common Core State Standards* (*CCSS*), and the Framework for 21st Century Learning that this lesson addresses, and Table 4.2 (p. 53) presents the key vocabulary. Vocabulary terms are provided for both teacher and student use. Teachers may choose to introduce some or all of the terms to students.

Table 4.1. Content Standards Addressed in STEM Road Map Module Lesson 1

NEXT GENERATION SCIENCE STANDARDS

PERFORMANCE OBJECTIVES

- MS-PS2–2 Plan an investigation to provide evidence that the change in an object's motion depends on the sum of the forces on the object and the mass of the object.

- MS-ETS1–2 Evaluate competing design solutions using a systematic process to determine how well they meet the criteria and constraints of the problem.

- MS-ETS1–3 Analyze data from tests to determine similarities and differences among several design solutions to identify the best characteristics of each that can be combined into a new solution to better meet the criteria for success.

SCIENCE AND ENGINEERING PRACTICES
Analyzing and Interpreting Data

- Analyze and interpret data to determine similarities and differences in findings.

Constructing Explanations and Designing Solutions

- Undertake a design project, engaging in the design cycle, to construct and/or implement a solution that meets specific design criteria and constraints.

- Apply scientific ideas or principles to design an object, tool, process, or system.

DISCIPLINARY CORE IDEAS
PS3.A: *Definitions of Energy*

- Temperature is not a measure of energy; the relationship between the temperature and the total energy of a system depends on the types, states, and amounts of matter present.

- Motion energy is properly called kinetic energy; it is proportional to the mass of the moving object and grows with the square of its speed.

- A system of objects may also contain stored (potential) energy, depending on their relative positions.

PS3.B: *Conservation of Energy and Energy Transfer*

- When the motion energy of an object changes, there is inevitably some other change in energy at the same time.

- The amount of energy transfer needed to change the temperature of a matter sample by a given amount depends on the nature of the matter, the size of the sample, and the environment.

- Energy is spontaneously transferred out of hotter regions or objects and into colder ones.

PS3.C: *Relationship Between Energy and Forces*

- When two objects interact, each one exerts a force on the other that can cause energy to be transferred to or from the object.

ESS3.A: *Natural Resources*

- Humans depend on Earth's land, ocean, atmosphere, and biosphere for many different resources. Minerals, fresh water, and biosphere resources are limited, and many are not renewable or replaceable over human lifetimes. These resources are distributed unevenly around the planet as a result of past geologic processes.

ESS3.C: *Human Impacts on Earth Systems*

- Typically as human populations and per-capita consumption of natural resources increase, so do the negative impacts on Earth unless the activities and technologies involved are engineered otherwise.

ETS1.A: *Defining and Delimiting Engineering Problems*

- The more precisely a design task's criteria and constraints can be defined, the more likely it is that the designed solution will be successful. Specification of constraints includes consideration of scientific principles and other relevant knowledge that is likely to limit possible solutions.

ETS1.B: *Developing Possible Solutions*

- A solution needs to be tested, and then modified on the basis of the test results in order to improve it.

ETS1.C: *Optimizing the Design Solution*

- Although one design may not perform the best across all tests, identifying the characteristics of the design that performed the best in each test can provide useful information for the redesign process – that is, some of the characteristics may be incorporated into the new design.

- The iterative process of testing the most promising solutions and modifying what is proposed on the basis of the test results leads to greater refinement and ultimately to an optimal solution.

CROSS-CUTTING CONCEPTS

Energy and Matter

- The transfer of energy can be tracked as energy flows through a designed or natural system.

- Energy may take different forms (e.g. energy in fields, thermal energy, energy of motion).

Continued

Table 4.1. (*continued*)

Cause and Effect
- Cause and effect relationships may be used to predict phenomena in natural or designed systems.

COMMON CORE STATE STANDARDS FOR MATHEMATICS
MATHEMATICAL PRACTICES

MP 1. Make sense of problems and persevere in solving them.

- MP 2. Reason abstractly and quantitatively.

- MP 3. Construct viable arguments and critique the reasoning of others.

- MP 4. Model with mathematics.

- MP 5. Use appropriate tools strategically.

COMMON CORE STATE STANDARDS FOR ENGLISH LANGUAGE ARTS
READING STANDARDS

- RL.8.1. Cite the textual evidence that most strongly supports an analysis of what the text says explicitly as well as inferences drawn from the text.

WRITING STANDARDS

- W.8.1. Write arguments to support claims with clear reasons and relevant evidence.

- W.8.1.B. Support claim(s) with logical reasoning and relevant evidence, using accurate, credible sources and demonstrating an understanding of the topic or text.

- W.8.1.C. Use words, phrases, and clauses to create cohesion and clarify the relationships among claim(s), counterclaims, reasons, and evidence.

- W.8.2. Write informative/explanatory texts to examine a topic and convey ideas, concepts, and information through the selection, organization, and analysis of relevant content.

- W.8.2.B. Develop the topic with relevant, well-chosen facts, definitions, concrete details, quotations, or other information and examples.

- W.8.2.C. Use appropriate and varied transitions to create cohesion and clarify the relationships among ideas and concepts.

- W.8.2.D. Use precise language and domain-specific vocabulary to inform about or explain the topic.

- W.8.7. Conduct short research projects to answer a question (including a self-generated question), drawing on several sources and generating additional related, focused questions that allow for multiple avenues of exploration.

- W.8.8. Gather relevant information from multiple print and digital sources, using search terms effectively; assess the credibility and accuracy of each source; and quote or paraphrase the data and conclusions of others while avoiding plagiarism and following a standard format for citation.

- W.8.9. Draw evidence from literary or informational texts to support analysis, reflection, and research.

SPEAKING AND LISTENING STANDARDS

- SL.8.1. Engage effectively in a range of collaborative discussions (one-on-one, in groups, and teacher-led) with diverse partners on grade 8 topics, texts, and issues, building on others' ideas and expressing their own clearly.

- SL.8.1.A. Come to discussions prepared, having read or researched material under study; explicitly draw on that preparation by referring to evidence on the topic, text, or issue to probe and reflect on ideas under discussion.

- SL.8.1.B. Follow rules for collegial discussions and decision-making, track progress toward specific goals and deadlines, and define individual roles as needed.

- SL.8.1.C. Pose questions that connect the ideas of several speakers and respond to others' questions and comments with relevant evidence, observations, and ideas.

- SL.8.1.D. Acknowledge new information expressed by others, and, when warranted, qualify or justify their own views in light of the evidence presented.

- SL.8.2. Analyze the purpose of information presented in diverse media and formats (for example, visually, quantitatively, orally) and evaluate the motives (for example, social, commercial, political) behind its presentation.

- SL.8.4. Present claims and findings, emphasizing salient points in a focused, coherent manner with relevant evidence, sound valid reasoning, and well-chosen details; use appropriate eye contact, adequate volume, and clear pronunciation.

FRAMEWORK FOR 21ST CENTURY LEARNING

Interdisciplinary themes (financial, economic, & business literacy; environmental literacy); Learning and Innovation Skills; Information, Media & Technology Skills; Life and Career Skills

Table 4.2. Key Vocabulary in Lesson 1

Key Vocabulary	Definition
British thermal unit (BTU)	a measure of energy defined as the amount of energy needed to change the temperature of 1 pound of water by 1 degree Fahrenheit
carbon-based fuels (or fossil fuels)	energy sources that were formed from the buried remains of plants and animals that lived millions of years ago (coal, crude oil, natural gas)

Continued

Table 4.2. (*continued*)

Key Vocabulary	Definition
electricity	the flow of electric energy that occurs when electrons move from one place to another
energy	the ability to do work
energy conservation	any behavior that results in the consumption of less energy
energy efficiency	using less energy to do a job, often using technological innovations
energy sustainability	the idea that each generation should meet its current energy needs without compromising the energy supply for future generations
finite energy source (or non-renewable energy source)	an energy resource that cannot be replenished within a short period of time (crude oil, natural gas, coal, uranium)
primary energy source	fuel source that occurs naturally and has not been converted to provide a usable source of energy; for example, crude oil, natural gas, wind, and solar radiation
renewable energy source	an energy resource that replenishes itself within a short period of time; for example, biomass, hydropower, geothermal, wind, and solar radiation
secondary energy source	a source of energy that has been produced from a primary energy source and is usable to consumers; for example, gasoline and electricity

TEACHER BACKGROUND INFORMATION

This lesson introduces students to renewable and non-renewable energy sources and the engineering design process (EDP). This section provides background on these topics and the basic chemistry of combustion, a topic that will be referred to throughout the module.

Renewable and Non-Renewable Energy Sources

Students may have preconceived notions about "green" energy and sustainability based upon the media and family beliefs. This module may challenge these preconceived notions by providing students the opportunity to think critically about energy sources and apply life cycle analyses to various energy sources to develop a deeper understanding of energy sources. Energy use in transportation and, in particular, motorsports, will provide a forum for students' investigation.

Students may benefit from a brief review of the two types of energy (potential and kinetic) and the various forms of energy before discussing further categorizations of energy sources. An energy classification graphic is included at the end of this lesson plan to aid in this.

Students may confuse primary energy sources with secondary energy sources, or energy carriers (for instance, they may identify electricity as a primary energy source). Electricity and gasoline are two examples of energy carriers, or secondary energy sources, since they are both made from the conversion of primary sources of energy such as crude oil, coal, wind, or solar radiation. Energy sources can be classified into two main groups: renewable and non-renewable.

Non-renewable, or finite, energy sources cannot be replenished within a short period of time. There are four major non-renewable energy resources:

1. Crude oil

2. Natural gas

3. Coal

4. Uranium (nuclear energy)

Oil, gas, and coal are considered fossil fuels because they were made from the remains of plants and animals that lived millions of years ago. Uranium is a non-renewable energy source but is not a fossil fuel, but rather is a naturally occurring element.

Renewable energy sources are those that regenerate fairly quickly. There are five renewable energy sources:

1. Biomass (includes wood, solid waste, landfill gas and biogas, ethanol, and biodiesel)

2. Hydropower

3. Geothermal

4. Wind

5. Solar

The U.S. Energy Information Agency (EIA) provides information about current U.S. energy consumption by source and by sector at www.eia.gov/energyexplained/us-energy-facts. You may wish to review this information or be prepared to share the graphics provided with students as you discuss energy usage in this lesson. According to the EIA, as of 2020, the transportation sector was the second-largest consumer of energy in the U.S. and the vast majority of the energy used in this sector was petroleum or crude oil.

Since oil is a non-renewable resource, has pollutant qualities, requires drilling operations, and because, as of 2021, the U.S. relied on foreign sources for about 40% of its oil (see the U.S. Energy Information at www.eia.gov/energyexplained/index.php?page=oil_imports for current data on U.S. oil imports), alternative energy sources for transportation are an area of interest for environmentalists and politicians. Fluctuating gas prices often spur renewed widespread interest in identifying alternative energy sources for automobiles as well. At the same time, however, there is little widespread public understanding of the total costs of various sources of energy

Chemistry of Combustion

Students will investigate the basic chemistry of combustion within this module. Oil products create a number of emissions when they undergo combustion, including:

- Carbon dioxide (CO_2)

- Carbon monoxide (CO)

- Sulfur dioxide (SO_2)

- Nitrogen oxides (NOX) and Volatile Organic Compounds (VOC)

- Particulate matter (PM)

- Lead and various air toxins such as benzene, formaldehyde, acetaldehyde, and 1,3-butadiene may be emitted when some types of petroleum are burned. (from http://environment-ecology.com/energy-and-environment/92-how-does-oil-impact-the-environment.html)

Essentially, all of these emissions have negative effects on the environment or on human health that students will investigate within this module. Laws requiring reformulated fuels have resulted in reduced emissions over the past decades.

The U.S. Energy Information Administration is a congressionally funded independent source of energy information and statistics and provides a wealth of information for consumers and policymakers on its website. The educator resource page provides a useful overview of renewable and non-renewable energy sources and can be accessed at www.eia.gov/kids/energy.cfm?page=6.

Engineering Design Process

Students should understand that engineers need to work in groups to accomplish their work, and that collaboration is important for designing solutions to problems. In this lesson, students will use the EDP, the same process that professional engineers use in their work. A graphic representation of the EDP is provided at the end of this lesson plan (p. 75). You may wish to provide each student with a copy of the EDP graphic or enlarge it and post it in a prominent place in your classroom for student reference throughout the module. Be prepared to review each step of the EDP with students and emphasize that the process is not a linear one – at any point in the process, they may need to return to a previous step. The steps of the process are as follows:

1. *Define.* Describe the problem you are trying to solve, identify what materials you are able to use, and decide how much time and help you have to solve the problem.

2. *Learn.* Brainstorm solutions and conduct research to learn about the problem you are trying to solve.

3. *Plan.* Plan your work, including making sketches and dividing tasks among team members if necessary.

4. *Try.* Build a device, create a system, or complete a product.

5. *Test.* Now, test your solution. This might be done by conducting a performance test, if you have created a device to accomplish a task, or by asking for feedback from others about their solutions to the same problem.

6. *Decide.* Based on what you found out during the Test step, you can adjust your solution or make changes to your device.

After completing all six steps, students can share their solution or device with others. This represents an additional opportunity to receive feedback and make modifications based on that feedback.

The following are additional resources about the EDP:

- www.sciencebuddies.org/engineering-design-process/engineering-design-compare-scientific-method.shtml

- www.pbslearningmedia.org/resource/phy03.sci.engin.design.desprocess/what-is-the-design-process

COMMON MISCONCEPTIONS

Students will have various types of prior knowledge about the concepts introduced in this lesson. Table 4.3 describes a common misconception students may have concerning these concepts. Because of the breadth of students' experiences, it is not possible to anticipate every misconception that students may bring as they approach this lesson. Incorrect or inaccurate prior understanding of concepts can influence student learning in the future, however, so it is important to be alert to misconceptions such as those presented in the table.

Table 4.3. Common Misconception About the Concepts in Lesson 1

Topic	Student Misconception	Explanation
Engineering design process (EDP)	Engineers use only scientific processes to solve problems in their work.	Experimental methods are used to test predictions and explanations about the world. The EDP, on the other hand, is used to create a solution to a problem. In reality, engineers and scientists may use both processes.

PREPARATION FOR LESSON 1

Review the teacher background information provided, assemble the materials for the lesson, make copies of the student handouts, and preview the video and websites recommended in the Learning Components section that follows. Have your students set up their STEM Research Notebooks (see pp. 27–28 for discussion and student instruction handout).

Prepare for the We've Bean Using Energy activity by preparing a paper bag filled with 100 beans and labeled with a different geographic area (see below) for each team of students (team size will vary depending on your class size; you should plan to divide students into six groups). White beans should be used to represent non-renewable energy sources and brown beans to represent renewable energy sources (make sure beans are mixed well in the bags). The distribution of beans for each geographic area is as follows:

- U.S.: 94 white (non-renewable) beans; 6 brown (renewable) beans
- China: 90 white beans; 10 brown beans
- Brazil: 55 white beans; 45 brown beans
- Denmark: 55 white beans; 45 brown beans
- Saudi Arabia: 99 white beans; 1 brown bean
- Global: 89 white beans; 11 brown beans

The final challenge for the module involves students making a presentation to a group of fictional investors. Begin to plan for these visitors by extending invitations to individuals such as school administrators, local engineers or energy industry representatives, local government officials, or other community volunteers.

LEARNING COMPONENTS
Introductory Activity/Engagement

Connection to the Challenge: Introduce students to the module challenge by telling students that they will have the opportunity to act as a race team and create a plan

for how their team powers its race car. Their challenge for this module will be to create a plan so that their race car has the least environmental impact possible. Tell them that during this unit, they will learn about various energy sources, about how a car's engine works, and about how to determine the impact of using various energy sources. Students will also need to be able to work to solve a problem and create a design in a group.

Begin each day of this lesson by directing students' attention to the module challenge, the Speed of Green Challenge. Remind students that they will work in teams to create a plan for a competitive automobile racing team that minimizes its car's environmental impact. Hold a brief class discussion each day of how students' learning in the previous days' lessons contributed to their ability to complete the challenge. You may wish to create a class list of key ideas on chart paper.

Science Class and Social Studies Connection: Ask students whether they believe that auto racing – like Indy Car and NASCAR – is environmentally friendly and to provide justifications for their responses. Next, introduce students to Leilani Münter and her goal for a carbon-free world by 2050 by showing students a video about Münter such as "Leilani Münter: A Vegan Hippie Chick with a Racecar" at www.you tube.com/watch?v=CqOM61vv5G0&feature=youtu.be. After watching the video, hold a class discussion about the term "carbon-free," asking students questions such as the following:

- What does "carbon-free" mean?

- What are some benefits of carbon-free auto racing?

- What are some challenges to carbon-free auto racing?

Introduce the driving question for the module: How can a motorsports race team power its car with minimal environmental impact? Have students brainstorm to create a class list of the information they think they will need in order to answer this question.

Mathematics Connection: Not applicable.

ELA Connection: Not applicable.

Activity/Exploration

Science and Social Studies Classes and Mathematics Connection: Review the definition of energy and the difference between potential and kinetic energy with students (see Energy graphic, attached at the end of this lesson plan). Tell students that they will consider where the energy they use daily in their homes and to power their vehicles comes from.

Divide students into groups of three to four and provide each group with a piece of paper or a whiteboard. Ask students to brainstorm about energy sources. Prompt them

by encouraging them to think about where the energy comes from to power their cars, turn on their lights, etc. Ask them to think about what they've seen in the news about sources of energy. Have students write down the energy sources they brainstormed on the paper or whiteboard.

Ask groups to share what energy sources they identified and create a class list (groups after the first one need only add sources that were not previously mentioned). The final list may include the following:

1. Crude oil*

2. Natural gas*

3. Coal

4. Uranium (nuclear energy)

5. Biomass (includes wood, solid waste, landfill gas and biogas, ethanol, and biodiesel)*

6. Hydropower

7. Geothermal

8. Wind*

9. Solar*

* These energy sources will be discussed in this module.

Students may need additional prompting to identify hydropower and geothermal as energy sources and, although they may include some items from the biomass category, they may not recognize these as biomass. Note: some students may identify "electricity" as an energy source. This provides an opportunity to distinguish the difference between primary energy sources and secondary sources.

Next, hold a class discussion about sources of energy students experience daily, asking students to identify what sources are used to power their cars and heat their homes and other buildings. These will likely be primarily non-renewable fossil fuels. Ask students what it means for an energy source to be non-renewable and what it means for an energy source to be renewable. Create class definitions for these terms and work as a class to categorize each energy source listed above as renewable or non-renewable.

We've Bean Using Energy Activity

Ask students what source of energy they think we use most in the U.S. – renewable or non-renewable. Tell students that they will participate in a game that will demonstrate

energy use around the world. Divide students into six teams. Distribute a We've Bean Using Energy activity sheet to each student and a paper bag filled with 100 beans and labeled with a geographic area to each team of about four to five students (see Preparation for Lesson 1, p. 58). Each group will represent a different geographic location with beans that approximately represent the proportion of non-renewable to renewable energy sources used:

U.S.: 94 white (non-renewable) beans; 6 brown (renewable) beans.

China: 90 white beans; 10 brown beans

Brazil: 55 white beans; 45 brown beans

Denmark: 55 white beans; 45 brown beans

Saudi Arabia: 99 white beans; 1 brown bean

Global: 89 white beans; 11 brown beans

Students will complete two cycles of the game. One cycle represents constant energy usage over 12 decades and the second represents increasing energy use over four decades. Students will use the following procedure:

Cycle 1: Constant Energy Use Over Time

1. Take turns drawing the number of beans indicated for the decade from the bag. You should remove the beans without looking in the bag.

2. After each draw, count the number of white beans (non-renewable energy) you drew and the number of brown beans (renewable energy) you drew.

3. Record these numbers on your data chart for Cycle 1: Constant Energy Use.

4. Set aside the white beans you drew but **replace the brown beans in the bag**. Continue these steps until all the white beans are gone.

5. Plot your data on a line graph (you will have two separate lines – one for non-renewable and one for renewable) with the decade on the x-axis and the number of beans on the y-axis.

Cycle 2: Repeat above procedure for Increasing Energy Use Over Time (increasing by 4% per decade)

Students will graph the results on a line graph (plotting both renewable and renewable on one graph, with the decade on the x-axis and number of beans on the y-axis).

An option is to use a graphing web tool such as: www.nces.ed.gov/nceskids/createa graph/default.aspx.

After teams have completed both cycles of the game, have each student group share their findings for their geographic area. Create a class chart displaying the geographic area, and the decade in which they ran out of non-renewable energy sources for both Cycles 1 and 2.

From the class data, have students identify the areas most and least dependent on non-renewable energy sources and compare this to the global average represented by the global team's data.

Next, introduce the concept of sustainability. Emphasize that a sustainable rate of energy use means that there will always be enough energy for next year's use. Or, in terms of this activity, there will always be enough beans in the bag to draw enough to meet energy needs.

Tell students that the U.S. Energy Information Administration projects that world energy consumption will increase by 28% by 2040 (www.eia.gov/todayinenergy/detail.php?id=32912). Ask students why they think that the demand for energy might increase each year and record student responses on a class list (for example, population growth, more people driving cars, more industry). Ask students if they think that energy demand changes in response to anything else (for example, weather conditions, more efficient appliances).

Next, show students the list of top energy-producing nations found at www.eia.gov/tools/faqs/faq.php?id=709&t=6Ask. Ask students if they think that it is important for Saudi Arabia and the United States (the top two producers as of 2020) to incorporate renewable energy sources given that they produce so much oil. Tell students that although much of Saudi Arabia's economy is dependent on oil revenues, it is beginning to focus more on renewable energy sources as their country's demand for energy increases because of a concern increasing internal demands might limit their available export supply (www.arabnews.com/news/517011).

Ask students from what country they think the U.S. gets most of its oil. Many students will be surprised to learn that in about 2015 the U.S. began to import more oil from Canada and Latin America than from the Middle East. As a class, review the U.S. petroleum imports charts available from the EIA at www.eia.gov/energyexplained/index.php?page=oil_imports.

Remind students that the focus of the module challenge is race cars. Ask students for their ideas about what energy source is typically associated with cars and other vehicles (oil). You may wish to show students graphs from the EIA's most recent Energy Review (accessible by clicking on the Energy Consumption by Sector data category at www.eia.gov/totalenergy/data/monthly) to emphasize the small role that renewable energy currently play in the U.S. transportation industry.

ELA Connection: Have students identify articles in current newspapers, television news reports, and online websites related to energy usage in the U.S. Have the class brainstorm to create a class list of how they can determine if information on a website is credible.

Explanation

Science and Social Studies Classes: Remind students that renewable energy currently plays a small role in the U.S. transportation industry. Ask them for their ideas about why renewable energy sources are not more commonly used to power vehicles, creating a list of students' responses. Tell students that they will work in teams to create vehicles powered by a renewable energy source in the Blown Away Design Challenge.

Blown Away Design Challenge

Tell students that they will work in teams to build vehicles that operate using a renewable energy source. They will have a limited set of materials and a limited amount of time. Ask students for their ideas about how they could organize their group work.

Introduce the engineering design process (see graphic at the end of this lesson plan). Review each of the elements with students and tell students that they will document their use of the EDP using the Engineer It! sheets (attached at the end of this lesson plan). Students should create a section for each step of the EDP and make notes about their work for each step, including labeled sketches and appropriate citations for any information they identify from research.

[Option: Students may create headings for each step of the EDP in their STEM Research Notebooks as an alternative to the Engineer It! handouts].

Tell students that they will learn about some careers related to energy and technology during this module. Emphasize that auto designers and other innovators frequently work in teams and use the EDP or similar processes to solve problems on a regular basis.

Distribute the Blown Away challenge description (at the end of this lesson plan) along with the EDP graphic to each student, and group students in groups of three to four. Each group should be allowed 1 minute per group to test their design with the fan before they redesign.

Mathematics Connection: Have students access the "This Week in Petroleum" page on the U.S. Energy Information website (www.eia.gov/petroleum/weekly). Have students provide an analysis of the types of charts and graphs provided, along with an explanation of why these types of graphics are appropriate for the data. Have students calculate percent changes in gasoline retail prices and oil stocks over the past week and year.

ELA Connection: Have students each search the internet for articles and information about the usefulness of renewable energy resources in transportation. Students should identify one source that supports the use of renewable energy for transportation and one that does not support its use. Have students work in teams to compare and contrast the sources of the information for the pro-renewable energy use information and the sources of the information that do not support the use of renewable energy sources in transportation. Have each team make a list of sources for each category. Have students highlight those sources they believe are most credible and circle those they believe are least credible. Have each team share one "credible" and one "not credible" source with the class and discuss their reasons for their decisions.

Elaboration/Application of Knowledge

Science and Social Studies Classes and ELA Connection: Have students respond to the questions in the prompt below, recording their responses in their STEM Research Notebooks.

STEM Research Notebook Prompt

- After creating a vehicle using wind energy, what do you think are the opportunities for using wind energy to power cars?

- What do you think are the challenges of using wind energy to power cars?

- You had the chance to use the engineering design process (EDP) in this lesson. Reflect on how using this process worked for your group. Did using the EDP make it easier to work as a group? What went well? What was a challenge? Were there any steps that were particularly challenging? How do you think that your group could improve its problem-solving work in the future?

Mathematics Connection: To introduce units of energy associated with energy, explore the Energy Information Administration (EIA) webpage "Energy Unit Basics" (www.eia.gov/kids/energy.cfm?page=about_energy_units-basics) as a class. Emphasize to students that in the U.S. the BTU, a measure of heat energy, is the most common unit used to compare fuel energies. Have students practice converting various units to BTUs (see www.eia.gov/kids/energy.cfm?page=about_energy_units-basics for conversion factors and a link to an energy calculator).

Evaluation/Assessment

Students may be assessed on the following performance tasks and other measures listed.

Performance Tasks

- We've Bean Using Energy activity handouts

- Engineer It! handout – Blown Away design challenge

- Participation in Blown Away challenge presentation (see Presentation Rubric, Appendix A)

Other Measures

- Teacher observations

- STEM Research Notebook entry

- Collaboration (see Appendix A for rubric)

INTERNET RESOURCES

EDP resources

- *www.sciencebuddies.org/engineering-design-process/engineering-design-compare-scientific-method.shtml*

- *www.pbslearningmedia.org/resource/phy03.sci.engin.design.desprocess/what-is-the-design-process*

"Energy Unit Basics"

- *www.eia.gov/kids/energy.cfm?page=about_energy_units-basics*

Environmental effects of petroleum use

- *www.eia.gov/kids/energy-sources/oil*

"Leilani Münter: A Vegan Hippie Chick with a Racecar" video

- *www.youtube.com/watch?v=CqOM61vv5G0&feature=youtu.be*

Online graphing tool

- *www.nces.ed.gov/nceskids/createagraph/default.aspx*

Renewable and non-renewable energy sources

- *www.eia.gov/kids/energy.cfm?page=6*

"This Week in Petroleum"

- *www.eia.gov/petroleum/weekly*

Top energy-producing nations

- *www.eia.gov/tools/faqs/faq.php?id=709&t=6Ask*

Saudi Arabia's use of renewable energy resources

- *www.arabnews.com/news/517011*

U.S. petroleum imports

- *www.eia.gov/energyexplaied/index.php?page=oil_imports*

U.S. energy consumption review

- *www.eia.gov/totalenergy/data/monthly/*

World energy consumption forecast

- *www.eia.gov/todayinenergy/detail.php?id=32912*

We've Bean Using Energy Student Handout
(Page 1 of 3)

Name: _____   Geographic Area: _____

In this activity, your group will simulate energy use for the geographic area marked on your bag. White beans represent non-renewable energy sources (coal, natural gas, coal, and uranium) that take millions of years to regenerate. Brown beans represent renewable energy sources (biomass, hydropower, wind, geothermal, and solar) that regenerate themselves within much shorter periods of time. The data record sheet gives the number of beans that should be removed from the bag for each decade.

Materials

1 bag of beans per group

1 data sheet per person

1 calculator per person

Procedure

Cycle 1: Constant Energy Use Over Time

1. Take turns drawing the number of beans indicated for the decade from the bag. You should remove the beans without looking in the bag.

2. After each draw, count the number of white beans (non-renewable energy) you drew and the number of brown beans (renewable energy) you drew.

3. Record these numbers on your data chart for Cycle 1: Constant Energy Use.

4. Set aside the white beans you drew but **replace the brown beans in the bag**. Continue these steps until all the white beans are gone.

5. Plot your data on a line graph (you will have two separate lines – one for non-renewable and one for renewable) on a graph using the decade on the x-axis and the number of beans on the y-axis.

Repeat above procedure for Cycle 2: Increasing Energy Use Over Time (increasing by 4% per decade).

We've Bean Using Energy Student Handout
(Page 2 of 3)

Answer the following questions:

1. For Cycle 1 (constant energy use), at what decade did you run out of non-renewable energy resources (white beans)? _____

2. For Cycle 2 (increasing energy use), at what decade did you run out of non-renewable energy resources (white beans)? _____

3. Look at your graphs. During which decade did you start using more renewables (brown beans) than non-renewables (white beans)?

   Cycle 1: _____

   Cycle 2: _____

We've Bean Using Energy Student Handout
(Page 3 of 3)

Data Record

Name: _____   Geographic Area: _____

Cycle 1: Constant Energy Use Over Time

Decade **(Energy needs – number of beans drawn)**	1 (10)	2 (10)	3 (10)	4 (10)	5 (10)	6 (10)	7 (10)	8 (10)	9 (10)	10 (10)	11 (10)	12 (10)	13 (10)	14 (10)
Non-renewable (white)														
Renewable														

Cycle 2: Increasing Energy Use Over Time (4% increase per decade)

Decade **(Energy needs – Number of beans drawn)**	1 (10)	2 (10)	3 (11)	4 (11)	5 (12)	6 (12)	7 (13)	8 (13)	9 (14)	10 (14)	11 (15)	12 (16)	13 (17)	14 (18)
Non-renewable (white)														
Renewable														

Potential Energy and Kinetic Energy

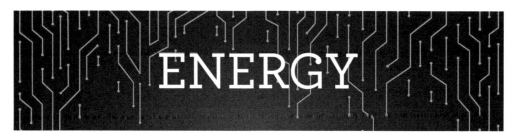

All energy can be classified as one of two types

POTENTIAL ENERGY
Stored energy, or the energy of position

KINETIC ENERGY
Energy of motion

Gravitational Potential Energy Energy stored in an object because of its position	**Mechanical Energy** The energy of a moving object
Elastic Potential Energy Energy stored in an object by applying force	**Thermal Energy** Also called heat. The internal energy in substances caused by the movement of atoms and molecules
Chemical Potential Energy Energy stored in bonds in atoms and molecules	**Sound Energy** Produced when an object vibrates – the movement of energy through substances in waves
Nuclear Potential Energy Energy stored in the bonds holding the nucleus of an atom together	**Electrical Energy** Energy produced by electrons moving through a substance

Blown Away Design Challenge Student Handout
(Page 1 of 2)

The windiest weather in the U.S. tends to be in the western plains, so these states have become a focus for work in harnessing wind energy. Today you are acting as vehicle engineers in the state of Nebraska. You have been challenged to create a prototype vehicle that can carry a given amount of weight at the maximum speed. Unfortunately, the wind has downed a power line outside of your lab, and your prototype is due TODAY, so you must use only the supplies you have on hand.

Your challenge is to build a wind-powered vehicle using the given supplies. You have 40 minutes to complete and test your design. Your design must meet the following requirements:

1. You may use only the materials supplied.

2. Each member of your team must track the team's design process using their own Engineer It! handout.

3. Your vehicle must be powered only by wind energy (supplied by the fan).

4. Your vehicle must be able to carry a load of ten paper clips at least 2 feet from the starting line.

5. The paper clip load must not blow off your vehicle.

6. When your team is ready to test its design it will have 1 minute to test using the wind source (the fan).

7. Your design will be judged by the distance traveled. In the case of a tie between teams' designs, additional paper clips will be added to each car and the trial repeated.

Blown Away Design Challenge Student Handout
(Page 2 of 2)

Materials:

- 5 drinking straws

- 3 index cards (4″ × 6″)

- 4 lifesaver mints

- 15 paper clips (10 of these must be used as your "load" and cannot be part of the car's design. Note: Your load can be attached to the vehicle however you like, but it must not be a part of the car's structure.)

- 4 small paper cups

- 1 plastic sandwich bag

- 4 rubber bands

- Ruler

- Scissors

- Sheet of paper

- 3 feet of string

- 1 roll masking tape

Engineer It! Student Handout
(Page 1 of 2)

Name: _____   Team Name: _____

Project/Activity: _____

Step 1:   Define   State the problem (what are you trying to do?):

Step 2:   Learn   What solutions can you and your team imagine? What did you learn from your research?

Step 3:   Plan   Make a sketch of your design here and label materials. How will you divide work among team members?

Step 4:   Try   Build it! Did everyone on your team have a chance to help?

Engineer It! Student Handout
(Page 2 of 2)

Name: _____   **Team Name:** _____

Step 5:   Try   Record the results of your test here. How did it work? Could it work better?

Step 6:   Try   This is your chance to use your test results to decide what changes to make. What would you change to make your boat work better?

Step 7:   **Share your design!** What features of your design will you point out to the class?

         NATIONAL SCIENCE TEACHING ASSOCIATION

Figure 4.1. Engineering Design Process

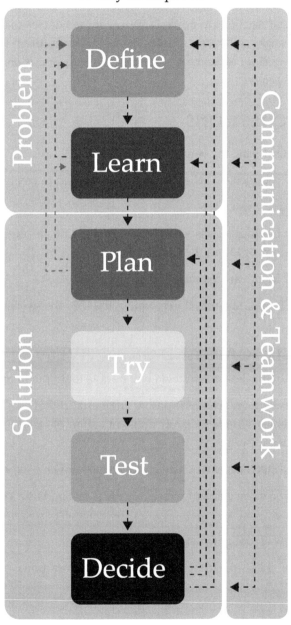

Lesson Plan 2:
From Fossils to Fuels

In this lesson, students will learn about the combustion of fossil fuels. Students will investigate the structure of straight-chain hydrocarbons and will apply their understanding of chemical reactions to power a Hero's engine device in a design challenge. Students will investigate oil from its biological formation through its use in passenger vehicles and will consider oil scarcity and energy in transportation from a geographic and historical perspective.

ESSENTIAL QUESTIONS

- What happens during the combustion of gasoline?

- How can the products of a chemical reaction be used to create motion?

- How is gasoline created?

- What are the byproducts associated with combusting gasoline and what are their effects on people and the environment?

- What energy inputs are necessary to produce gasoline?

- What is OPEC and how was it involved in the U.S. energy crisis in the 1970s?

ESTABLISHED GOALS AND OBJECTIVES

At the conclusion of this lesson, students will be able to do the following:

- Explain that chemical reactions power engines and that most modern passenger vehicles in the U.S. rely on combustion of fossil fuel (gasoline) to power engines

- Identify the difference between an endothermic and an exothermic reaction

- Identify carbon as an element critical for life forms and as a key element of fossil fuels

- Create models of straight-chain hydrocarbons

- Identify several uses of simple straight-chain hydrocarbons

- Apply their understanding of chemical reactions to create and power a Hero's engine type device

- Explain the processes by which oil is created in the earth

- Identify energy costs associated with producing and transporting gasoline

NATIONAL SCIENCE TEACHING ASSOCIATION

- Identify environmental impacts associated with producing and transporting gasoline

- Identify benefits, disadvantages, and costs of using gasoline as a fuel source for automobiles

- Identify causes of the 1970s energy crisis in the U.S.

TIME REQUIRED

6 days (approximately 45 minutes each day; see Tables 3.6–3.7, pp. 43–44)

MATERIALS

Required Materials for Lesson 2

- STEM Research Notebooks

- computer with internet access for viewing videos

Additional Materials for Making Hydrocarbons activity (for each pair of students)

- 1 small box of raisins (about 20 raisins)

- 20 mini marshmallows

- 25 toothpicks

- 8 red jelly beans or gumdrops

Additional Materials for Heal-Free Hero's Engine Activity (per team of 3–4 students)

- 2 8 ounce plastic cups (clear)

- 1 tablespoon vinegar

- 1 tablespoon baking soda

- thermometer

- watch or timer

- safety glasses (1 per student)

- disposable non-latex gloves (1 per student)

Additional Materials for Be a Hero! Design Challenge (for each team of 3–4 students)

- plastic film canister

- 3 seltzer tablets

- thread

The Speed of Green, Grade 8

- wire coat hanger

- 5″ × 5″ Styrofoam block

- masking tape

- rubber band

- water

- plastic cup for water

- plastic container or bowl for waste

- safety glasses (1 per student)

- disposable non-latex gloves (1 per student)

- Optional: Access to device to make holes in plastic

Additional Materials for Fossils to Fuels Timeline (for each team of 3–4 students unless otherwise noted)

- masking tape (1 roll for class)

- 1 piece of colored 8½″ × 11″ paper

- set of markers

- scissors

Additional Materials for Boyles Law & Charles Law demonstrations (Optional – 1 per class):

- 4 non-latex balloons

- ruler

- ice bath

- 6 large books (to make two stacks each approximately eight inches tall)

SAFETY NOTES

1. Caution students not to eat any materials used for activities.

2. Students should use caution when handling scissors or other pointed objects, as the sharp points and blades can cut or puncture skin.

3. Remind students that personal protective equipment (safety glasses or goggles, aprons, and gloves) must be worn during the setup, hands-on, and takedown segments of the Heat-Free Hero's Engine activity and the Be a Hero! design challenge.

4. Caution students to take care in using glass thermometers as glass can break and cut or puncture skin.

5. Caution students not to eat seltzer tablets.

6. Immediately wipe up any spilled water or other liquids on the floor to avoid a slip-and-fall hazard.

7. Tell students to use care when bending wire hangers to avoid puncturing skin.

CONTENT STANDARDS AND KEY VOCABULARY

Table 4.4 lists the content standards from the *NGSS, CCSS*, and the Framework for 21st Century Learning that this lesson addresses, and Table 4.5 presents the key vocabulary. Vocabulary terms are provided for both teacher and student use. Teachers may choose to introduce some or all of the terms to students.

Table 4.4 Content Standards Addressed in STEM Road Map Module Lesson 2

NEXT GENERATION SCIENCE STANDARDS
PERFORMANCE OBJECTIVES

- MS-PS1–2. Analyze and interpret data on the properties of substances before and after the substances interact to determine if a chemical reaction has occurred.

- MS-PS1–3. Gather and make sense of information to describe that synthetic materials come from natural resources and impact society.

- MS-PS2–2. Plan an investigation to provide evidence that the change in an object's motion depends on the sum of the forces on the object and the mass of the object.

- MS-PS3–2. Develop a model to describe that when the arrangement of objects interacting at a distance changes, different amounts of potential energy are stored in the system.

- MS-PS3–5. Construct, use, and present arguments to support the claim that when the kinetic energy of an object changes, energy is transferred to or from the object.

- MS-ETS1–1. Define the criteria and constraints of a design problem with sufficient precision to ensure a successful conclusion, taking into account relevant scientific principles and potential impacts on people and the natural environment that may limit possible solutions.

- MS-ETS1–2. Evaluate competing design solutions using a systematic process to determine how well they meet the criteria and constraints of the problem.

Continued

Table 4.4. *(continued)*

- MS-ETS1–3. Analyze data from tests to determine similarities and differences among several design solutions to identify the best characteristics of each that can be combined into a new solution to better meet the criteria for success.

SCIENCE AND ENGINEERING PRACTICES
Developing and Using Models
- Develop and use a model to describe phenomena.

Obtaining, Evaluating, and Communicating Information
- Gather, read, and synthesize information from multiple appropriate sources and assess the credibility, accuracy, and possible bias of each publication and methods used, and describe how they are supported or not supported by evidence.

Analyzing and Interpreting Data
- Analyze and interpret data to determine similarities and differences in findings.

Constructing Explanations and Designing Solutions
- Undertake a design project, engaging in the design cycle, to construct and/or implement a solution that meets specific design criteria and constraints.
- Apply scientific ideas or principles to design an object, tool, process or system.

Planning and Carrying Out Investigations
- Plan an investigation individually and collaboratively, and in the design: identify independent and dependent variables and controls, what tools are needed to do the gathering, how measurements will be recorded, and how many data are needed to support a claim.
- Conduct an investigation and evaluate the experimental design to produce data to serve as the basis for evidence that can meet the goals of the investigation.

Engaging in Argument from Evidence
- Construct and present oral and written arguments supported by empirical evidence and scientific reasoning to support or refute an explanation or a model for a phenomenon or a solution to a problem.

DISCIPLINARY CORE IDEAS
PS1.A: *Structure and Properties of Matter*
- Substances are made from different types of atoms, which combine with one another in various ways. Atoms form molecules that range in size from two to thousands of atoms.
- Each pure substance has characteristic physical and chemical properties (for any bulk quantity under given conditions) that can be used to identify it.

- Gases and liquids are made of molecules or inert atoms that are moving about relative to each other.

- The changes of state that occur with variations in temperature or pressure can be described and predicted using these models of matter.

PS1.B: *Chemical Reactions*

- Substances react chemically in characteristic ways. In a chemical process, the atoms that make up the original substances are regrouped into different molecules, and these new substances have different properties from those of the reactants.

PS3.A: *Definitions of Energy*

- Temperature is not a measure of energy; the relationship between the temperature and the total energy of a system depends on the types, states, and amounts of matter present.

- Motion energy is properly called kinetic energy; it is proportional to the mass of the moving object and grows with the square of its speed.

- A system of objects may also contain stored (potential) energy, depending on their relative positions.

PS3.B: *Conservation of Energy and Energy Transfer*

- When the motion energy of an object changes, there is inevitably some other change in energy at the same time.

- The amount of energy transfer needed to change the temperature of a matter sample by a given amount depends on the nature of the matter, the size of the sample, and the environment.

- Energy is spontaneously transferred out of hotter regions or objects and into colder ones.

PS3.C: *Relationship Between Energy and Forces*

- When two objects interact, each one exerts a force on the other that can cause energy to be transferred to or from the object.

ESS3.A: *Natural Resources*

- Humans depend on Earth's land, ocean, atmosphere, and biosphere for many different resources. Minerals, fresh water, and biosphere resources are limited, and many are not renewable or replaceable over human lifetimes. These resources are distributed unevenly around the planet as a result of past geologic processes.

ESS3.C: *Human Impacts on Earth Systems*

- Typically as human populations and per-capita consumption of natural resources increase, so do the negative impacts on Earth unless the activities and technologies involved are engineered otherwise.

Continued

Table 4.4. *(continued)*

ETS1.A: *Defining and Delimiting Engineering Problems*

- The more precisely a design task's criteria and constraints can be defined, the more likely it is that the designed solution will be successful. Specification of constraints includes consideration of scientific principles and other relevant knowledge that is likely to limit possible solutions.

ETS1.B: *Developing Possible Solutions*

- A solution needs to be tested, and then modified on the basis of the test results in order to improve it.

ETS1.C: *Optimizing the Design Solution*

- Although one design may not perform the best across all tests, identifying the characteristics of the design that performed the best in each test can provide useful information for the redesign process – that is, some of the characteristics may be incorporated into the new design.

- The iterative process of testing the most promising solutions and modifying what is proposed on the basis of the test results leads to greater refinement and ultimately to an optimal solution.

CROSS-CUTTING CONCEPTS
Patterns

- Macroscopic patterns are related to the nature of microscopic and atomic-level structure.

Scale, Proportion, and Quantity

- Time, space, and energy phenomena can be observed at various scales using models to study systems that are too large or too small.

Systems and System Models

- Models can be used to represent systems and their interactions—such as inputs, processes and outputs—and energy and matter flows within systems.

Energy and Matter

- The transfer of energy can be tracked as energy flows through a designed or natural system.

- Energy may take different forms (e.g. energy in fields, thermal energy, energy of motion).

Cause and Effect

- Cause and effect relationships may be used to predict phenomena in natural or designed systems.

COMMON CORE STATE STANDARDS FOR MATHEMATICS
MATHEMATICAL PRACTICES

- MP 1. Make sense of problems and persevere in solving them.

- MP 2. Reason abstractly and quantitatively.

- MP 3. Construct viable arguments and critique the reasoning of others.

- MP 4. Model with mathematics.

- MP 5. Use appropriate tools strategically.

COMMON CORE STATE STANDARDS FOR ENGLISH LANGUAGE ARTS
READING STANDARDS

- RL.8.1. Cite the textual evidence that most strongly supports an analysis of what the text says explicitly as well as inferences drawn from the text.

- RL.8.9. Analyze a case in which two or more texts provide conflicting information on the same topic and identify where the texts disagree on matters of fact or interpretation.

WRITING STANDARDS

- W.8.3. Write narratives to develop real or imagined experiences or events using effective technique, relevant descriptive details, and well-structured event sequences.

- W.8.3.A. Engage and orient the reader by establishing a context and point of view and introducing a narrator and/or characters; organize an event sequence that unfolds naturally and logically.

- W.8.3.D. Use precise words and phrases, relevant descriptive details, and sensory language to capture the action and convey experiences and events.

- W.8.7. Conduct short research projects to answer a question (including a self-generated question), drawing on several sources and generating additional related, focused questions that allow for multiple avenues of exploration.

- W.8.8. Gather relevant information from multiple print and digital sources, using search terms effectively; assess the credibility and accuracy of each source; and quote or paraphrase the data and conclusions of others while avoiding plagiarism and following a standard format for citation.

- W.8.9. Draw evidence from literary or informational texts to support analysis, reflection, and research

SPEAKING AND LISTENING STANDARDS

- SL.8.1. Engage effectively in a range of collaborative discussions (one-on-one, in groups, and teacher-led) with diverse partners on grade 8 topics, texts, and issues, building on others' ideas and expressing their own clearly.

- SL.8.1.A. Come to discussions prepared, having read or researched material under study; explicitly draw on that preparation by referring to evidence on the topic, text, or issue to probe and reflect on ideas under discussion.

- SL.8.1.B. Follow rules for collegial discussions and decision-making, track progress toward specific goals and deadlines, and define individual roles as needed.

Continued

Table 4.4. (*continued*)

- SL.8.1.C. Pose questions that connect the ideas of several speakers and respond to others' questions and comments with relevant evidence, observations, and ideas.

- SL.8.1.D. Acknowledge new information expressed by others, and, when warranted, qualify or justify their own views in light of the evidence presented.

- SL.8.2. Analyze the purpose of information presented in diverse media and formats (for example, visually, quantitatively, orally) and evaluate the motives (for example, social, commercial, political) behind its presentation.

- SL.8.4. Present claims and findings, emphasizing salient points in a focused, coherent manner with relevant evidence, sound valid reasoning, and well-chosen details; use appropriate eye contact, adequate volume, and clear pronunciation.

FRAMEWORK FOR 21ST CENTURY LEARNING

Interdisciplinary themes (financial, economic, & business literacy; environmental literacy); Learning and Innovation Skills; Information, Media & Technology Skills; Life and Career Skills

Table 4.5. Key Vocabulary in Lesson 2

Key Vocabulary	Definition
chemical reaction	when two or more substances (reactants) interact to create different substances (products)
combustion	a chemical reaction that produces heat and light
endothermic reaction	a chemical reaction that absorbs energy from the surrounding environment and results in a drop in temperature
ethanol	a fuel made from vegetation such as sugar cane, potatoes, or corn
exothermic reaction	a chemical reaction that releases energy in the form of heat, light, electricity, or sound
fuel	a substance that releases usable energy through a chemical reaction
gasoline	a fuel made from crude oil and other petroleum liquids
hydrocarbons	compounds made of hydrogen and carbon; the main components of petroleum and natural gas that produce heat when burned
internal combustion engine	an engine in which a fuel reacts with air in a combustion reaction to produce mechanical energy
life cycle analysis	a "cradle to grave" study of materials that helps to weigh the pros and cons of using the materials

Key Vocabulary	Definition
octane rating	a measure of the performance of fuel; higher octane ratings indicate that the fuel can withstand more compression before igniting
oil	a liquid made from petroleum
Otto cycle	the cycle involved in the four-stroke combustion cycle in engines
petroleum	a liquid mixture of hydrocarbons found deep below Earth's surface; it can be extracted and refined to produce fuels such as gasoline, kerosene, and diesel oil
pressure	a measure of the force that molecules exert on the surfaces surrounding them; force per unit area
primary source of information	an artifact or information created at the time an event happened by people directly involved with the event
product (of chemical reaction)	the new substance resulting from a chemical reaction
reactant	the atoms and molecules that interact in a chemical reaction
secondary source	an artifact or information created by a person who did not participate in an event directly
viscosity	a property of liquids indicating how fast they flow; how thick a liquid is
volume	the amount of space occupied by a liquid, solid, or gas

TEACHER BACKGROUND INFORMATION

This lesson focuses on combustion reactions and the life cycle of fossil fuels. An optional component of this lesson is a discussion of gas pressure and gas volume and therefore Charles's Law and Boyle's Law will also be discussed in this section.

Combustion Reactions

In chemical reactions, atoms and molecules (reactants) interact with each other to create new substances (products). This change in substance is caused by bonds breaking in the reactants and the atoms rearranging to form new bonds to create the products. Students should have a basic understanding of atoms, molecules, and elements in the periodic table before undertaking this lesson.

Fuel-powered engines use combustion reactions. A combustion reaction occurs when fuel reacts quickly with oxygen. A complete combustion reaction produces carbon dioxide and water vapor as well as heat and light. Since these reactions produce heat, they are known as exothermic reactions. The generalized reaction can be expressed as: Fuel + $O_2 \rightarrow CO_2 + H_2O$

Many common items that combust, including vehicle fuels such as gasoline and natural gas, contain hydrocarbons, compounds that contain only the elements carbon (C) and hydrogen (H). Octane is a major component of gasoline used in everyday vehicles (note that the gasoline used to power cars is a complex mixture of hundreds of different hydrocarbons and the blend of hydrocarbons can be adjusted to accommodate altitude and season). When a heat source is applied, octane reacts with oxygen in the following reaction:

$$2C_8H_{18} + 25O_2 \longrightarrow 16CO_2 + 18H_2O$$

Ethanol is the primary hydrocarbon in race car fuel (and most vehicle gasoline is 10% ethanol, resulting in the name "gasohol"). The chemical reaction for the combustion of ethanol is:

$$C_2H_5OH + 3O_2 \longrightarrow 2CO_2 + 3H_2O$$

You may choose to share these chemical equations with students, or you may choose to use the reaction of methane and oxygen as a simpler example of an equation for the combustion of a fossil fuel:

$$CH_4 + 2O_2 \longrightarrow CO_2 + 2H_2O$$

Most common internal combustion automobile engines can be described as Otto cycle, or four-cycle, engines. The steps below provide a simple outline of the internal combustion cycle (for an example of how pistons in a combustion cycle work, see www.energyeducation.ca/encyclopedia/Piston):

1. Air and gasoline enter the engine (the reactants).

2. The engine compresses the air and gasoline mixture to increase the energy that will be produced in the reaction.

3. A spark plug ignites the compressed air and gasoline mixture, causing a combustion reaction in the form of an explosion. This explosion forces down the engine's piston, which turns a crankshaft. The crankshaft then rotates a transmission, which rotates the wheels of the vehicle. The continued repetition of this cycle is what moves the vehicle down the road.

4. The byproducts (carbon dioxide and carbon monoxide*) are released as exhaust.
    *If pure gasoline vapor is burned with a hot flame and ample oxygen, nearly pure carbon dioxide and water are the products of combustion. In reality,

the gasoline combustion is incomplete and pressure inside the car's cylinder results in various combinations of nitrogen and oxygen. Additionally, impurities in the gas, including sulfur, react to form additional byproducts.

Life Cycle Analysis

In this lesson, student teams will conduct a life cycle analysis (LCA) of gasoline as a fuel for vehicles by creating a timeline of gasoline from its formation through its use to power vehicles. This framework will be used throughout the module to assess the impact of various energy sources. The life cycle analysis framework accounts for energy production, distribution, and use and recognizes the various points where energy inputs are required, along with environmental impacts of production, distribution, and use.

LCA is a tool used by governmental agencies, businesses, researchers, and energy producers to gain an understanding of the full range of environmental effects of various products. The LCA framework for this module will take a "cradle to grave" approach, accounting for the various steps of energy production from resource formation to extraction, refinement, transportation, delivery to consumer, and use. Resources are provided within the lesson to scaffold student understanding of this process and to create a framework in which energy sources can be compared with one another based on their respective LCAs. Conducting accurate energy analyses requires information and mathematical skills that are complex beyond the scope of middle school curriculum, and therefore the focus will be on a qualitative understanding that fuels not only produce energy, but also have a variety of energy and environmental costs associated with their production. More information about life cycle assessments of energy sources is available at www.worldenergy.org/wp-content/uploads/2012/10/PUB_Comparison_of_Energy_Systens_using_lifecy cle_2004_WEC.pdf.

Charles's Law and Boyle's Law

An option for this lesson is to introduce students to the concepts of gas pressure and gas volume using gas laws (Charles's Law and Boyle's Law). This will be a very cursory overview of the kinetic theory of gases from a qualitative perspective and provides a general background for an understanding of the ideal gas law (a combination of Charles's Law and Boyle's Law):

$PV = nRT$ where P=pressure; V=volume; n= moles of gas; R=ideal gas constant; and T=temperature

The ideal gas law explains the relationship between pressure and temperature in gases and will be introduced to students in high school chemistry. If you would like

more background on the ideal gas law, visit www.khanacademy.org/science/chem istry/gases-and-kinetic-molecular-theory/ideal-gas-laws/v/ideal-gas-equation-pv-nrt. The University of Colorado's PhET interactive simulations site (https://phet.colo rado.edu) provides online simulations of gas laws that may be useful to help students visualize concepts.

In order to understand Charles's Law and Boyle's Law, students will need to understand the difference between gas volume and gas pressure. This may be a difficult distinction for some students to make. Students should understand that a gas is composed of gas molecules that are in constant motion. Volume refers to the amount of space these molecules occupy, and pressure refers to the force with which the molecules strike the walls of the surrounding container.

Pressure is caused by gas molecules hitting the walls of the container. With a smaller volume, the gas molecules will hit the walls more frequently, and so the pressure increases. Boyles Law states: *For a fixed mass of gas at constant temperature, the volume is inversely proportional to the pressure.* Using a balloon as an example, students will see that when the volume is reduced (by squeezing the balloon) the pressure increases until the balloon pops.

Charles's Law relates the temperature of a gas to volume. Since gases are molecules in motion, adding heat to a gas causes the molecules to move faster and therefore to occupy more space. Charles's Law states: *For a fixed mass of gas at constant pressure, the volume is directly proportional to the kelvin temperature.*

Know, Learned, Evidence, Wonder, Scientific Principle (KLEWS) Charts

You may wish to use Know, Learned, Evidence, Wonder, Scientific Principle (KLEWS) charts throughout this module. These charts are used to access and assess student prior knowledge, encourage students to think critically about the topic under discussion, and track student learning throughout the module. Using KLEWS charts challenges students to connect evidence and scientific principles with their learning. The topic should be listed at the top of each chart, and the chart should consist of five columns – one for each KLEWS component. It may be helpful to create class charts and post these charts in a prominent place in the classroom so that students can refer to them throughout the module. For more information about KLEWS charts, see the NSTA Books and Resources article "Evidence Helps the KLW get a KLEW" at www.nsta.org/journals/science-and-children/science-and-children-february-2006/methods-and-strategies-evidence.

COMMON MISCONCEPTIONS

Students will have various types of prior knowledge about the concepts introduced in this lesson. Table 4.6 describes a common misconception students may have

Table 4.6. Common Misconception About the Concepts in Lesson 2

Topic	Student Misconception	Explanation
Oil and gasoline	Pollution related to oil and gasoline spills comes only from oil spills from tankers and other large-scale events.	While large-scale spills such the 1989 Exxon Valdez oil spill can cause devastating effects to the environment, consumer-based activities also result in releases of oil and gasoline into the environment. For example, the Environmental Protection Agency estimates that 200 million gallons of oil are released into the environment each year through improper disposal of oil in automobile oil changes (www.nationalgeographic.com/science/article/110601-green-motor-oil-recycling). In addition, gasoline is spilled when consumers overfill or improperly fill automobile or boat gas tanks and when improperly maintained cars leak oil and gasoline.

concerning these concepts. Because of the breadth of students' experiences, it is not possible to anticipate every misconception that students may bring as they approach this lesson. Incorrect or inaccurate prior understanding of concepts can influence student learning in the future, however, so it is important to be alert to misconceptions such as those presented in the table.

PREPARATION FOR LESSON 2

Review the teacher background information provided, assemble the materials for the lesson, duplicate student handouts, and preview videos included within the Learning Components.

Students will investigate and discuss the 1970s U.S. energy crisis in this lesson. To prepare for discussions, review the historical events surrounding the crisis. For information, see www.history.state.gov/milestones/1969-1976/oil-embargo.

Students will participate in a team design challenge to create a version of a Hero's engine powered by carbon dioxide (see Design Challenge: Be a Hero! activity at the end of this lesson plan). Students should use the EDP (Engineer It! handouts are provided at the end of Lesson 1) and the understanding of the chemical reaction that they gain from a preliminary lab activity, Heat-Free Hero's Engine (activity handouts are attached at the end of this lesson plan). Students may have multiple solutions to this challenge; however, the key is to cause the film canister to spin. This requires that the canister have holes in it and that it be suspended in such a way that it can turn freely. You may pre-drill holes in the sides of the canisters or provide the means for students to create their own holes (a nail and a hammer or a drill).

For the Fossils to Fuels Timeline activity, identify a large open space on a wall (about 5–7 feet). Place a picture of the sun at the beginning of the space and a picture of the sun and sky at the end. Students will work in teams of three to four students each for this activity; these teams should continue to work together throughout the remainder of the module.

For a science, social studies, and mathematics connection during the Elaboration/ Application of Knowledge phase of the lesson, students will explore reasons for fluctuations in gasoline prices. Links to sample articles are provided within the lesson; however, these will not reflect the most current economic conditions, and it is recommended that you identify some current articles relating to gasoline prices.

LEARNING COMPONENTS
Introductory Activity/Engagement

Connection to the Challenge: Begin each day of this lesson by directing students' attention to the module challenge, the Speed of Green Challenge. Remind students that they will work in teams to create plans for ways to minimize the environmental impact of powering a race car. Hold a brief class discussion each day of how students' learning in the previous days' lessons contributed to their ability to complete the challenge. You may wish to create a class list of key ideas on chart paper.

Science Social Studies Classes and Mathematics Connection: Show students a video about how an engine works such as "Science Please: The Internal Combustion Engine" at www.youtube.com/watch?v=5tN6eynMMNw. After viewing the video, ask students to share their understanding of how an engine works. Next, show the video again; ask students to identify where chemical reactions take place.

Explain to students that chemical reactions take place whenever two or more substances interact to form new substances. Introduce the concept of hydrocarbons as compounds that are made entirely of hydrogen and carbon and are the main component of fuels including petroleum and natural gas because they release large amounts of heat when burned.

Explain to students that all life forms are carbon based and that there is an entire branch of chemistry, organic chemistry, that focuses on the study of carbon. Ask students for their ideas about the connection between life forms being carbon based and fuels being carbon based. Tell students that fuels such as gasoline and natural gas were once living organisms.

Next, distribute the Fuel Figures Activity (attached at the end of this lesson plan) to each student. Give students 5 minutes to match the numbers to the facts. Review answers as a group, discussing each fact.

Ask students to consider if they think that motorsports can be "green" (i.e., use renewable instead of non-renewable energy sources). Remind them of the Leilani

Münter video from Lesson 1. Tell students that innovations in passenger cars often start in the motorsports industry because new technologies are often developed much more quickly in motorsports than in other vehicle product development.

In 2008, the American Le Mans series held its first "Green Challenge" that awarded scores for fuel type, speed, and efficiency. Show the video about the Michelin Green X Challenge at the American Le Mans series at www.youtube.com/watch?v=YA2alyO1lSM. Ask students to consider why developing alternatives to gasoline might be important (e.g., gasoline is a finite resource, the U.S. may not be able to produce enough for its own needs, pollution).

Social Studies Class and ELA Connection: Introduce students to the 1970s oil crisis by reviewing an overview of the crisis on a website such as the National Museum of American History "Energy Crisis" page at www.americanhistory.si.edu/american-enterprise-exhibition/consumer-era/energy-crisis. Next, as a class read aloud President Jimmy Carter's Crisis of Confidence Speech from July 15, 1979 (can be accessed at www.1977energycrisis.weebly.com/primary-sources.html). Have students work in teams of three to four to compare and contrast the two sources, creating a list of similarities and differences between the two. Have student teams share their ideas with the class. Introduce the terms *primary source of information* and *secondary source of information* and ask students to classify each of the above sources as either primary or secondary.

Activity/Exploration

Science Class: Ask students to share what they know about carbon. Answers may include:

- All living things contain carbon.

- Carbon compounds make good fuels.

- There are many different compounds that contain carbon.

Tell students that carbon is unique in its ability to bond to other carbon atoms, and it can form long chains and rings. This results in some very complex compounds, like DNA, which can contain tens of billions of carbon atoms.

Display a periodic table and ask students to identify where carbon is on the table. Next, ask students to identify how many electrons carbon has (six). Tell students that of these six electrons, two are in an inner shell (closer to the nucleus) and four are in the outer shell, also known as its valence shell.

Explain to students that carbon atoms can form four bonds because it has four valence electrons (its outermost layer of electrons). Atoms are most stable when they have eight valence electrons (the octet rule), so they will form bonds (or share electrons) with other atoms in order to have eight valence electrons. Since students will be

working with hydrocarbons, they need only know that carbon forms four bonds to be stable in hydrocarbons and that carbons will bond to each other in straight lines and in rings. In the following activity, students will make models of simple straight-chain hydrocarbons.

Making Hydrocarbons Activity

Have students work in pairs for this activity. Distribute the Making Hydrocarbons student handout to each student and a set of materials to each student pair. Have students follow directions to create hydrocarbon models.

Next, students will experience a simple chemical reaction and observe its effects in preparation for a design challenge (the Be a Hero! Design Challenge). The Heat-Free Hero's Engine activity will provide an example of the type of reaction they will use in their design challenge and serves as a preliminary activity for the design challenge. Heat-Free Hero's Engine student handouts are attached at the end of this lesson plan.

Heat-Free Hero's Engine Activity

Students should work in teams of three to four to complete the Heat-Free Hero's Engine activity.

Distribute a Heat-Free Hero's Engine student handout to each student and a set of materials to each team.

Tell students that they will have a chance to create a chemical reaction in class. Ask if they think they will use hydrocarbons and why or why not. Tell students that reactions involving hydrocarbons are known as combustion reactions, meaning that they can create large amounts of heat and are therefore not safe in the classroom. Use the combustion graphic (attached at the end of this lesson) to illustrate what happens in such reactions. Introduce the term *exothermic* to describe reactions that release heat.

Explain to students that they will create their own engine using a chemical reaction, but that the reaction they will use does not create heat; instead, it is an endothermic reaction. Ask students what they think endothermic means (a reaction that uses up heat instead of creating it during a reaction). Students will observe the temperature change that occurs during the chemical reaction:

$$NaHCO_3 + HC_2H_3O_2 \rightarrow NaC_2H_3O_2 + H_2O + CO_2$$

Making these observations will help students understand that heat is not the cause for the engine movement in the design challenge where they will create a CO_2 powered "engine" using the EDP (see Explanation section).

Science and Social Studies Classes and Mathematics Connection: Students will create a timeline for fossil fuels extending from their formation in the earth to their use and associated emissions into the atmosphere.

Fossils to Fuels Timeline

Distribute the Fossils to Fuels student handout to each student. Students should work together in their teams for this activity. Assign each team one of the following research questions:

1. How is oil formed in the earth?

2. How is oil removed from the earth?

3. Refining oil: what is that and how is it done?

4. From the refinery to your car: How does gasoline get to the gas station and how is it used in your car?

5. Emissions from your car: What does gasoline produce after it is burned and what effects does this have on the environment?

Instruct students to investigate their topic online. The following websites may be useful to them:

- www.eia.gov/kids

- www.need.org/need-students/energy-information-resources/

- www.energy.gov/sites/prod/files/2013/04/f0/MS_Oil_Studyguide_draft1.pdf

After students have completed their research, each team should attach a picture or graphic to the timeline, placing it chronologically relative to other teams' entries.

Next, ask students to indicate each place on the timeline where energy is consumed (e.g., steps of the refining process, transporting fuel). Attach an energy input arrow (attached at the end of this lesson) at each point where students indicate that energy is used. Tell students that for each gallon of gasoline produced, a certain amount of energy is used.

Explain the concept of life cycle analyses to students (see Teacher Background section, p. 87). You can introduce the concept of net energy production to your students at this point if you wish. This can be conceptualized as the amount of energy available from the end product minus the energy used to produce the product. Tell students that gasoline has about an 81% efficiency of output relative to the energy required to produce it. This would mean that it takes about 19 BTUs from outside energy sources to create gasoline with energy of 100 BTUs (100–19 =81).] Alternatively, to simplify, you could say that producing each 100 gallons of gasoline uses energy inputs equal to the number of arrows on your timeline.

Next, ask students if anything comes out of the system along the way (e.g., pollutants). Have students indicate where pollutants or byproducts might be released or

where there is a possibility for other environmental impacts. Use the environmental impact markers (attached at the end of this lesson plan) to indicate where students identify environmental impacts. Count the number of environmental impact symbols and summarize the findings form this life cycle analysis. For example, for every 100 gallons of gas produced, 12 outside energy inputs are needed, and there are 9 environmental impacts.

Tell students that they will evaluate other fuels in a similar way during this module and then introduce the Energy Source STEM Research Notebook Entry student handouts (attached at the end of this lesson plan). Tell students that they will complete one of these for each fuel source discussed during the module. Tell students that their Fossils to Fuels Timeline serves as the LCA for gasoline. Have students complete an Energy Source STEM Research Notebook Entry for gasoline.

ELA Connection: As a homework assignment, have students conduct an interview with a parent, relative, or other adult about the 1973 oil crisis. Tell students that their goal is to understand how the oil crisis affected individuals. To prepare for this, students should each create an interview guide to elicit information about the oil crisis. For example, students may ask questions about the crisis such as:

- What are your memories of the oil crisis?

- How did the oil crisis affect your family?

- How did the oil crisis affect your community?

- What were your fears about the oil crisis?

- Do you think this could happen again? Why or why not?

Students should also ask questions that provide information about life in the 1970s versus life now. For example,

- What kind of car did you or your family drive then?

- How were cars different then than now?

- What are some of the major differences you see in the way you lived in the 1970s as compared to the way a person the same age lives now?

Explanation

Science Class: Students will apply their learning from the Heat-Free Hero's Engine activity to explain their observations in the Be a Hero! Design Challenge.

Be a Hero! Design Challenge

Tell students that they will work in teams to create a Hero's engine type device, using what they learned about chemical reactions in the Heat-Free Hero's Engine activity. Review the steps of the EDP with students. Distribute the Be a Hero! Design Challenge handouts and an Engineer It! handout (attached at the end of the Lesson 1 lesson plan) to each student. Review the information about the Hero's engine provided on the student handout and the challenge rules. Distribute a set of materials to each team and have each team work together to create a Hero's engine using the materials provided.

Social Studies Class and ELA Connection: Show students a map of the world and identify the nations that are currently members of OPEC (see the OPEC website for a current list of member countries: www.opec.org/opec_web/en/about_us/25.htm).

Have students use the results of the interview they conducted to write a narrative essay about the oil crisis from the perspective of the person they interviewed.

Mathematics Connection: Have students create a graphical representation of their life cycle analysis for gasoline to represent net energy production (a bar graph or pie chart may be useful for this – the following graphing tool may be useful: www.nces.ed.gov/nceskids/graphing/classic/bar.asp).

Elaboration/Application of Knowledge

Science Class (Optional): An option for this lesson is to introduce Charles's Law and Boyle's Law using the procedure described in the following paragraphs.

Place two stacks of books (each about eight inches tall) parallel to each other, leaving about ten inches between the stack. Blow up a balloon and place it between two stacks of books; adjust the stacks of books so that the balloon's sides just touch the sides of the books. Measure the distance between the books and record this measurement. Next, place the balloon in an ice bath and tell students that you are going to leave it there for a few minutes to see what happens.

While the balloon cools, ask students to explain what happened in their Hero's engine devices. Ask them what came out of the film can (they should be able to conclude that this was a gas – review states of matter if necessary). Ask students to explain why the gas didn't stay inside the container like the liquid did. Lead students to understand that gases are composed of molecules in motion and that they increased the volume of gas in the film container.

Blow up another balloon as a demonstration. Ask students what made the balloon grow larger. Lead students to an understanding that gas molecules are in constant motion and therefore collide with each other and the surfaces around them. By blowing up the balloon, you added gas molecules. Point out to students that particles also move in solids and liquids, but that the extent to which they move is different (i.e., in gases, particles move freely in all directions; in liquids, particles vibrate and slide past each other; in solids, particles vibrate but generally do not move from one place to another).

Ask students if they saw any evidence of pressure in their Hero's engines. Ask students what happened (a gas was created and gas pressure escaped through the holes).

Ask students if they think that temperature has any influence on gas volume, or the amount of space the gas molecules take up. Ask students to hypothesize whether the ice bath balloon will be larger, smaller, or the same size than it was initially. Remove the balloon and place it between the stacks of books. Ask students to observe whether the balloon still touches the books like it did when it was at room temperature. Move the books so that they touch the sides of the balloon and measure the new distance. Explain to students that this is an example of Charles's Law. Charles's law says that the volume of a fixed amount of gas will vary in direct proportion to the temperature. Ask them what happened to the gas particles in the balloon when it was chilled (they move more slowly and therefore hit the walls of the balloon less often and do not push it out as far as they did at room temperature). Ask students what will happen when the balloon returns to room temperature (it will return to its original size) and what would happen if you heated the balloon to an even higher temperature (it would expand).

Ask students to consider other examples of gas volume and temperature. Prompt them to consider what happens to car tires in the winter (they begin to appear more "flat"). How about in the summer (they appear more "full"). Ask students what this has to do with volume (the air molecules are moving less in the cold and therefore taking up less space). Ask students if they know how air in tires is measured (tire pressure). Lead students to a definition of gas pressure as the force that moving molecules put on the surrounding container. Ask them if they think that the volume and pressure are related.

Use one of the inflated balloons and ask students if it is possible to change the pressure inside the balloon. How? Lead students to understand that if you decrease the size of the balloon by squeezing part of it, you increase the pressure of the gas molecules against the walls of the balloon. Ask students what happens to the volume (amount of space the gas occupies) when you put pressure on the balloon (it decreases). Gas pressure will cause the balloon to pop when you reduce the size of the balloon enough. Lead students to understand that as volume decreases, pressure increases. This is Boyle's Law, which says that there is an inverse relationship between volume and pressure.

Science and Social Studies Classes and Mathematics Connection: Discuss the phenomenon of fluctuating gasoline prices and why prices fluctuate on a daily basis for this product but not for other consumer products. Show students a graph of gasoline prices such as that found at www.gasbuddy.com/gb_retail_price_chart.aspx. Ask students to share their ideas about why gasoline prices fluctuate, creating a class list of students' ideas.

Assign each student team one of the articles you identified (see Teacher Preparation, p. 90) or one of the following articles or websites to explore to find reasons for gasoline price fluctuations:

- www.npr.org/2015/02/19/387539924/as-oil-prices-tank-firms-large-and-small-feel-the-pain

- www.eia.gov/tools/faqs/faq.cfm?id=1&t=10

- www.auto.howstuffworks.com/fuel-efficiency/fuel-consumption/gas-price.htm

After teams have reviewed their assigned resources, have each team report to the class what they learned about gasoline price fluctuations, creating a class list.

Social Studies Class and ELA Connection: Have students synthesize the information from their interviews and their research to create a response to the prompt below in their STEM Research Notebooks. Remind students that their use of language is important since they are trying to convince residents not to panic while providing them with factual information and realistic suggestions about actions they can take.

STEM Research Notebook Prompt

It is November 1973. As mayor of Happytown, U.S.A., you are concerned about the confusion and panic that is resulting from gasoline shortages and the long lines at local gas stations. People are angry and frightened and some of them even think it is your fault. Your job is to explain the gasoline shortage to the town's residents and tell them how they can best conserve gasoline. You have 5 minutes to speak on the local radio station to provide residents with information.

Evaluation/Assessment

Students may be assessed on the following performance tasks and other measures listed.

Performance Tasks

- Fuel Figures handout

- Making Hydrocarbons activity handout

- Heat-Free Hero's Engine activity handout

- Be a Hero! Design Challenge

- Engineer It! – Be a Hero! handouts

- Fossils to Fuels Timeline

- Energy Source STEM Research Notebook entry for gasoline

Other Measures

- Teacher observations

- Collaboration (See rubric in Appendix A)

INTERNET RESOURCES

"Evidence Helps the KLW get a KLEW"

- *www.nsta.org/journals/science-and-children/science-and-children-february-2006/ methods-and-strategies-evidence*

Graphing tool

- *www.nces.ed.gov/nceskids/graphing/classic/bar.asp*

Green oil recycling

- *www.nationalgeographic.com/science/article/110601-green-motor-oil-recycling*

Life cycle analyses of energy sources

- *www.worldenergy.org/wp-content/uploads/2012/10/PUB_Comparison_of_Energy_ Systens_using_lifecycle_2004_WEC.pdf*

Ideal gas laws

- *www.khanacademy.org/science/chemistry/gases-and-kinetic-molecular-theory/ideal-gas-laws/v/ideal-gas-equation-pv-nrt*

Michelin Green X Challenge at the American Le Mans series video

- *www.youtube.com/watch?v=YA2alyO1lSM*

National Museum of American History "Energy Crisis"

- *www.americanhistory.si.edu/american-enterprise-exhibition/consumer-era/energy-crisis*

OPEC

- *www.opec.org/opec_web/en/about_us/25.htm*

Oil embargo information

- *www.history.state.gov/milestones/1969-1976/oil-embargo*

PhET Simulations

- *https://phet.colorado.edu*

Pistons

- *www.energyeducation.ca/encyclopedia/Piston*

President Jimmy Carter's Crisis of Confidence Speech, July 15, 1979

- *www.1977energycrisis.weebly.com/primary-sources.html*

Resources about oil

- *www.eia.gov/kids*

- *www.need.org/need-students/energy-information-resources/*

- *www.energy.gov/sites/prod/files/2013/04/f0/MS_Oil_Studyguide_draft1.pdf*

Resources for gasoline price fluctuations

- *www.fuelfix.com/blog/2015/02/19/three-more-oil-service-firms-cutting-hundreds-of-jobs-wages/*

- *www.npr.org/2015/02/19/387539924/as-oil-prices-tank-firms-large-and-small-feel-the-pain*

- *www.eia.gov/tools/faqs/faq.cfm?id=1&t=10*

- *www.auto.howstuffworks.com/fuel-efficiency/fuel-consumption/gas-price.htm*

"Science Please: The Internal Combustion Engine" video

- *www.youtube.com/watch?v=5tN6eynMMNw*

Fuel Figures Student Handout

Name: _____

Match the numbers in the bank below to the gasoline facts. Use each number only once.

1. Number of gallons of gasoline used per day in 2021 _____

2. Percentage of motor gasoline consumed in the U.S. that is ethanol, a biofuel additive _____

3. Number of light duty vehicles (cars, SUVs, and small trucks) in use in the U.S. _____

4. Average fuel economy – miles per gallon of gas – of light duty vehicles in the U.S. _____

5. Percentage of energy used in the U.S. that comes from petroleum _____

6. Percentage of petroleum consumed in the U.S. that comes from other countries _____

7. Pounds of carbon dioxide produced from burning 1 gallon of gasoline _____

8. Percentage of U.S. petroleum consumption that is in the transportation sector _____

9. Gallons of fuel an Indy Car race car uses per lap (2 ½ miles) at the Indianapolis Motor Speedway _____

10. Gallons of fuel put into an Indy Car race car in an average pit stop _____

11. Percent of gasoline in each gallon of fuel used in an Indy Car race car _____

75	1.3
0	21.5
33	1.3
369 million	10
36	210 million
40	19.6

NATIONAL SCIENCE TEACHING ASSOCIATION

FUEL FIGURES ANSWER KEY

1. Number of gallons of gasoline used per day in 2021 (369 million). This is more than one gallon per person every day.

2. Percentage of motor gasoline consumed in the U.S. that is ethanol, a biofuel additive (10)

3. Number of light duty vehicles (cars, SUVs, and small trucks) in use in the U.S. (210 million)

4. Average fuel economy – miles per gallon of gas – of light duty vehicles in the U.S. (21.5)

5. Percentage of energy used in the U.S. that comes from petroleum (36)

6. Percentage of petroleum consumed in the U.S. that comes from other countries (33)

7. Pounds of carbon dioxide produced from burning 1 gallon of gasoline (19.6)

8. Percentage of U.S. petroleum consumption that is in the transportation sector (75)

9. Gallons of fuel an Indy Car uses per lap (2 ½ miles) at the Indianapolis Motor Speedway (1.3)

10. Gallons of fuel put into an Indy Car in an average pit stop (40)

11. Percent of gasoline in each gallon of fuel used in an Indy Car (0) Indy Cars run on pure methanol, or wood alcohol

Making Hydrocarbons Student Handout
(Page 1 of 3)

In this activity, you and a partner will create models of hydrocarbons, chemical compounds that are made of only hydrogen and carbon. These compounds compose the fuels we use in our everyday life. Keep in mind that carbon forms FOUR bonds and carbons can bond with each other!

Materials

1 box raisins (carbon atoms)
20 mini marshmallows (hydrogen atoms)
25 toothpicks (bonds)
8 red jelly beans or gumdrops (oxygen)

Procedure

1. Read each chemical formula on page 3.

2. Build a model of the compound using the materials provided.

3. After you have completed your model, draw the structure (see the example on page 2).

4. After you have completed your structures, fill in the "I am . . ." column for each, using the Hydrocarbon Use choices below.

5. Now, rebuild your methane model.

6. Build two oxygen molecules (O_2); these will each be two red candies connected with a toothpick

7. Now build the products ($CO_2 + 2H_2O$) for this reaction:

    $CH_4 + 2O_2 \longrightarrow CO_2 + 2H_2O$

    Will this reaction happen if methane is exposed to air (which contains O_2)? _____

    What else would you need to add for this reaction to happen? _____

NATIONAL SCIENCE TEACHING ASSOCIATION

Making Hydrocarbons Student Handout
(page 2 of 3)

Hydrocarbon Uses (Match these uses with the hydrocarbons in the table):

a) A component of gasoline; its name became popular in the mid-1960s when fuel companies began advertising high levels of it in their gasoline.

b) A popular choice for grills and home heating.

c) The main component of natural gas and released from cows as part of their digestive process.

d) A component of gasoline.

e) Used in fuel for lighters, as an ingredient of gasoline, and as a propellant in aerosol sprays like deodorant.

f) The second-largest component of natural gas; used to produce ethylene in the chemical industry.

Making Hydrocarbons Student Handout
(Page 3 of 3)

Name: _____

Hydrocarbon Name	Chemical Formula	Chemical Structure	I am . . . .
Decane	$C_{10}H_{22}$		
Methane	CH_4		
Ethane	C_2H_6		
Propane	C_3H_8		
Butane	C_4H_{10}		
Octane	C_8H_{18}		

Heat-Free Hero's Engine Student Handout
(Page 1 of 3)

A Greek mathematician and engineer named Hero is credited with describing the first steam engine, known as Hero's Engine. This early engine connected a pan of water to a ball with pipes coming out of it. The water was boiled and the steam entered the ball, exiting through the pipes and causing the ball to spin. You will be challenged to create a Hero's engine without a heat source. Instead, you will use a chemical reaction between a seltzer tablet and water to power your engine.

Source: NASA Gallery (Public domain). Retrieved from https://images.nasa.gov/details-9513982

This activity is an introduction to the design challenge where you will explore the type of chemical reaction you will use in the challenge.

Seltzer tablets contain an acid and baking soda; when you add this to water it creates a chemical reaction that is very similar to what happens when baking soda (sodium bicarbonate) and vinegar (acetic acid) react. In order to understand the reaction that will power your engine, you will first observe the reaction between baking soda and vinegar. This reaction can be expressed as:

$$NaHCO_3 + HC_2H_3O_2 \rightarrow NaC_2H_3O_2 + H_2O + CO_2$$

or

Sodium bicarbonate + acetic acid → sodium acetate + water + carbon dioxide

Materials:

2 small cups (clear)
1 tablespoon vinegar
1 tablespoon baking soda
Thermometer
Watch or timer

Heat-Free Hero's Engine Student Handout
(Page 2 of 3)

Procedure:

1. Designate one person to read the temperature, one person to record the temperature,* and one persons to be timekeeper.

2. Pour 1 tablespoon of vinegar into a clear plastic cup.

3. Place a thermometer in the vinegar. Record the temperature under Time 0.

4. While the thermometer is in the cup, add ½ teaspoon of baking soda to the vinegar.

5. Read the temperature on the thermometer every 15 seconds.

6. Record your observations about what you see happening in the cup.

*Be sure to record the units for your temperature measurement. Are you measuring temperature in degrees Fahrenheit or degrees Celsius?

4

Heat-Free Hero's Engine Student Handout
(Page 3 of 3)

Name: _____

Time Elapsed (seconds)	0	15	30	45	60	75
Temperature (F or C)						

What did you observe when the baking soda was added to the vinegar?

_____

_____

What was the overall temperature change in the cup?

_____

_____

How is this reaction different than boiling water?

_____

_____

How is this reaction similar to boiling water?

_____

_____

How could this reaction power a Hero's engine?

_____

_____

Design Challenge: Be a Hero! Student Handout

Your design team will create an engine similar to a Hero's engine. Remember that a working engine creates energy that moves parts like the crankshaft in a car. A Hero's engine has a rotating part.

Your team will use the EDP and the following materials to create a Hero's engine powered by a chemical reaction very similar to the reaction between baking soda and vinegar you created in the last activity.

Materials:

Plastic film canister
3 seltzer tablets
Thread
Wire coat hanger
5" × 5" Styrofoam block
Masking tape
Rubber band
Water
Option: Access to device to make holes in plastic

Rules:

1. Each team member must track the team's use of the EDP on their own handout (remember, the lab activity with baking soda and vinegar was part of your background research!)

2. The engine must create rotation

3. The rotation may not be initiated by a person (it must be powered by a chemical reaction)

From Fossils to Fuels Timeline Student Handout
(Page 1 of 2)

Name: _____ Team Name: _____

You and your team are going to dig into one of the topics below. Follow your teacher's directions for deciding which topic you will investigate, and then use this guide to help you create a timeline entry for your topic.

- How is oil formed in the earth?

- How is oil removed from the earth?

- Refining oil – what is that and how is it done?

- From the refinery to your car: How does gas get to the gas station and how is it used in your car?

- Emissions from your car: What does gas produce after it is burned and what affect does this have on the environment?

Write your team's question here:

_____

Your team's goals are to:

1. Answer your team's question.

2. Create a picture or graphic representing the process you are describing.

3. Complete your Fossils to Fuels Timeline handout (each team member completes one).

3. Present your answer to the class.

Remember that you are working as a team. Think about what each team member should do. For instance, who will create the picture? Who will present the information to the class? Make sure that everyone on your team participates!

Brainstorm and Research: What do you already know about this topic?

Where did you go to find more information? If you used websites, books, or articles record your sources here:

From Fossils to Fuels Timeline Student Handout
(Page 2 of 2)

Name: _____   Team Name: _____

Write down what you think are the five most important facts you found:

Write the answer to your team's question in no more than four sentences in this space:

On a blank sheet of paper, draw a picture or create a graphic that represents your team's answer to the question.

Fossils to Fuels Timeline Energy Input Arrows

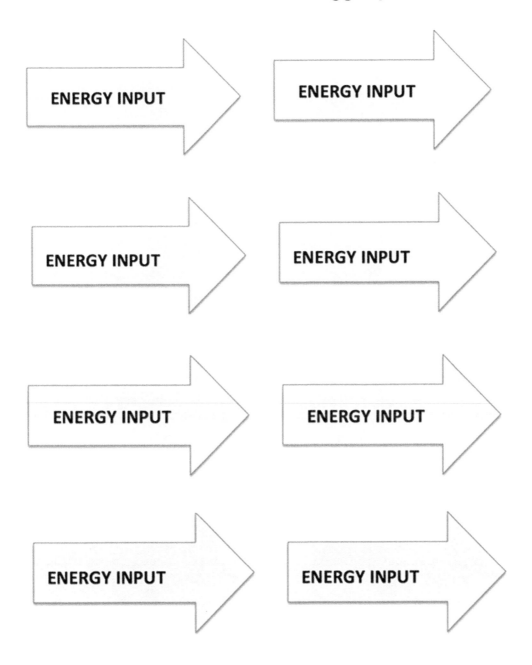

Fossils to Fuels Timeline Environmental Impact Markers

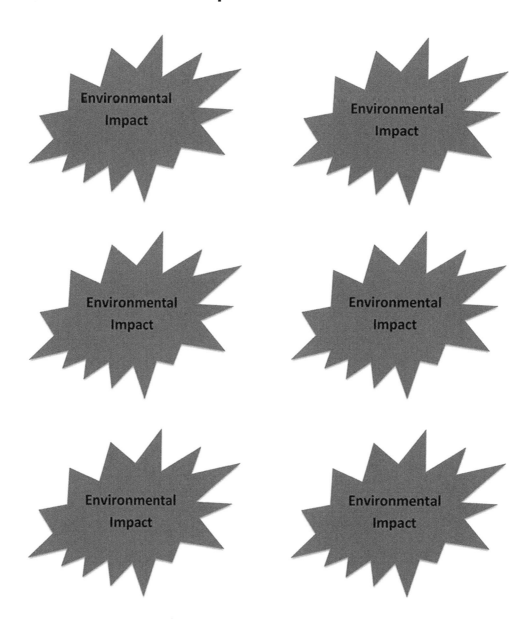

Energy Source STEM Research Notebook Entry Student Handout

(Page 1 of 2)

Name: _____   Primary Energy Source: _____

Pros & Cons	
Advantages to using this source to power a race car:	**Disadvantages to using this source to power a race car:**

This Energy Source is (circle one):   Renewable   Non-Renewable

Average price per unit:

$_____ /_____

Energy Source STEM Research Notebook
Entry Student Handout
(Page 2 of 2)

What technologies are necessary to use this fuel in racing?

Record any other thoughts here:

Combustion Graphic

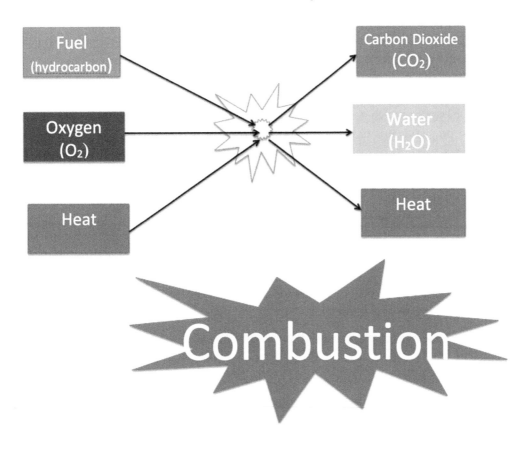

Lesson Plan 3:
Gas, Naturally

This lesson focuses on the use of natural gas as fuel for vehicles. Students will participate in an interactive demonstration of the greenhouse effect as an introduction to the atmospheric processes associated with fossil fuels. Students will participate in an inquiry activity in which they will use decomposing organic material to mimic the conditions under which natural gas is created. Student teams will investigate the history and pros and cons of using natural gas for vehicle fuel and will create LCAs for natural gas.

ESSENTIAL QUESTIONS

- How is natural gas created?

- How is natural gas used to fuel vehicles?

- What is the greenhouse effect?

- What energy inputs and environmental impacts are associated with using natural gas to power vehicles?

- What chemical reaction is used to create biofuels?

ESTABLISHED GOALS AND OBJECTIVES

At the conclusion of this lesson, students will be able to do the following:

- Identify natural gas as a fossil fuel

- Explain how natural gas is formed

- Explain how natural gas can be used to power vehicles

- Analyze the implications of using natural gas as a power source for vehicles

- Demonstrate a conceptual understanding of the greenhouse effect

- Simulate the creation of natural gas

TIME REQUIRED

- 3 days (approximately 45 minutes each day; see Table 3.7, p. 44)

MATERIALS

Required Materials for Lesson 3

- STEM Research Notebooks

- computer with internet access for viewing videos
- stick-on nametags (1 per student)

Additional Materials for Gas It Up! (for each group of 2–3 students unless otherwise indicated)

- 3 small-necked glass bottles
- 3 large non-latex balloons
- 1 funnel
- 3 cups soil
- 1½ cups of a mixture of fruit/vegetable scraps
- 1 gallon-size Zipper-seal plastic bag
- duct tape
- permanent marker
- ruler
- safety glasses (1 per student)
- disposable non-latex gloves (1 per student)

Additional Materials for Life Cycle Analysis of Natural Gas (for each team of 3–4 students)

- 1 set of markers
- scissors
- tape or glue
- 1 piece of 22"×28" poster board (optional, see Preparation for Lesson 3, p. 125)
- 6 pieces of colored paper (optional, see Preparation for Lesson 3, p. 125)

SAFETY NOTES

1. Caution students not to eat any materials used for activities.

2. Students should use caution when handling scissors, as the sharp points and blades can cut or puncture skin.

3. Remind students that personal protective equipment (safety glasses or goggles, aprons, and gloves) must be worn during the setup, hands-on, and takedown segments of the Gas It Up! activity.

4. Caution students to take care in handling glass bottles as glass can break and cut or puncture skin.

5. Immediately wipe up any spilled water or soil on the floor to avoid a slip-and-fall hazard.

CONTENT STANDARDS AND KEY VOCABULARY

Table 4.7 lists the content standards from the *NGSS*, *CCSS*, and the *Framework for 21st Century Learning* that this lesson addresses, and Table 4.8 presents the key vocabulary. Vocabulary terms are provided for both teacher and student use. Teachers may choose to introduce some or all of the terms to students.

Table 4.7. Content Standards Addressed in STEM Road Map Module Lesson 3

NEXT GENERATION SCIENCE STANDARDS
PERFORMANCE OBJECTIVES

- MS-PS1–2. Analyze and interpret data on the properties of substances before and after the substances interact to determine if a chemical reaction has occurred.

- MS-PS1–3. Gather and make sense of information to describe that synthetic materials come from natural resources and impact society.

- MS-PS3–5. Construct, use, and present arguments to support the claim that when the kinetic energy of an object changes, energy is transferred to or from the object.

SCIENCE AND ENGINEERING PRACTICES
Developing and Using Models

- Develop and use a model to describe phenomena.

Obtaining, Evaluating, and Communicating Information

- Gather, read, and synthesize information from multiple appropriate sources and assess the credibility, accuracy, and possible bias of each publication and methods used, and describe how they are supported or not supported by evidence.

Analyzing and Interpreting Data

- Analyze and interpret data to determine similarities and differences in findings.

Constructing Explanations and Designing Solutions

- Undertake a design project, engaging in the design cycle, to construct and/or implement a solution that meets specific design criteria and constraints.

- Apply scientific ideas or principles to design an object, tool, process or system.

Planning and Carrying Out Investigations

- Plan an investigation individually and collaboratively, and in the design: identify independent and dependent variables and controls, what tools are needed to do the gathering, how measurements will be recorded, and how many data are needed to support a claim.

- Conduct an investigation and evaluate the experimental design to produce data to serve as the basis for evidence that can meet the goals of the investigation.

Engaging in Argument from Evidence

- Construct and present oral and written arguments supported by empirical evidence and scientific reasoning to support or refute an explanation or a model for a phenomenon or a solution to a problem.

DISCIPLINARY CORE IDEAS

PS1.A: *Structure and Properties of Matter*

- Substances are made from different types of atoms, which combine with one another in various ways. Atoms form molecules that range in size from two to thousands of atoms.

- Each pure substance has characteristic physical and chemical properties (for any bulk quantity under given conditions) that can be used to identify it.

- Gases and liquids are made of molecules or inert atoms that are moving about relative to each other.

- The changes of state that occur with variations in temperature or pressure can be described and predicted using these models of matter.

PS1.B: *Chemical Reactions*

- Substances react chemically in characteristic ways. In a chemical process, the atoms that make up the original substances are regrouped into different molecules, and these new substances have different properties from those of the reactants.

PS3.B: *Conservation of Energy and Energy Transfer*

- When the motion energy of an object changes, there is inevitably some other change in energy at the same time.

- The amount of energy transfer needed to change the temperature of a matter sample by a given amount depends on the nature of the matter, the size of the sample, and the environment.

- Energy is spontaneously transferred out of hotter regions or objects and into colder ones.

ESS3.A: *Natural Resources*

- Humans depend on Earth's land, ocean, atmosphere, and biosphere for many different resources. Minerals, fresh water, and biosphere resources are limited, and many are not renewable or replaceable over human lifetimes. These resources are distributed unevenly around the planet as a result of past geologic processes.

Continued

Table 4.7. (*continued*)

ESS3.C: *Human Impacts on Earth Systems*
- Typically as human populations and per-capita consumption of natural resources increase, so do the negative impacts on Earth unless the activities and technologies involved are engineered otherwise.

CROSS-CUTTING CONCEPTS
Patterns
- Macroscopic patterns are related to the nature of microscopic and atomic-level structure.

Scale, Proportion, and Quantity
- Time, space, and energy phenomena can be observed at various scales using models to study systems that are too large or too small.

Systems and System Models
- Models can be used to represent systems and their interactions—such as inputs, processes and outputs—and energy and matter flows within systems.

Energy and Matter
- The transfer of energy can be tracked as energy flows through a designed or natural system.
- Energy may take different forms (e.g. energy in fields, thermal energy, energy of motion).

Cause and Effect
- Cause and effect relationships may be used to predict phenomena in natural or designed systems.

Stability and Change
- Explanations of stability and change in natural or designed systems can be constructed by examining the changes over time and forces at different scales.

Structure and Function
- Structures can be designed to serve particular functions by taking into account properties of different materials, and how materials can be shaped and used.

COMMON CORE STATE STANDARDS FOR MATHEMATICS
MATHEMATICAL PRACTICES
- MP 1. Make sense of problems and persevere in solving them.
- MP 2. Reason abstractly and quantitatively.
- MP 3. Construct viable arguments and critique the reasoning of others.
- MP 4. Model with mathematics.
- MP 5. Use appropriate tools strategically.

MATHEMATICAL CONTENT

- 8.F.B.4. Construct a function to model a linear relationship between two quantities. Determine the rate of change and initial value of the function from a description of a relationship or from two (x, y) values, including reading these from a table or from a graph. Interpret the rate of change and initial value of a linear function in terms of the situation it models, and in terms of its graph or a table of values.

- 8.F.B.5. Describe qualitatively the functional relationship between two quantities by analyzing a graph (for example, where the function is increasing or decreasing, linear or nonlinear). Sketch a graph that exhibits the qualitative features of a function that has been described verbally.

COMMON CORE STATE STANDARDS FOR ENGLISH LANGUAGE ARTS
READING STANDARDS

- RL.8.1. Cite the textual evidence that most strongly supports an analysis of what the text says explicitly as well as inferences drawn from the text.

- RL.8.9. Analyze a case in which two or more texts provide conflicting information on the same topic and identify where the texts disagree on matters of fact or interpretation.

WRITING STANDARDS

- W.8.1. Write arguments to support claims with clear reasons and relevant evidence.

- W.8.1.A. Introduce claim(s), acknowledge and distinguish the claim(s) from alternate or opposing claims, and organize the reasons and evidence logically.

- W.8.1.B. Support claim(s) with logical reasoning and relevant evidence, using accurate, credible sources and demonstrating an understanding of the topic or text.

- W.8.1.C. Use words, phrases, and clauses to create cohesion and clarify the relationships among claim(s), counterclaims, reasons, and evidence.

- W.8.1.E. Provide a concluding statement or section that follows from and supports the argument presented.

- W.8.2. Write informative/explanatory texts to examine a topic and convey ideas, concepts, and information through the selection, organization, and analysis of relevant content.

- W.8.2.A. Introduce a topic clearly, previewing what is to follow; organize ideas, concepts, and information into broader categories; include formatting (for example, headings), graphics (for example, charts, tables), and multimedia when useful to aiding comprehension.

- W.8.2.B. Develop the topic with relevant, well-chosen facts, definitions, concrete details, quotations, or other information and examples.

- W.8.2.C. Use appropriate and varied transitions to create cohesion and clarify the relationships among ideas and concepts.

- W.8.2.D. Use precise language and domain-specific vocabulary to inform about or explain the topic.

Continued

Table 4.7. *(continued)*

- W.8.3. Write narratives to develop real or imagined experiences or events using effective technique, relevant descriptive details, and well-structured event sequences.

- W.8.3.A. Engage and orient the reader by establishing a context and point of view and introducing a narrator and/or characters; organize an event sequence that unfolds naturally and logically.

- W.8.3.D. Use precise words and phrases, relevant descriptive details, and sensory language to capture the action and convey experiences and events.

- W.8.7. Conduct short research projects to answer a question (including a self-generated question), drawing on several sources and generating additional related, focused questions that allow for multiple avenues of exploration.

- W.8.8. Gather relevant information from multiple print and digital sources, using search terms effectively; assess the credibility and accuracy of each source; and quote or paraphrase the data and conclusions of others while avoiding plagiarism and following a standard format for citation.

- W.8.9. Draw evidence from literary or informational texts to support analysis, reflection, and research.

SPEAKING AND LISTENING STANDARDS

- SL.8.1 Engage effectively in a range of collaborative discussions (one-on-one, in groups, and teacher-led) with diverse partners on grade 8 topics, texts, and issues, building on others' ideas and expressing their own clearly.

- SL.8.1.A. Come to discussions prepared, having read or researched material under study; explicitly draw on that preparation by referring to evidence on the topic, text, or issue to probe and reflect on ideas under discussion.

- SL.8.1.B. Follow rules for collegial discussions and decision-making, track progress toward specific goals and deadlines, and define individual roles as needed.

- SL.8.1.C. Pose questions that connect the ideas of several speakers and respond to others' questions and comments with relevant evidence, observations, and ideas.

- SL.8.1.D. Acknowledge new information expressed by others, and, when warranted, qualify or justify their own views in light of the evidence presented.

- SL.8.2. Analyze the purpose of information presented in diverse media and formats (for example, visually, quantitatively, orally) and evaluate the motives (for example, social, commercial, political) behind its presentation.

- SL.8.4. Present claims and findings, emphasizing salient points in a focused, coherent manner with relevant evidence, sound valid reasoning, and well-chosen details; use appropriate eye contact, adequate volume, and clear pronunciation.

FRAMEWORK FOR 21ST CENTURY LEARNING

Interdisciplinary themes (financial, economic, & business literacy; environmental literacy); Learning and Innovation Skills; Information, Media & Technology Skills; Life and Career Skills

Table 4.8. Key Vocabulary in Lesson 3

Key Vocabulary	Definition
archaea	microbes that cannot live in the presence of oxygen and are responsible for methanogenesis
carbon footprint	the amount of greenhouse gas emissions caused by an individual, group, organization, or event
compressed natural gas	methane stored at high pressure that can be used in place of gasoline, diesel fuel, or propane
global warming	the term used to describe a gradual increase in the average temperature of Earth's atmosphere and oceans over time
greenhouse effect	the process in which heat from Earth's surface is absorbed by atmospheric gases and re-radiated to the Earth
greenhouse gas	gas that traps heat in Earth's atmosphere including water vapor, carbon dioxide, methane, nitrous oxide, and ozone
liquefied natural gas	natural gas that has been converted to liquid form for storage or transport
methane	a hydrocarbon that is the primary component of natural gas
methanogenesis	the formation of methane by methanogens
methanogens	microbes that produce methane as a byproduct of metabolism; also known as archaea
microbes	microscopic organisms
natural gas	a fossil fuel formed when buried plants, gases, and animal remains are exposed to heat and pressure over thousands of years
renewable natural gas	a biogas (methane) obtained from biomass

TEACHER BACKGROUND INFORMATION

This lesson introduces natural gas as a potential fuel source for vehicles.

Natural Gas

Natural gas is a mixture of hydrocarbons composed primarily of methane (CH_4) that, as of 2021, supplied about 38% of the energy used in the United States, although only about 3% of this was used for transportation fuel (see www.eia.gov/energyexplained/natural-gas/use-of-natural-gas.php for the most current data). In 2021, natural gas was used to power about 175,000 vehicles in the U.S. and about 23 million around the world. The majority of natural gas used in the U.S. is produced domestically and most

is drawn from wells or extracted during crude oil production. The U.S. Department of Energy Alternative Fuels Data Center provides information on natural gas at www.afdc.energy.gov/vehicles/natural_gas.html. The data provided about natural gas use in this lesson is from this site and from the Energy Information Administration website, www.eia.gov/kids/energy.cfm?page=natural_gas_home-basics.

Hydraulic fracturing, commonly known as fracking, is a process by which natural gas is mined by fracturing subsurface rock with a hydraulically pressurized liquid. The process of fracking has been a source of contention in recent years because of the need to transport large quantities of water, the toxicity of some chemicals used in fracking fluid, the potential for surface water and soil contamination, and the potential for earthquakes in areas where fracking is conducted. For more information on the debate over fracking and environmental concerns, see the following resources:

- www.nytimes.com/2013/03/14/opinion/global/the-facts-on-fracking.html

- www.sierraclub.org/policy/energy/fracking

Because of the gaseous state of natural gas, it must be either compressed or liquefied for use in vehicles. Compressed natural gas (CNG) is stored in highly pressurized cylinders (3,000 to 3,600 pounds per square inch). CNG-powered vehicles typically have fuel economy similar to that of gasoline-powered vehicles. Liquefied natural gas (LNG) is produced when natural gas is purified and cooled to extremely cold temperatures (-260°F). LNG is denser than CNG and therefore provides a longer range of operation because more volume can be stored in a tank. The tanks, however, must be double-walled and vacuum insulated in order to maintain the cold temperatures and are typically used in medium and heavy-duty vehicles such as trucks.

Fuel economy and range are important considerations for using natural gas in passenger vehicles because of the relatively limited availability of CNG and LNG fueling stations. In 2022 there were 872 CNG fueling stations and 59 LNG fueling stations in the U.S. and Canada (www.afdc.energy.gov/fuels/natural_gas_locations.html).

For a comprehensive discussion of the pros and cons of using natural gas as vehicle fuel, see the U.S. Department of Energy's publication "Issues affecting adoption of natural gas fuel in light- and heavy-duty vehicles" (Whyatt, 2010) at www.energy.gov/sites/default/files/2022-10/Chapter_14-Natural_Gas.pdf.

The benefits of natural gas include potential savings in fuel costs (see the U.S. Department of Energy Alternative Fuels Data Center at www.afdc.energy.gov/data), reduction in foreign oil imports, and reduced vehicle emissions (Whyatt, 2010). Challenges to using natural gas as a vehicle fuel include the cost of vehicles, competition from hybrid vehicles, the limited selection of vehicles, the limited fueling infrastructure, and the space requirements for CNG fuel storage relative to gasoline (Whyatt, 2010).

COMMON MISCONCEPTIONS

Students will have various types of prior knowledge about the concepts introduced in this lesson. Table 4.9 describes a common misconception students may have concerning these concepts. Because of the breadth of students' experiences, it is not possible to anticipate every misconception that students may bring as they approach this lesson. Incorrect or inaccurate prior understanding of concepts can influence student learning in the future, however, so it is important to be alert to misconceptions such as those presented in the table.

Table 4.9. Common Misconception About the Concepts in Lesson 3

Topic	Student Misconception	Explanation
Natural gas	Natural gas has a bad odor.	Natural gas has no odor; gas distribution companies add a substance (mercaptan) to gas so that gas leaks are detectable.

PREPARATION FOR LESSON 3

Review the teacher background information provided, assemble the materials for the lesson, duplicate student handouts, and preview videos included within the Learning Components.

The Gas It Up! activity requires fruit and vegetable scraps that should be assembled ahead of time (about 1½ cups for each group of 2–3 students). You may wish to work with your school's cafeteria to collect these. Students will need to collect data approximately every second day for seven days; plan for time for students to collect data (observe and measure their balloons) and to complete the activity on or around the seventh day after you begin it.

Identify a current news article about natural gas fracking that highlights the public debate about this practice in terms of its environmental implications.

Be prepared with an open space in which to conduct the Greenpeople Effect activity. This activity requires students to line up on either side of an open area (with at least ten feet between students). Prepare stick-on nametags, ten labeled as "Heat" and the remainder as "Greenhouse Gas."

In Lesson 2, students used a timeline (the Fossils to Fuels Timeline activity) as the basis of their LCA for gasoline. For the remainder of this module, students will use a similar approach using the basic framework provided in the Life Cycle Analysis student handouts provided in this lesson. Students should work in teams to create an LCA for each type of energy source introduced in this lesson through Lesson 6 (they will create LCAs for natural gas, biofuel, biodiesel [optional], solar energy, and wind). You may wish to have teams create their final LCAs using the Life Cycle Analysis handouts

provided, or you may wish to have teams use these handouts as working drafts for LCAs that they create on pieces of poster board. If you choose the latter option, you should be prepared to provide each team with a piece of 22″×28″ white poster board and markers. For LCAs created on poster board you may wish to enlarge the energy input and environmental impact symbols (provided as part of the Life Cycle Analysis student handout). You may also wish to provide students with pieces of colored paper, scissors, and glue so that they can describe each step of the cycle on a piece of paper that they glue onto their posters. Choose which option you plan to have your students use and prepare materials accordingly.

If you have not already contacted individuals to act as fictional investors for students' final challenge, you may wish to do so now.

LEARNING COMPONENTS
Introductory Activity/Engagement

Connection to the Challenge: Begin each day of this lesson by directing students' attention to the module challenge, the Speed of Green Challenge. Remind students that they will work in teams to create plans for ways to minimize the environmental impact of powering a race car. Hold a brief class discussion each day of how students' learning in the previous days' lessons contributed to their ability to complete the challenge. You may wish to create a class list of key ideas on chart paper.

Science Class: Introduce the Pat Patrick racing natural gas initiative by showing a video such as "Patrick Racing Natural Gas Initiative – Racing Engine Powered By Natural Gas" at www.youtube.com/watch?v=ynXky7JefZI#t=14. Hold a class discussion, asking questions such as the following:

- The racing industry is a place where innovations for consumer cars are tried out; why do you think this is?

- What do you know about natural gas?

- Do you think that natural gas could be used for race cars? Why or why not?

Ask students what they remember about hydrocarbon reactions (they are combustion reactions). Tell students that natural gas is composed mostly of methane, CH_4, the simplest hydrocarbon they made in Lesson 1. Remind them of the model they made with raisins, marshmallows, and jelly beans in Lesson 1 (you may wish to have them repeat this) to demonstrate the following reaction:

$$CH_4 + 2O_2 \rightarrow CO_2 + 2H_2O + energy$$

Tell students that in 2021, natural gas was used to power about 175,000 vehicles in the U.S. and about 23 million around the world. Refer to the timeline students created in

Lesson 3 and ask students to point out if and where natural gas played a role in the development of transportation in the U.S.

Social Studies Class and ELA Connection: Share the news article you identified (see Teacher Preparation, p. 125) about the use of hydraulic fracturing (fracking) to extract natural gas. Have students read this article and hold a class discussion about the pros and cons of extracting natural gas using this method.

Mathematics Connection: Not applicable.

Activity/Exploration

Science Class and Mathematics Connection: Students will investigate natural gas as a transportation fuel and the greenhouse effect in the following activities:

- Life Cycle Analysis – natural gas

- Greenpeople Effect activity

- Gas It Up! investigation

Life Cycle Analysis – Natural Gas

To introduce the history and production of natural gas, show students a video about the source of natural gas such as "The History of Natural Gas" at www.youtube.com/watch?v=BXi14Dr0Cj4. As a class or in student teams, create a LCA of natural gas production and transportation similar to that used for the gasoline production timeline (see Life Cycle Analysis student handout attached at the end of this lesson plan). Use the energyiInput ane Environmentil Impact symbols to mark points in the production and transportation timeline that require energy inputs or have the potential for environmental impacts.

Ask students if they think that any gas escapes into the atmosphere during natural gas production. (Estimates are that 1% of the gas is lost as emissions while another 2.8% is burned in methane flares, and 4.2% is combusted in equipment [Skone et al., 2014]).

Ask students which they think has fewer emissions when burned – gasoline or methane. Remind them of the byproducts of gasoline discussed in Lesson 2 and review the methane combustion reaction equation. Tell students that natural gas is the cleanest burning fossil fuel. Gasoline is a much more complicated hydrocarbon and therefore has more byproducts than the relatively simple methane.

$$\text{Gasoline combustion: } 2\ C_8H_{18} + 25\ O_2 \rightarrow 16\ CO_2 + 18\ H_2O$$

$$\text{Natural gas combustion: } CH_4 + 2O_2 \rightarrow CO_2 + 2H_2O$$

Point out to students that even though natural gas has few byproducts when burned, it does release byproducts into the atmosphere. Ask students what is released into the atmosphere when gas (CH_4, or methane) is removed from the earth and used as fuel. Ask students if they have heard of greenhouse gases, and tell them that methane is one of the major greenhouse gases. Have students share their ideas about what the greenhouse effect is. Prompt students by asking them how a greenhouse is used to grow plants (it traps heat).

Explain to students that the greenhouse effect happens when certain gases collect in Earth's atmosphere. These gases allow the sun's light to shine onto Earth, but they trap the heat that is reflected back into the atmosphere. This is important because it allows Earth to be warm enough to sustain life; without the greenhouse effect scientists estimate that the average temperature of the Earth would drop from 57°F to −.4°F (you may wish to have students visit www.nationalgeographic.org/article/greenhouse-effect-our-planet to read more about the greenhouse effect). Point out to students that since the early 1800s people have been releasing large amounts of greenhouse gases into the atmosphere; however, scientists believe that these emissions are increasing the greenhouse effect, which results in increases in the Earth's temperature. Greenhouse gases include carbon dioxide, methane, nitrous oxide, fluorinated gases, and ozone.

Tell students that in spite of the fact that natural gas burns relatively cleanly compared to other fossil fuels, leaks can occur during its extraction and delivery that result in the release of carbon dioxide, a greenhouse gas that is one of the products of burning methane.

Greenpeople Effect

This interactive activity allows students to gain a conceptual understanding of the greenhouse effect and how chemicals interact in the atmosphere. Gather students in an area in which half the class can line up on either side of the area with at least ten feet of open space between the groups. Label one end of the room as "Sun" and the other as "Earth" (the middle of the room represents the atmosphere). Use the following procedure:

- Assign students roles by distributing stick-on nametags to 15 students: ten students wearing nametags labeled as "Heat" and five students wearing nametags labeled with "Greenhouse Gas" (the remaining students will become Greenhouse Gases in the second part of the activity).

- Have students labeled "Heat" line up on the Sun side of the room and students labeled with "Greenhouse Gas" on the Earth side of the room.

- Tell students that the sun produces heat that reaches the Earth, so the "Heat" students should walk toward the Earth side of the room.

- After the Heat students reach the Earth side of the room, have the Greenhouse Gas students move to the center of the room (Earth's atmosphere).

- Remind students that heat is reflected from the Earth's surface back into space, so the "Heat" students should begin to return back to the Sun side of the room; however, each Greenhouse Gas will "capture" one Heat student by standing side by side and remaining in the middle of the room.

- Have the remaining Heat students return to the Sun side of the room.

- Have the captured Heat students line up on the Earth side of the room and count them.

- Have students return to their original positions.

- Tell students that there is suddenly a large increase in the amount of greenhouse gases given off from the Earth; ask students for their ideas about why this might happen (for example, increase in numbers of cars, factories, natural gas leaks).

- Give the remaining students "Greenhouse Gas" nametags and have them stand on the Earth side of the room.

- Repeat the activity by having the Heat students move to the Earth side of the room.

- Have the newly increased number of Greenhouse Gas students move to the middle of the room (atmosphere).

- Tell the Heat students to move back to the Sun side of the room. The Greenhouse Gas students should each capture one Heat student.

- Now have the Heat students line up on the Earth side of the room and count how many Heat students are on the Earth side. Compare this number to the first count.

Tell students that this is scientists' understanding of how the greenhouse effect results in increasing global temperatures – by increasing the amount of heat that is trapped in the atmosphere.

Next, have students watch a video about the greenhouse effect such as "The Greenhouse Effect" produced by the Environmental Protection Agency at www.youtube.com/watch?v=VYMjSule0Bw. Show students the combustion reaction graphic from Lesson 2. Ask students what greenhouse gases are produced from combustion reactions (carbon dioxide and water).

NASA provides a "Climate Time Machine" web tool that you may wish to share with your students to illustrate the increase in the concentration of carbon dioxide in the atmosphere over time. See https://climate.nasa.gov/interactives/climate-time-machine.

Next, ask students if they can think of any other source of methane besides the methane that comes from deep within the Earth? Show students a video about methane emissions from farming such as "Cow Farts Blow Up a Barn" at www.youtube.com/watch?v=gpa8Oz9DRbY.

Ask students how they think that farmers might be able to capture that gas for energy production (it is sometimes captured from manure via large "digester" tanks) and if they think it would be possible to capture enough methane to run a car.

If students did not identify landfills as a source of methane, tell them that this is another source. Hold a class discussion about solid waste and methane, asking the following questions:

- How many pounds of trash do you think each person in the U.S. creates each day? (over 4 pounds as of 2022).

- What happens to trash in a landfill? (it decays)

- What do they think is produced as the trash decays? (gas)

- Is there a similarity between trash decaying and natural gas forming in below the Earth's surface? (Natural gas below the Earth is from decaying plants and animals; much of our trash is plant and animal matter).

Tell students that they are going to see what happens to decaying food in the Gas It Up! activity.

Gas It Up! Activity

Introduce the activity by telling students that they are going to produce methane. They will attempt to capture methane from decomposing plants and will determine what, if any, effect, the surrounding environment has on methane production.

Ask students for their ideas about what happens when food gets old. Introduce the concept of decomposition. Ask students what they think makes food decay or decompose. Lead students to an understanding that microscopic organisms, or microbes, cause food decomposition. In fact, it is microbes in the digestive systems of cows that produce the methane that cows release. The kind of microorganisms that cause methane to be produced are called methanogens and are a type of microbe called archaea. These microbes can resist extreme temperatures and function without oxygen.

Point out to students that they cannot see microbes without a microscope. Ask for their ideas about how they will be able to tell if the microbes are present (by the production of methane gas). After students have concluded that gas emission provides evidence of microbes doing their work, ask students for their ideas about how we can detect methane gas since it is not visible to the human eye (by capturing it in a way that it can be measured). Tell students that they will capture the gas in a balloon.

Ask students for their ideas about how they will know that gas is being produced (the balloon will inflate).

Next, ask students to make a hypothesis about what type of environmental conditions (for example, heat, cold, light, dark) would cause decomposing plant material to produce methane the quickest. Distribute the Gas It Up! student handouts to each student and have them record their predictions. Assemble students in teams of two to three and distribute a set of materials to each team. Working in their teams, students will have a chance to test their predictions over the next seven class periods.

Social Studies Class: Students will investigate the advantages and benefits of using natural gas to power vehicles in the Gas-Powered Cars activity.

Gas-Powered Cars

Ask students to think about what they have learned about gases (gases are made of molecules constantly in motion). Be sure to distinguish between the fuel gasoline and gases as air-like substances such as methane. Ask students for their ideas about how much space they think it would take to store enough natural gas to run a car. Explain that in order to store enough gas to allow the car to travel reasonable distances, natural gas is usually highly compressed when used in vehicles. This is called compressed natural gas (CNG). Explain that some vehicles use liquefied natural gas (LNG) that provides enough gas for longer distance travel (it takes up 1/600th the volume of natural gas), but that this requires the gas to be kept at extremely cold temperatures that requires special storage units.

Have student teams research the pros and cons of natural gas vehicles and choose one side or the other (pro or con) to represent; you may wish to assign teams a position in order to ensure that each side is represented equally. Distribute the presentation rubric (in Appendix A) to teams and review the requirements as a class. Each team should create a brief (two to three minute) presentation that incorporates some visual content (for example, students can draw pictures, print photographs or graphics from a website, or create a PowerPoint presentation).

ELA Connection: Have students create advertisements for natural gas cars. They will need to use persuasive and informational language for this task and should highlight the various benefits (for example, cost and environmental impact) of natural gas-powered vehicles. Have students choose a medium for this activity (for example, print ad, radio ad, TV commercial, website, or social media) and create an advertisement appropriate to this medium.

Explanation

Science Class: Students should continue to collect data for the Gas It Up! activity approximately every second day for seven days and complete the activity on or

around the seventh day. As a class, discuss students' observations at each observation and create a class chart of students' observations and the circumference of their balloons. Discuss whether or not students' predictions were accurate.

Have students create Energy Source STEM Research Notebook entries for natural gas using the handout from Lesson 2.

Social Studies Class: After the Gas-Powered Cars presentations, have the class vote about whether they think that expanding natural gas use in vehicles is a good idea. Have students identify the closest CNG fueling stations to the school and their homes (see www.afdc.energy.gov/fuels/natural_gas_locations.html for locations of CNG fueling stations in the U.S.). Based on the availability of fueling stations, ask students whether they think that a natural gas vehicle is a good idea for their families and how the availability of fueling stations might affect decisions on the use of natural gas-powered vehicles.

Mathematics Connection: Have students conduct calculations to compare the cost of fueling a gasoline-powered vehicle versus a natural gas-powered vehicle. Students should calculate fuel efficiency (for example, miles per gallon) for each type of vehicle and cost per mile. Current costs for gasoline and natural gas can be found on the EIA website (www.eia.gov). Students will need to understand that compressed natural gas is measured in gasoline gallon equivalents (GGE). One GGE produces the same amount of energy as one gallon of gasoline.

ELA Connection: Have students present the advertisements they created for natural gas-powered cars. Students should explain the benefits of natural gas-powered cars they emphasized and how this would appeal to consumers, what medium they created the advertisement for, and how they crafted their message to suit this medium.

Elaboration/Application of Knowledge

Science and Social Studies Classes: Hold a class discussion about the possible environmental effects of fracking to extract natural gas. Emphasize to students that one concern is an increased frequency of earthquakes in areas where natural gas is extracted using this method. Show students a map of areas where hydraulic fracturing is currently being used to extract natural gas (for example, the Inside Climate News page "Map: The Fracking Boom State by State" at https://insideclimatenews.org/news/20150120/map-fracking-boom-state-state).

As a class, look for evidence of recent earthquakes in these areas, using the United States Geological Survey's "Recent Earthquake Survey" tool at www.earthquaketrack.com/p/united-states/recent).

As an optional extension of students' exploration of the greenhouse effect, have students explore the greenhouse effect PhET simulation found at https://phet.colorado.edu/en/simulations/greenhouse-effect/about.

Mathematics Connection: Have students graph their findings from the Gas It Up! activity and determine the rate of change of the size of their balloons.

Introduce the term *carbon footprint* to students and discuss how an individual's carbon footprint is related to his or her daily activities and consumer choices. Challenge students to consider their own carbon footprints. Have students work in groups of two to three to make lists of their daily activities that might result in carbon emissions (for example, riding the bus to school, heating their homes). Have each team share items from its list with the class, creating a class list of activities that contribute to their carbon footprints.

Next, have students calculate their carbon footprints using an online carbon footprint calculator such as www.carbonglobe.com/carbon-footprint-calculator.php. Have students share their findings with the class and calculate a class average for carbon footprint.

ELA Connection: Have students create a print media message that encourages people to reduce their carbon footprints and suggests how to do this. Ask students for their ideas about what makes people read printed messages (for example, interesting or provocative slogans, eye-catching graphics). Students should include reasons why and at least two ways that individuals can reduce their carbon footprints.

Evaluation/Assessment

Students may be assessed on the following performance tasks and other measures listed.

Performance Tasks

- Life Cycle Analysis – natural gas

- Participation in Greenpeople Effect activity

- Gas It Up! activity handout

- Energy Source STEM Research Notebook Entry – Natural Gas

- Gas-Powered Cars presentations (see Appendix A for presentation rubric)

Other Measures

- Teacher observations

- Collaboration (see Appendix A for rubric)

INTERNET RESOURCES

Alternative Fuels Data Center

- *https://afdc.energy.gov/data*

Carbon footprint calculator

- *www.carbonglobe.com/carbon-footprint-calculator.php*

"Car Farts Blow Up a Barn" video

- *www.youtube.com/watch?v=gpa8Oz9DRbY*

CNG fueling stations

- *www.afdc.energy.gov/fuels/natural_gas_locations.html*

Gasoline and natural gas costs

- *www.eia.gov*

Greenhouse effect

- *www.nationalgeographic.org/article/greenhouse-effect-our-planet*
- *https://phet.colorado.edu/en/simulations/greenhouse-effect/about*

Hydraulic fracturing

- *www.nytimes.com/2013/03/14/opinion/global/the-facts-on-fracking.html*
- *www.sierraclub.org/policy/energy/fracking*

"Map: The Fracking Boom State by State"

- *https://insideclimatenews.org/news/20150120/map-fracking-boom-state-state*

NASA's "Climate Time Machine"

- *https://climate.nasa.gov/interactives/climate-time-machine*

Natural gas

- *www.afdc.energy.gov/vehicles/natural_gas.html*
- *www.eia.gov/kids/energy.cfm?page=natural_gas_home-basic*

Natural gas in transportation

- *www.afdc.energy.gov/vehicles/natural_gas.html*

Natural gas usage rates

- *www.eia.gov/energyexplained/natural-gas/use-of-natural-gas.php*

"Patrick Racing Natural Gas Initiative - Racing Engine Powered By Natural Gas" video

- *www.youtube.com/watch?v=ynXky7JefZI#t=14*

"The Greenhouse Effect" video

- *www.youtube.com/watch?v=VYMjSule0Bw*

"The History of Natural Gas" video

- *www.youtube.com/watch?v=BXi14Dr0Cj4*

U.S. Department of Energy, "Issues Affecting Adoption of Natural Gas Fuel in Light- and Heavy-Duty Vehicles"

- *https://www.energy.gov/sites/default/files/2022-10/Chapter_14-Natural_Gas.pdf*

U.S. Geological Survey's "Recent Earthquake Survey"

- *www.earthquaketrack.com/p/united-states/recent*

Life Cycle Analysis Student Handout

Primary Energy Source: _____

Name: _____

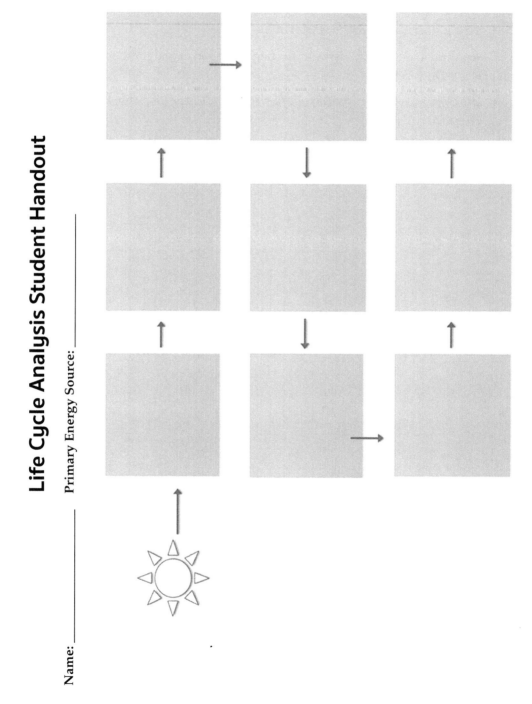

Use another sheet of paper if you need more space

Life Cycle Analysis Student Handout, Page 2

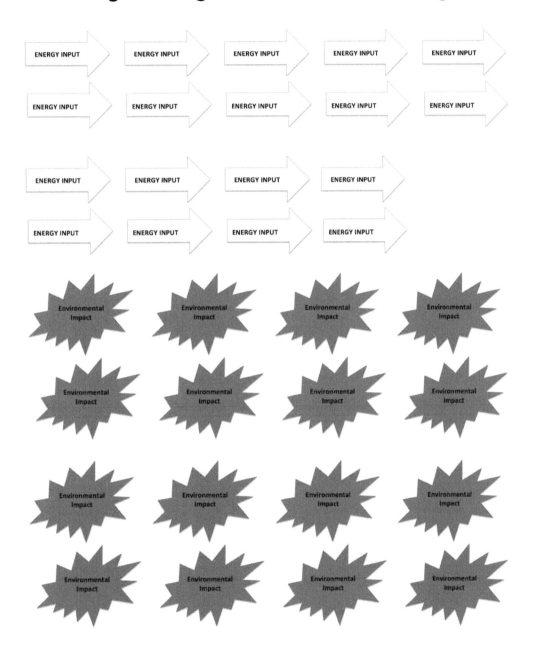

Gas It Up! Student Handout
(Page 1 of 4)

Materials and Instructions

Materials:

- 3 small-necked glass bottles
- 3 large balloons
- Disposable gloves
- 1 funnel
- 3 cups soil
- 1½ cups of a mixture of fruit/vegetable scraps
- Gallon-size Zipper-seal plastic bag
- Duct tape
- Permanent marker
- Ruler

Instructions:

1. Mix the soil and fruit/vegetable scraps thoroughly in a Zipper-seal plastic bag.

2. Divide the mixture evenly between the three bottles, using the funnel to help you put the contents into the bottle.

3. Stretch a balloon over the opening of each bottle and secure it with duct tape.

4. Mark the initial level of the mixture on the bottle and mark the date.

5. Decide on three locations to place your bottle for observation (for instance, in sunlight, in artificial light, near a heat source, in a refrigerator, in a dark place, etc.)

6. Label the bottom of each bottle with the name of your group and the location.

7. Place the bottles upright in each of the locations.

8. Record on your data sheet where you placed each bottle.

9. Make a prediction about what you think will happen to the balloon circumferences and the heights of the mixtures in the bottles after seven days. Record your predictions on your data sheet.

Gas It Up! Student Handout
(Page 2 of 4)

10. Observe the bottles every other day for seven days. When you make your observation, mark the mixture level and the date. Measure the mixture levels and the balloon circumference and record the measurements on your data sheet.

11. After seven days, answer the "Analyze" questions and graph your results.

12. After your measurements are complete, dispose of your mixtures outside and away from flames.

Gas It Up! Student Handout
(Page 3 of 4)
Data Sheet

Name: _____   Team Name: _____

	PREDICT What do you expect to observe about the material and the balloon after 7 days?	Observations			
		DAY 1	DAY 3	DAY 5	DAY 7
Bottle 1 **Location:**	Balloon Circumference: Mixture Height:	Balloon Circumference: Mixture Height:	Balloon Circumference: Mixture Height:	Balloon Circumference: Mixture Height:	Balloon Circumference: Mixture Height:
Bottle 2 **Location:**	Balloon Circumference: Mixture Height:	Balloon Circumference: Mixture Height:	Balloon Circumference: Mixture Height:	Balloon Circumference: Mixture Height:	Balloon Circumference: Mixture Height:
Bottle 3 **Location:**	Balloon Circumference: Mixture Height:	Balloon Circumference: Mixture Height:	Balloon Circumference: Mixture Height:	Balloon Circumference: Mixture Height:	Balloon Circumference: Mixture Height:

4

Gas It Up! Student Handout
(Page 4 of 4)
Data Sheet

Analyze

1. In which locations did the balloons inflate the most? Why?

2. In which locations did the balloons inflate the least? Why?

3. Graph your results. Use the day of measurement on the x-axis and the balloon circumference on the y-axis. Use different colors for each of the three different locations.

4. Based on your graph, what was the relationship between the levels of the mixtures and what happened to the balloons?

Lesson Plan 4:
From Photosynthesis to Fuel: Biofuels

Students will investigate biofuels in this lesson, with a focus on biofuels as fuels formed from geologically recent carbon fixation. Ethanol will be the focus of the lesson as an example of the use of plants to create fuel. Students will investigate fermentation of glucose using yeast, the basic chemical reaction associated with producing ethanol. Students will create a LCA for ethanol and participate in an inquiry activity in which they will observe fermentation reactions.

ESSENTIAL QUESTIONS

- What are the sources of biofuels?

- How are biofuels produced?

- What are the advantages and disadvantages of biofuel as a fuel source for cars?

- What energy inputs and environmental impacts are associated with using biofuel to power vehicles?

- What are the implications for food production associated with using biofuels to fuel vehicles?

ESTABLISHED GOALS AND OBJECTIVES

At the conclusion of this lesson, students will be able to do the following:

- Identify the difference between fossils fuels and biofuels

- Explain how biofuel is formed

- Analyze the implications of using biofuels as a power source for vehicles

- Identify and discuss the environmental and food production implications of using corn as an ethanol source

- Explain the chemistry of fermentation reactions and apply this understanding to creating ethanol

- Create a line graph using findings from an investigation

TIME REQUIRED

2 days (approximately 45 minutes each day; see Table 3.8, p. 44)

MATERIALS

Required Materials for Lesson 4

- STEM Research Notebooks

- computer with internet access for viewing videos

Additional Materials for Fermentable Fuels (for each group of 2–3 students unless otherwise indicated)

- 3 snack-size Zipper-seal plastic bags

- 2 sandwich-size Zipper-seal plastic bags

- 1 ruler (metric)

- 1 tsp. table sugar (1 packet)

- 1/8 cup breakfast cereal (NOTE: sugary cereals will ferment more quickly than low-sugar cereals)

- 1 slice of canned sliced beets

- ¾ cup warm tap water

- 3 tsp. yeast

- measuring spoon – 1 tsp.

- measuring cup – ¼ cup

- permanent marker

- paper towels (4–5 full-size towels per group)

- safety goggles (1 for each student)

Additional Materials for Life Cycle Analysis of Biofuels (for each team of 3–4 students)

- 1 set of markers

- scissors

- tape or glue

- 1 piece of 22″×28″ poster board (optional, see Preparation for Lesson 3, p. 125)

- 6 pieces of colored paper (optional, see Preparation for Lesson 3, p. 125)

SAFETY NOTES

1. Caution students not to eat any materials used for activities.

2. Students should use caution when handling scissors, as the sharp points and blades can cut or puncture skin.

3. Remind students that personal protective equipment (safety glasses or goggles, aprons, and gloves) must be worn during the setup, hands-on, and takedown segments of the Fermentable Fuels activity.

4. Caution students to take care in handling glass bottles as glass can break and cut or puncture skin.

5. Immediately wipe up any spilled water or other liquids on the floor to avoid a slip-and-fall hazard.

CONTENT STANDARDS AND KEY VOCABULARY

Table 4.10 lists the content standards from the *NGSS*, *CCSS*, and the Framework for 21st Century Learning that this lesson addresses, and Table 4.11 presents the key vocabulary. Vocabulary terms are provided for both teacher and student use. Teachers may choose to introduce some or all of the terms to students.

Table 4.10. Content Standards Addressed in STEM Road Map Module Lesson 4

NEXT GENERATION SCIENCE STANDARDS
PERFORMANCE OBJECTIVES

- MS-PS1–2. Analyze and interpret data on the properties of substances before and after the substances interact to determine if a chemical reaction has occurred.

- MS-PS1–3. Gather and make sense of information to describe that synthetic materials come from natural resources and impact society.

- MS-PS3–2. Develop a model to describe that when the arrangement of objects interacting at a distance changes, different amounts of potential energy are stored in the system.

- MS-PS3–5. Construct, use, and present arguments to support the claim that when the kinetic energy of an object changes, energy is transferred to or from the object.

SCIENCE AND ENGINEERING PRACTICES
Developing and Using Models

- Develop and use a model to describe phenomena.

Obtaining, Evaluating, and Communicating Information

- Gather, read, and synthesize information from multiple appropriate sources and assess the credibility, accuracy, and possible bias of each publication and methods used, and describe how they are supported or not supported by evidence.

Analyzing and Interpreting Data

- Analyze and interpret data to determine similarities and differences in findings.

Constructing Explanations and Designing Solutions

- Undertake a design project, engaging in the design cycle, to construct and/or implement a solution that meets specific design criteria and constraints.

- Apply scientific ideas or principles to design an object, tool, process, or system.

Planning and Carrying Out Investigations

- Plan an investigation individually and collaboratively, and in the design: identify independent and dependent variables and controls, what tools are needed to do the gathering, how measurements will be recorded, and how many data are needed to support a claim.

- Conduct an investigation and evaluate the experimental design to produce data to serve as the basis for evidence that can meet the goals of the investigation.

Engaging in Argument from Evidence

- Construct and present oral and written arguments supported by empirical evidence and scientific reasoning to support or refute an explanation or a model for a phenomenon or a solution to a problem.

DISCIPLINARY CORE IDEAS

PS1.A: *Structure and Properties of Matter*

- Substances are made from different types of atoms, which combine with one another in various ways. Atoms form molecules that range in size from two to thousands of atoms.

- Each pure substance has characteristic physical and chemical properties (for any bulk quantity under given conditions) that can be used to identify it.

- Gases and liquids are made of molecules or inert atoms that are moving about relative to each other.

- The changes of state that occur with variations in temperature or pressure can be described and predicted using these models of matter.

PS1.B: *Chemical Reactions*

- Substances react chemically in characteristic ways. In a chemical process, the atoms that make up the original substances are regrouped into different molecules, and these new substances have different properties from those of the reactants.

PS3.A: *Definitions of Energy*

- Temperature is not a measure of energy; the relationship between the temperature and the total energy of a system depends on the types, states, and amounts of matter present.

Continued

Table 4.10. (*continued*)

- Motion energy is properly called kinetic energy; it is proportional to the mass of the moving object and grows with the square of its speed.

- A system of objects may also contain stored (potential) energy, depending on their relative positions.

PS3.B: *Conservation of Energy and Energy Transfer*

- When the motion energy of an object changes, there is inevitably some other change in energy at the same time.

- The amount of energy transfer needed to change the temperature of a matter sample by a given amount depends on the nature of the matter, the size of the sample, and the environment.

- Energy is spontaneously transferred out of hotter regions or objects and into colder ones.

ESS3.A: *Natural Resources*

- Humans depend on Earth's land, ocean, atmosphere, and biosphere for many different resources. Minerals, fresh water, and biosphere resources are limited, and many are not renewable or replaceable over human lifetimes. These resources are distributed unevenly around the planet as a result of past geologic processes.

ESS3.C: *Human Impacts on Earth Systems*

- Typically as human populations and per-capita consumption of natural resources increase, so do the negative impacts on Earth unless the activities and technologies involved are engineered otherwise.

ETS1.A: *Defining and Delimiting Engineering Problems*

- The more precisely a design task's criteria and constraints can be defined, the more likely it is that the designed solution will be successful. Specification of constraints includes consideration of scientific principles and other relevant knowledge that is likely to limit possible solutions.

ETS1.B: *Developing Possible Solutions*

- A solution needs to be tested, and then modified on the basis of the test results in order to improve it.

ETS1.C: *Optimizing the Design Solution*

- Although one design may not perform the best across all tests, identifying the characteristics of the design that performed the best in each test can provide useful information for the redesign process – that is, some of the characteristics may be incorporated into the new design.

- The iterative process of testing the most promising solutions and modifying what is proposed on the basis of the test results leads to greater refinement and ultimately to an optimal solution.

CROSS-CUTTING CONCEPTS

Patterns

- Macroscopic patterns are related to the nature of microscopic and atomic-level structure.

Scale, Proportion, and Quantity

- Time, space, and energy phenomena can be observed at various scales using models to study systems that are too large or too small.

Systems and System Models

- Models can be used to represent systems and their interactions—such as inputs, processes and outputs—and energy and matter flows within systems.

Energy and Matter

- The transfer of energy can be tracked as energy flows through a designed or natural system.

- Energy may take different forms (e.g. energy in fields, thermal energy, energy of motion).

Cause and Effect

- Cause and effect relationships may be used to predict phenomena in natural or designed systems.

Stability and Change

- Explanations of stability and change in natural or designed systems can be constructed by examining the changes over time and forces at different scales.

Structure and Function

- Structures can be designed to serve particular functions by taking into account properties of different materials, and how materials can be shaped and used.

COMMON CORE STATE STANDARDS FOR MATHEMATICS
MATHEMATICAL PRACTICES

- MP 1. Make sense of problems and persevere in solving them.

- MP 2. Reason abstractly and quantitatively.

- MP 3. Construct viable arguments and critique the reasoning of others.

- MP 4. Model with mathematics.

- MP 5. Use appropriate tools strategically.

MATHEMATICAL CONTENT

- 8.F.B.4. Construct a function to model a linear relationship between two quantities. Determine the rate of change and initial value of the function from a description of a relationship or from two (x, y) values, including reading these from a table or from a graph. Interpret the rate of change and initial value of a linear function in terms of the situation it models, and in terms of its graph or a table of values.

Continued

Table 4.10. (*continued*)

- 8.F.B.5. Describe qualitatively the functional relationship between two quantities by analyzing a graph (for example, where the function is increasing or decreasing, linear or nonlinear). Sketch a graph that exhibits the qualitative features of a function that has been described verbally.

COMMON CORE STATE STANDARDS FOR ENGLISH LANGUAGE ARTS
READING STANDARDS

- RL.8.1. Cite the textual evidence that most strongly supports an analysis of what the text says explicitly as well as inferences drawn from the text.

- RL.8.9. Analyze a case in which two or more texts provide conflicting information on the same topic and identify where the texts disagree on matters of fact or interpretation.

WRITING STANDARDS

- W.8.1. Write arguments to support claims with clear reasons and relevant evidence.

- W.8.1.A. Introduce claim(s), acknowledge and distinguish the claim(s) from alternate or opposing claims, and organize the reasons and evidence logically.

- W.8.1.B. Support claim(s) with logical reasoning and relevant evidence, using accurate, credible sources and demonstrating an understanding of the topic or text.

- W.8.1.C. Use words, phrases, and clauses to create cohesion and clarify the relationships among claim(s), counterclaims, reasons, and evidence.

- W.8.1.E. Provide a concluding statement or section that follows from and supports the argument presented.

- W.8.2. Write informative/explanatory texts to examine a topic and convey ideas, concepts, and information through the selection, organization, and analysis of relevant content.

- W.8.2.A. Introduce a topic clearly, previewing what is to follow; organize ideas, concepts, and information into broader categories; include formatting (for example, headings), graphics (for example, charts, tables), and multimedia when useful to aiding comprehension.

- W.8.2.B. Develop the topic with relevant, well-chosen facts, definitions, concrete details, quotations, or other information and examples.

- W.8.2.C. Use appropriate and varied transitions to create cohesion and clarify the relationships among ideas and concepts.

- W.8.2.D. Use precise language and domain-specific vocabulary to inform about or explain the topic.

- W.8.3. Write narratives to develop real or imagined experiences or events using effective technique, relevant descriptive details, and well-structured event sequences.

- W.8.3.A. Engage and orient the reader by establishing a context and point of view and introducing a narrator and/or characters; organize an event sequence that unfolds naturally and logically.

- W.8.3.D. Use precise words and phrases, relevant descriptive details, and sensory language to capture the action and convey experiences and events.

- W.8.7. Conduct short research projects to answer a question (including a self-generated question), drawing on several sources and generating additional related, focused questions that allow for multiple avenues of exploration.

- W.8.8. Gather relevant information from multiple print and digital sources, using search terms effectively; assess the credibility and accuracy of each source; and quote or paraphrase the data and conclusions of others while avoiding plagiarism and following a standard format for citation.

- W.8.9. Draw evidence from literary or informational texts to support analysis, reflection, and research.

SPEAKING AND LISTENING STANDARDS

- SL.8.1. Engage effectively in a range of collaborative discussions (one-on-one, in groups, and teacher-led) with diverse partners on grade 8 topics, texts, and issues, building on others' ideas and expressing their own clearly.

- SL.8.1.A. Come to discussions prepared, having read or researched material under study; explicitly draw on that preparation by referring to evidence on the topic, text, or issue to probe and reflect on ideas under discussion.

- SL.8.1.B. Follow rules for collegial discussions and decision-making, track progress toward specific goals and deadlines, and define individual roles as needed.

- SL.8.1.C. Pose questions that connect the ideas of several speakers and respond to others' questions and comments with relevant evidence, observations, and ideas.

- SL.8.1.D. Acknowledge new information expressed by others, and, when warranted, qualify or justify their own views in light of the evidence presented.

- SL.8.2. Analyze the purpose of information presented in diverse media and formats (for example, visually, quantitatively, orally) and evaluate the motives (for example, social, commercial, political) behind its presentation.

- SL.8.4. Present claims and findings, emphasizing salient points in a focused, coherent manner with relevant evidence, sound valid reasoning, and well-chosen details; use appropriate eye contact, adequate volume, and clear pronunciation.

FRAMEWORK FOR 21ST CENTURY LEARNING

Interdisciplinary themes (financial, economic, & business literacy; environmental literacy); Learning and Innovation Skills; Information, Media & Technology Skills; Life and Career Skills

Table 4.11. Key Vocabulary in Lesson 4

Key Vocabulary	Definition
biodiesel	fuel made from vegetable oils, animal fats, or greases
biofuel	fuels, such as ethanol and biodiesel, produced from animal or plant material
biomass	biological material from living or recently living organisms
cellulosic ethanol	a biofuel produced using wood, grass, or inedible parts of plants
diesel	a fuel refined from crude oil and that is about 33% more efficient than gasoline
ethanol	an alcohol that is found in alcoholic beverages and is also used as a motor fuel, mainly as an additive to gasoline
fermentation	chemical reactions that convert sugar to acids, gases, and/or alcohol
fracking	hydraulic fracturing
hydraulic fracturing	a technique in which rock below the Earth's surface is fractured by a pressurized liquid composed of water, sand, and chemicals; also known as fracking

TEACHER BACKGROUND INFORMATION
Microbes

This lesson includes a discussion of microbes in the context of fermentation. The term microbe was coined to denote organisms visible only by microscope; however, with current knowledge the term has become less precise. Some organisms historically called "microbes" – for example, certain fungi – may actually be visible with the human eye. In addition, viruses must enter living cells to reproduce, calling into question whether they should be grouped with bacteria as microbes. The American Microbiological Society discusses these nuances in an online article, "What Counts as a Microbe?" (www.asm.org/Articles/2021/April/What-Counts-as-a-Microbe) that you may wish to review. The article concludes that the term "'microbe' is a convenient and practical term to introduce novices to the multitudes of the microbial world" and is therefore used in this lesson to refer to bacteria, fungi, and viruses.

Biofuels

In this lesson, students will consider biomass as energy sources for vehicles. This category of renewable fuels includes wood/wood waste; municipal solid waste; landfill gas/biogas; ethanol; biodiesel. The emphasis of this lesson will be on ethanol, although biodiesel is also an example of a biomass fuel source and may be introduced as an option.

As discussed in Lesson 3, natural gas that is extracted from below the Earth's surface is a fossil fuel and is considered a non-renewable energy source. Renewable natural gas is a relatively newly tapped source of fuel. Students investigated this type of gas – gas is produced from decaying organic materials – in the Gas It Up! activity in Lesson 3 and should therefore be aware that this type of gas can be captured from landfills, plant waste, and livestock. The methane production from decomposing plant matter is caused by methanogens, anaerobic microbes classified as archaea.

Ethanol has a rich history as a fuel in the United States. Henry Ford's Model T, designed in 1908, ran on a mixture of gasoline and ethanol. When Prohibition began in 1919, however, ethanol was considered an alcoholic beverage and was banned until 1933 when Prohibition ended. Ethanol use increased somewhat during World War II when oil and gasoline were in short supply; however, interest in its use spiked in the 1970s when oil embargoes and shortages began to affect consumers. Since the 1970s, ethanol use has been supported by tax credits and by environmental legislation calling for cleaner burning fuels. For a timeline of the history of ethanol in the U.S., see www.eia.gov/kids/energy.cfm?page=tl_ethanol.

Today, nearly all gasoline sold in the U.S. contains ethanol. Most gasoline-powered vehicle engines in the U.S. can run on fuel mixtures of up to 10% ethanol and 90% gasoline (called E10, or gasohol). Flexible fuel vehicles (FFV) use E85 fuel with up to 85% ethanol content. This fuel is most widely available in the Midwest; however, there are limited fueling sources for E85 nationwide (www.eia.gov/kids/energy.cfm?page=biofuel_home-basics#biofuel_ethanol_home-basics).

Advantages to ethanol include that it is biodegradable, non-toxic, burns more cleanly than gasoline, is considered carbon neutral since the plants from which it is derived absorb carbon dioxide, is renewable, and reduces the amount of gasoline vehicles use. Disadvantages to ethanol use include that it has less energy per unit than gasoline, it requires large amounts of farmland to produce plants, evaporates quickly in high temperatures, fertilizers and pesticides are used on crops grown to produce ethanol, and the fermentation process required to produce it requires heat and therefore another energy source (coal and natural gas are used as heat sources).

Ethanol, chemical formula is C_2H_5OH, is a product of the fermentation of carbohydrates like sugar and starch. Yeast is used to convert carbohydrates into a mixture of ethanol and carbon dioxide. Plants such as sugar beets and sugar cane contain natural sugar. Other crops like corn, wheat, and barley contain starch that can be converted to sugar. The following steps are involved in making ethanol by a dry-milling process:

1. The plants are ground.

2. Sugar is dissolved from the material, or the starch is converted into sugar.

3. Yeast is added to feed on the sugar, producing ethanol and carbon dioxide as byproducts.

4. The ethanol is purified.

For a video tour of an ethanol plant, see www.youtube.com/watch?v=npJ1N-1K84E.

A wet milling process can also be used in which grains are soaked in dilute sulfurous acid to facilitate separation of the grain into its constituent parts. This process is used by many large-scale ethanol producers, and produces byproducts such as high fructose corn syrup.

The basic chemical reaction that occurs is called starch fermentation. Students should understand that grains are treated to extract the carbohydrates (sugars or starches) and that the yeast then "eats" the carbohydrate, producing ethanol and carbon dioxide.

Biodiesel is a biofuel alternative to diesel fuel. Diesel fuel is derived from petroleum by the refining process, typically provides better gas mileage than gasoline, and is often used in freight trucks, and in other large vehicles such as farm and construction vehicles. Diesel produces carbon dioxide, a greenhouse gas, when burned. Biodiesels, manufactured from vegetable oils and/or animal fats, can be used in existing diesel engines with no modifications necessary. Other advantages to biodiesels include the following:

- They are generally less toxic than petroleum-based fuels.

- They are biodegradable.

- They produce fewer air pollutants than diesel fuels when burned.

- They are made from plants that consume carbon dioxide, which offsets the carbon dioxide produced while making and using biodiesel (i.e., it is carbon neutral).

- They tend to provide significantly better gas mileage than gasoline.

Disadvantages to biodiesels include the following:

- They slightly increases emissions of nitrogen oxides, known to contribute to smog and ozone.

- In some parts of the world, natural forests and vegetation have been cleared to grow plants to produce biodiesel (soybeans and palm oil trees).

- The crops used to produce them require the use of fertilizers and pesticides.

- They are more expensive than petroleum diesels.

- They can harm rubber parts in engines.

- They don't perform well in low temperatures.

- The distribution infrastructure is currently underdeveloped.

The chemical reactions to produce biodiesels involve reacting vegetable or animal fats with methanol or ethanol (short-chain alcohols). The transesterification reactions used to produce biodiesels are beyond the scope of a middle school course; however, if you choose to introduce biodiesels you may wish to explain to students that the reactions rely on chemical catalysts or enzymes to accelerate the reaction.

COMMON MISCONCEPTIONS

Students will have various types of prior knowledge about the concepts introduced in this lesson. Table 4.12 describes a common misconception students may have concerning these concepts. Because of the breadth of students' experiences, it is not possible to anticipate every misconception that students may bring as they approach this lesson. Incorrect or inaccurate prior understanding of concepts can influence student learning in the future, however, so it is important to be alert to misconceptions such as those presented in the table.

Table 4.12. Common Misconception About the Concepts in Lesson 4

Topic	Student Misconception	Explanation
Biofuels	Because biofuels are made from plant matter they are without environmental costs.	Producing biofuels requires a number of activities that can result in emissions of substances into the atmosphere and long-term stress on land; for example, biofuel production may require land clearing that can involve burning and associated atmospheric emissions and can disrupt ecosystems.

PREPARATION FOR LESSON 4

Review the teacher background information provided, assemble the materials for the lesson, make copies of the student handouts, and preview the videos recommended in the Learning Components section below.

If you have not already contacted individuals to act as the fictional investors for students' final challenge, you should do so.

LEARNING COMPONENTS
Introductory Activity/Engagement

Connection to the Challenge: Begin each day of this lesson by directing students' attention to the module challenge, the Speed of Green Challenge. Remind students

that they will work in teams to create plans for ways to minimize the environmental impact of powering a race car. Hold a brief class discussion each day of how students' learning in the previous days' lessons contributed to their ability to complete the challenge. You may wish to create a class list of key ideas on chart paper.

Science Class: Remind students that their ultimate challenge for the module is to create a race plan to power a race car with minimal environmental impact. Introduce students to the Eco-Marathon, as an example of a challenge in which high school and college students work in teams to build actual cars. The Eco-Marathon is a contest in which students create energy-efficient vehicles. Tell students that, although they will not be building cars, it may be useful to consider how these students approached their challenge. Show students a video overview of the 2014 Eco-Marathon (for example, "Shell Eco-marathon Americas – 2014 Overview" at www.youtube.com/ watch?v=CADL6Aucj68). After showing the video, ask students for their ideas about what fuel the 2014 winning team used to fuel their prototype car (it was a gasoline-powered car). Ask students to guess how many miles per gallon the car achieved (2,824 miles per gallon). Ask students if they think that gasoline has a low environmental impact in this case. Next, ask students to brainstorm about how a car could get that sort of fuel economy, reminding students that an average passenger car gets around 25–30 miles per gallon.

Show students the video "2,824 Miles Per Gallon - 2014 Shell Eco-marathon Winners" at www.youtube.com/watch?v=E3Sepx2h_Tw or a similar video identified by using the search terms "2014 Shell Eco-marathon winners," and ask students to watch for the innovations the team used that enabled such high fuel economy. Ask students for their ideas about how the innovations they saw in the video could be useful in a race car.

Point out to students that most cars today are powered by a combination of gasoline and ethanol. Ask students what they know about ethanol and where it comes from (corn). Tell students that adding ethanol to gasoline has benefits and costs. Ask students to brainstorm about the benefits (for example, burns cleanly and reduces greenhouse gas emissions, is a renewable energy source, decreases the amount of gasoline we use) and the problems with using ethanol (for example, it has less energy than gasoline, using farmland to grow plants for fuel reduces the amount of land available for growing food for people to eat).

Tell students that in this lesson they will consider fuels that come from biomass, like ethanol. Introduce the term *biofuel*. Remind students of their Gas It Up! activity (students should be measuring and recording data every second day until the end of seven days). Tell students that the material they used is a type of biomass, and the gas produced by that material is considered a biofuel. The biofuels students will consider in this lesson are ethanol and biodiesel (optional).

Social Studies Class: To introduce biofuels, ask students the following questions:

- What might cattle farms and landfills have in common?

- Can landfills produce anything useful to the community?

Introduce the idea that biofuels are fuels such as methane that are produced by living or recently living animals and plants. Ask students to revisit the questions above, keeping this information in mind.

Remind students of their discussion in Lesson 3 about cattle producing methane during their digestive process and that methane is also produced in landfills. Some farms and some landfills are able to harness this methane as a power source.

Mathematics Connection: Not applicable.

ELA Connection: Not applicable.

Activity/Exploration

Science Class and Mathematics Connection: Students will focus their investigation on ethanol as an example of biomass fuel in this lesson. They will construct a life cycle analysis of ethanol, and explore ethanol creation through an inquiry activity, Fermentable Fuels. As an option, you may introduce biodiesel as another biomass fuel option.

Life Cycle Analysis – Ethanol

Show students a video that provides an overview of the production of ethanol such as "Video Tour of an Ethanol Plant" at www.youtube.com/watch?v=npJ1N-1K84E, asking students to watch for the following while they watch:

- Steps in the production process

- Energy inputs necessary for production and transportation

- Environmental impacts

Student teams should use this information and their own internet research to conduct a life cycle analysis of ethanol using the Life Cycle Analysis handouts (at the end of Lesson 3).

Fermentable Fuels

Distribute the Fermentable Fuels instructions and handout to each student and a set of materials to each team. Have students work in teams to complete the investigation.

Ask students to recall what they observed in the Gas It Up! activity. Ask them what was happening to the vegetable and fruit mixture in their bottles. They should have

evidence that a gas (methane) was produced. Ask students if they recall what happens to food as it decays (it produces a gas). Remind students that microbes are "eating" the waste and producing methane as a byproduct.

Ask students if they can name any microbes (they may mention bacteria and viruses). Introduce the concept that there are many different types of microbes. Bacteria, viruses, fungi, and archaea are a few types of microbes. Archaea are known for their ability to withstand extreme temperatures and function without oxygen. These microbes produce methane as a byproduct of digesting plants in the digestive system of cows and are responsible for the methane cows emit.

Ask students if they've ever seen bread made. What makes it rise? (yeast). Tell students that yeast is a type of microbe known as a fungus. Yeast is responsible for the chemical reaction that turns sugars and grains into alcohol. Introduce the concept of fermentation to students as a type of chemical reaction in which sugars and starches are turned into alcohol. This is how alcohol beverages like beer are made. The same process is used to create ethanol as a fuel. Students will observe a simple process of fermentation in this activity.

You may wish to introduce the chemical reaction for fermentation:

$$C_6H_{12}O_6 + \text{Yeast} \rightarrow 2\,C_2H_5OH + 2\,CO_2$$

$$\text{(glucose)} \qquad\qquad \text{(ethanol)} + \text{(carbon dioxide)}$$

Yeast uses the glucose (sugar) as food. Yeast contains chemical compounds (enzymes) that break down the sugars so that the yeast can use them. Tell students that in contrast to the bacteria that were acting in the Gas It Up! activity, yeast will act fairly quickly to produce ethanol and carbon dioxide.

Biodiesels (Optional)

You may wish to introduce biodiesels to your student as another alternative biomass fuel. The chemical reactions associated with biodiesel production are complex and beyond the scope of a middle school course. The Mythbusters video, "Cooking Oil as Economical Diesel Fuel" at www.youtube.com/watch?v=QEX1YFXYTdI provides an overview of biodiesel.

Students will need a basic understanding of diesel fuel and diesel fueled vehicles in order to create a life cycle analysis. The U.S. Department of Energy's "Biofuel Basics" at www.energy.gov/eere/bioenergy/biofuel-basics and the Alternative Fuels Data Center page on biofuel-powered vehicles (https://afdc.energy.gov/vehicles/how-do-biodiesel-cars-work) may be helpful to students in creating life cycle analyses for biodiesels.

Social Studies Class: If methane is harvested from landfills in your geographic region, have students investigate how much power is produced this way. The Environmental

Protection Agency (EPA) provides information about and a locator map for landfill gas energy at www.epa.gov/lmop/project-and-landfill-data-state. Hold a class discussion about landfill gas and how students think this might impact people's opinions of having landfills located near their communities.

ELA Connection: Have students research the history of ethanol in the U.S. and choose a pro-ethanol or anti-ethanol stance regarding the use of ethanol as a fuel.

Explanation

Science Class: After students have completed their ethanol (and biodiesel if students completed these) LCAs, have several students share their LCAs. As a class, compare and contrast the analyses, focusing on differences in energy inputs and environmental impacts students identified.

Have students create Energy Source STEM Research Notebook entries for ethanol (and for biodiesel if this was introduced) using the Energy Source STEM Research Notebook Entry handout from Lesson 2.

Social Studies Class: Students should understand that although biofuels are considered renewable fuels there are disadvantages to using them, including diverting farmland away from food production. Have students conduct research to find out how much farmland is currently being used for ethanol production.

Mathematics Connection: Have students graph the results of their Fermentable Fuels inquiry and determine the rate of change in the size of each bag. You may wish to have students analyze their graphs to decide whether the gas production was linear or exponential based upon the shape of their graphs.

Explain to students the difference between linear and exponential functions. Students should understand that linear functions can be expressed as $y = mx + b$ while exponential functions are expressed as $y = a \cdot b^x$. Variables in linear functions do not have exponents.

ELA Connection: Based on the research students conducted about the history of ethanol, have each student write a persuasive essay stating and supporting a position for or against the use of ethanol as a vehicle fuel.

Elaboration/Application of Knowledge

Science Class: Have students use their learning from this lesson and the results from the Gas It Up! and Fermentable Fuels activity to craft an argument for the use of biofuels as opposed to petroleum-based fuels.

As an optional extension, have students investigate fermentation with a variety of breakfast cereals with varying sugar contents and varying grains using the Fermentable Fuels handouts as a guide.

Social Studies Class: Have students report their findings on the amount of land used for ethanol production. As a class, discuss the implications of using agricultural land for crops for fuel production. Hold a class discussion about the justifications for using corn for ethanol production, and discuss the role of government subsidies in the use of agricultural land and the choice of crops.

Mathematics Connection: Have students from several teams share the graphs they created from the Fermentable Fuels activity. Compare and contrast the graphs and discuss the reasons for differences in various teams' data and graphs.

ELA Connection: Choose five students who adopted a pro-ethanol stance and five students who adopted an anti-ethanol stance and have these students hold a tag team debate, with the remainder of the class acting as the audience who will vote for one side or the other at the conclusion of the debate. In a tag team debate, each side has a set amount of time (for example, 5 minutes) to present its side of the debate. Each student should be limited to a certain amount of time to speak (for example, 1 minute) before "tagging" the next speaker on his or her team to take over. After each side has presented its argument, have the class vote on which position they found most convincing.

Hold a class discussion about the debate, focusing on how arguments could be improved by the use of evidence and persuasive language.

Evaluation/Assessment

Students may be assessed on the following performance tasks and other measures listed.

Performance Tasks

- Fermentable Fuels activity handout

- Fermentable Fuels graph

- Life Cycle Analysis – biofuels

- Life Cycle Analysis – biodiesels (optional)

- Energy Source STEM Research Notebook Entry – biofuels

- Energy Source STEM Research Notebook Entry – biodiesel (optional)

Other Measures

- Teacher observations

- STEM Research Notebook entries

- Collaboration (see Appendix A for rubric)

INTERNET RESOURCES

Alternative Fuel Data Center, "How do Diesel Vehicles Work Using Biodiesel?"

- *https://afdc.energy.gov/vehicles/how-do-biodiesel-cars-work*

Biofuel Basics

- *www.energy.gov/eere/bioenergy/biofuel-basics*

"Cooking Oil as Economical Diesel Fuel" video

- *www.youtube.com/watch?v=QEX1YFXYTdI*

Ethanol fueling stations

- *www.eia.gov/kids/energy.cfm?page=biofuel_home-basics#biofuel_ethanol_home-basics*

History of ethanol

- *www.eia.gov/kids/energy.cfm?page=tl_ethanol*

Locator map for landfill gas energy

- *www.epa.gov/lmop/project-and-landfill-data-state*

Shell Eco-marathon Americas – 2014 Overview

- *www.youtube.com/watch?v=CADL6Aucj68*
- *www.youtube.com/watch?v=E3Sepx2h_Tw*

"Video Tour of an Ethanol Plant"

- *www.youtube.com/watch?v=npJ1N-1K84E*

"What Counts as a Microbe?" video

- *www.asm.org/Articles/2021/April/What-Counts-as-a-Microbe*

Fermentable Fuels Student Handout
(Page 1 of 4)

In this activity, you will create a fermentation reaction. This is the reaction that is used to create ethanol from biomass like corn.

This is the chemical reaction that will occur:

$$C_6H_{12}O_6 + Yeast \rightarrow 2\ C_2H_5OH + 2\ CO_2$$
$$(glucose - sugar) \rightarrow (ethanol) + (carbon\ dioxide)$$

You will observe this reaction with three different sources of sugar: table sugar, breakfast cereal, and beets.

Materials

3 snack-size Zipper-seal plastic bags	¾ cup warm tap water
2 sandwich-size Zipper-seal plastic bags	3 tsp. yeast
1 ruler (metric)	measuring spoon – 1 tsp.
1 tsp. table sugar (1 packet)	measuring cup – ¼ cup
1/8 cup breakfast cereal	permanent marker
1 slice of beet	paper towels (4–5 full size towels per group)
	safety goggles (1 for each student)

Procedure

1. Place the breakfast cereal in one of the sandwich-size Zipper-seal plastic bags. Seal the bag and crush the cereal until it is a fine powder. Why do you think you do this?

2. Measure 1 tsp. of the crushed cereal and put it into one of the snack-size Zipper-seal plastic bags. Label the bag "cereal."

3. Place the beet slice in one of the sandwich-size Zipper-seal plastic bags. Seal the bag and crush the beet. NOTE: beet juice can stain clothes; be sure to use caution when handling the beets.

4. Measure 1 tsp. of the crushed beet and put it into one of the snack-size Zipper-seal plastic bags. Label the bag "beet."

5. Make sure your measuring spoon is clean and dry. Measure 1 tsp. sugar and put it into one of the snack-size Zipper-seal plastic bags. Label the bag "sugar."

Fermentable Fuels Student Handout
(Page 2 of 4)

6. Add 1 tsp. yeast into each of the three snack-size bags.

7. Add ¼ cup of warm water to the "cereal" bag. Zip the bag closed, removing as much air as possible. Mix the bag gently and lay on a flat surface.

8. Add ¼ cup of warm water to the "beet" bag. Zip the bag closed, removing as much air as possible. Mix the bag gently and lay on a flat surface.

9. Add ¼ cup of warm water to the "sugar" bag. Zip the bag closed, removing as much air as possible. Mix the bag gently and lay on a flat surface.

10. Cover the bags with several layers of paper towels (yeast works best in the dark).

11. Observe what happens at 15 minute intervals during class and at the start of your next class session and record your observations on your data sheet.

** This reaction will produce carbon dioxide and the bags will expand – they could even pop! If the bag becomes too inflated, release some of the gas and note this in your observations.

Fermentable Fuels Student Handout

(Page 3 of 4)

Data Sheet

Name: _____

For each observation, record the time and what you see happening in each bag. Record the height of each bag from the tabletop (in mm) and note anything else you see happening in the bag.

Sugar Source	Time 1 _____	Time 2 _____	Time 3 _____	Time 4 _____
Table Sugar	Bag Height: Observations:	Bag Height: Observations:	Bag Height: Observations:	Bag Height: Observations:
Breakfast Cereal	Bag Height: Observations:	Bag Height: Observations:	Bag Height: Observations:	Bag Height: Observations:
Beets	Bag Height: Observations:	Bag Height: Observations:	Bag Height: Observations:	Bag Height: Observations:

Fermentable Fuels Student Handout
(Page 4 of 4)

1. Did any of the bags inflate? _____ If so, what is filling them up?

_____

_____

2. What is happening to the liquid in the bags?

_____

_____

3. How did the yeast respond to the different kinds of food?

_____

_____

4. If you observed a difference between what is happening in the bags, why do you think this is?

_____

_____

5. What kind of sugar source would create the most ethanol the fastest?

_____

6. Corn is the main source of sugar used to produce ethanol. Why do you think this is?

_____

_____

Lesson Plan 5:
Speed from the Sun

In this lesson, students will consider solar energy as a power source for vehicles. Students will investigate the role of photovoltaic cells in solar energy and solar power as a direct source of energy. They will also learn about electric cars and consider the role of solar power in these cars, and will investigate batteries as energy storage devices.

ESSENTIAL QUESTIONS

- What is solar energy?

- What are the advantages and disadvantages of solar energy?

- How can a vehicle be powered using solar energy?

- How does a photovoltaic cell work?

- What energy sources do electric cars use?

- What is the history of electric cars in the U.S.?

- How can we use a solar cell to power a device?

- How can energy be stored?

- How does a battery work?

ESTABLISHED GOALS AND OBJECTIVES

At the conclusion of this lesson, students will be able to do the following:

- Identify the differences between a primary energy source and a secondary energy source or energy carrier

- Demonstrate a conceptual understanding of how photovoltaic cells capture solar energy

- Apply a basic understanding of electrical circuits to create a circuit that powers a battery using solar energy

- Identify and describe several careers associated with solar energy

- Describe the flow of electrons within a battery

- Apply their understanding of electron flows within a battery and their understanding of simple circuits to create a battery

- Analyze the implications of using solar energy as a power source for vehicles

- Apply the EDP to solve a problem

TIME REQUIRED

4 days (approximately 45 minutes each day; see Table 3.8–3.9, pp. 44–45)

MATERIALS

Required Materials for Lesson 5

- STEM Research Notebooks

- computer with internet access for viewing videos

Additional Materials for PV Cell Simulation Challenge (one for the class)

- 4 plastic buckets

- 25–30 small balls (ping-pong balls or other similarly sized balls)

- 2 dice

- chalk or masking tape

- bell

- 40 feet of string or rope

- PV cell for demonstration

Additional Materials for Solar Circuits Activity (1 for each group of 2–3 students):

- mini PV cell (approximately 1.5 volt, 80 × 60 mm)*

- direct current motor*

- small propeller to attach to motor

- wires with alligator clips

- 1 piece of black construction paper

- * Note that there are many varieties of motors and mini PV cells; you should ensure that the motors and cells will work together. See, for example, Solar Schoolhouse at https://solarschoolhouse.org or the National Energy Education Development Project at https://shop.need.org/collections/hands-on-kits

Additional Materials for Lemon Power Activity – optional (one for each pair of students)

- 2 lemons

- 4 copper wires with alligator clips

- 4 galvanized nails (zinc coating)

- 4 pieces of copper wire (16 gauge, about 2″ long)

- digital clock or timer (normally powered by a 1.5 V watch-type battery)

- 1 knife

- paper towels

- safety goggles (1 per student)

- voltmeter or multimeter

Additional Materials for Life Cycle Analysis of Solar Energy (for each team of 3–4 students)

- 1 set of markers

- scissors

- tape or glue

- 1 piece of 22″ × 28″ poster board (optional, see Preparation for Lesson 3, p. 125)

- 6 pieces of colored paper (optional, see Preparation for Lesson 3, p. 125)

SAFETY NOTES

1. Caution students not to eat any materials used for activities.

2. Students should use caution when handling scissors and knives, as the sharp points and blades can cut or puncture skin.

3. Students should use caution when handling nails, as sharp ends can cut or puncture skin; for the Lemon Power activity, demonstrate to students how to carefully push the nail into the lemon, keeping hands and fingers free of the pointed end of the nail.

4. Students should use caution when handling wires, as sharp ends can cut or puncture skin; for the Lemon Power activity, demonstrate to students how to carefully push the wire into the lemon.

5. Remind students that personal protective equipment (safety glasses or goggles, aprons, and gloves) must be worn during the setup, hands-on, and take-down segments of the Solar Circuits and Lemon Power activities.

6. Caution students of the risk of shock when using electricity in activities, even when voltage is low.

7. Caution students to keep their hands away from the spinning propeller in the Solar Circuits activity.

8. Immediately wipe up any spilled water or other liquids on the floor to avoid a slip-and-fall hazard.

CONTENT STANDARDS AND KEY VOCABULARY

Table 4.13 lists the content standards from the *NGSS*, *CCSS*, and the Framework for 21st Century Learning that this lesson addresses, and Table 4.14 presents the key vocabulary. Vocabulary terms are provided for both teacher and student use. Teachers may choose to introduce some or all of the terms to students.

Table 4.13. Content Standards Addressed in STEM Road Map Module Lesson 5

NEXT GENERATION SCIENCE STANDARDS
PERFORMANCE OBJECTIVES

- MS-PS1–2. Analyze and interpret data on the properties of substances before and after the substances interact to determine if a chemical reaction has occurred.

- MS-PS1–3. Gather and make sense of information to describe that synthetic materials come from natural resources and impact society.

- MS-PS3–2. Develop a model to describe that when the arrangement of objects interacting at a distance changes, different amounts of potential energy are stored in the system.

- MS-PS3–5. Construct, use, and present arguments to support the claim that when the kinetic energy of an object changes, energy is transferred to or from the object.

SCIENCE AND ENGINEERING PRACTICES
Developing and Using Models

- Develop and use a model to describe phenomena.

Obtaining, Evaluating, and Communicating Information

- Gather, read, and synthesize information from multiple appropriate sources and assess the credibility, accuracy, and possible bias of each publication and methods used, and describe how they are supported or not supported by evidence.

Analyzing and Interpreting Data

- Analyze and interpret data to determine similarities and differences in findings.

Continued

Table 4.13. (*continued*)

Constructing Explanations and Designing Solutions

- Undertake a design project, engaging in the design cycle, to construct and/or implement a solution that meets specific design criteria and constraints.

- Apply scientific ideas or principles to design an object, tool, process, or system.

Planning and Carrying Out Investigations

- Plan an investigation individually and collaboratively, and in the design: identify independent and dependent variables and controls, what tools are needed to do the gathering, how measurements will be recorded, and how many data are needed to support a claim.
- Conduct an investigation and evaluate the experimental design to produce data to serve as the basis for evidence that can meet the goals of the investigation.

Engaging in Argument from Evidence

- Construct and present oral and written arguments supported by empirical evidence and scientific reasoning to support or refute an explanation or a model for a phenomenon or a solution to a problem.

DISCIPLINARY CORE IDEAS

PS1.A: *Structure and Properties of Matter*

- Substances are made from different types of atoms, which combine with one another in various ways. Atoms form molecules that range in size from two to thousands of atoms.

- Each pure substance has characteristic physical and chemical properties (for any bulk quantity under given conditions) that can be used to identify it.

- Gases and liquids are made of molecules or inert atoms that are moving about relative to each other.

- The changes of state that occur with variations in temperature or pressure can be described and predicted using these models of matter.

PS1.B: *Chemical Reactions*

- Substances react chemically in characteristic ways. In a chemical process, the atoms that make up the original substances are regrouped into different molecules, and these new substances have different properties from those of the reactants.

PS3.A: *Definitions of Energy*

- Temperature is not a measure of energy; the relationship between the temperature and the total energy of a system depends on the types, states, and amounts of matter present.

- Motion energy is properly called kinetic energy; it is proportional to the mass of the moving object and grows with the square of its speed.

- A system of objects may also contain stored (potential) energy, depending on their relative positions.

PS3.B: *Conservation of Energy and Energy Transfer*

- When the motion energy of an object changes, there is inevitably some other change in energy at the same time.

- The amount of energy transfer needed to change the temperature of a matter sample by a given amount depends on the nature of the matter, the size of the sample, and the environment.

- Energy is spontaneously transferred out of hotter regions or objects and into colder ones.

ESS3.A: *Natural Resources*

- Humans depend on Earth's land, ocean, atmosphere, and biosphere for many different resources. Minerals, fresh water, and biosphere resources are limited, and many are not renewable or replaceable over human lifetimes. These resources are distributed unevenly around the planet as a result of past geologic processes.

ESS3.C: *Human Impacts on Earth Systems*

- Typically as human populations and per-capita consumption of natural resources increase, so do the negative impacts on Earth unless the activities and technologies involved are engineered otherwise.

ETS1.A: *Defining and Delimiting Engineering Problems*

- The more precisely a design task's criteria and constraints can be defined, the more likely it is that the designed solution will be successful. Specification of constraints includes consideration of scientific principles and other relevant knowledge that is likely to limit possible solutions.

ETS1.B: *Developing Possible Solutions*

- A solution needs to be tested, and then modified on the basis of the test results in order to improve it.

ETS1.C: *Optimizing the Design Solution*

- Although one design may not perform the best across all tests, identifying the characteristics of the design that performed the best in each test can provide useful information for the redesign process – that is, some of the characteristics may be incorporated into the new design.

- The iterative process of testing the most promising solutions and modifying what is proposed on the basis of the test results leads to greater refinement and ultimately to an optimal solution.

CROSS-CUTTING CONCEPTS

Patterns

- Macroscopic patterns are related to the nature of microscopic and atomic-level structure.

Continued

Table 4.13. (*continued*)

Scale, Proportion, and Quantity

• Time, space, and energy phenomena can be observed at various scales using models to study systems that are too large or too small.

Systems and System Models

• Models can be used to represent systems and their interactions—such as inputs, processes and outputs and energy and matter flows within systems.

Energy and Matter

• The transfer of energy can be tracked as energy flows through a designed or natural system.

• Energy may take different forms (e.g. energy in fields, thermal energy, energy of motion).

Cause and Effect

• Cause and effect relationships may be used to predict phenomena in natural or designed systems.

Stability and Change

• Explanations of stability and change in natural or designed systems can be constructed by examining the changes over time and forces at different scales.

Structure and Function

• Structures can be designed to serve particular functions by taking into account properties of different materials, and how materials can be shaped and used.

COMMON CORE STATE STANDARDS FOR MATHEMATICS
MATHEMATICAL PRACTICES

• MP 1. Make sense of problems and persevere in solving them.

• MP 2. Reason abstractly and quantitatively.

• MP 3. Construct viable arguments and critique the reasoning of others.

• MP 4. Model with mathematics.

• MP 5. Use appropriate tools strategically.

MATHEMATICAL CONTENT

• 8.F.B.4. Construct a function to model a linear relationship between two quantities. Determine the rate of change and initial value of the function from a description of a relationship or from two (x, y) values, including reading these from a table or from a graph. Interpret the rate of change and initial value of a linear function in terms of the situation it models, and in terms of its graph or a table of values.

- 8.F.B.5. Describe qualitatively the functional relationship between two quantities by analyzing a graph (for example, where the function is increasing or decreasing, linear or nonlinear). Sketch a graph that exhibits the qualitative features of a function that has been described verbally.

COMMON CORE STATE STANDARDS FOR ENGLISH LANGUAGE ARTS
READING STANDARDS

- RL.8.1. Cite the textual evidence that most strongly supports an analysis of what the text says explicitly as well as inferences drawn from the text.

- RL.8.9. Analyze a case in which two or more texts provide conflicting information on the same topic and identify where the texts disagree on matters of fact or interpretation.

WRITING STANDARDS

- W.8.1. Write arguments to support claims with clear reasons and relevant evidence.

- W.8.1.A. Introduce claim(s), acknowledge and distinguish the claim(s) from alternate or opposing claims, and organize the reasons and evidence logically.

- W.8.1.B. Support claim(s) with logical reasoning and relevant evidence, using accurate, credible sources and demonstrating an understanding of the topic or text.

- W.8.1.C. Use words, phrases, and clauses to create cohesion and clarify the relationships among claim(s), counterclaims, reasons, and evidence.

- W.8.1.E. Provide a concluding statement or section that follows from and supports the argument presented.

- W.8.2. Write informative/explanatory texts to examine a topic and convey ideas, concepts, and information through the selection, organization, and analysis of relevant content.

- W.8.2.A. Introduce a topic clearly, previewing what is to follow; organize ideas, concepts, and information into broader categories; include formatting (for example, headings), graphics (for example, charts, tables), and multimedia when useful to aiding comprehension.

- W.8.2.B. Develop the topic with relevant, well-chosen facts, definitions, concrete details, quotations, or other information and examples.

- W.8.2.C. Use appropriate and varied transitions to create cohesion and clarify the relationships among ideas and concepts.

- W.8.2.D. Use precise language and domain-specific vocabulary to inform about or explain the topic.

- W.8.3. Write narratives to develop real or imagined experiences or events using effective technique, relevant descriptive details, and well-structured event sequences.

- W.8.3.A. Engage and orient the reader by establishing a context and point of view and introducing a narrator and/or characters; organize an event sequence that unfolds naturally and logically.

Continued

Table 4.13. (*continued*)

- W.8.3.D. Use precise words and phrases, relevant descriptive details, and sensory language to capture the action and convey experiences and events.

- W.8.7. Conduct short research projects to answer a question (including a self-generated question), drawing on several sources and generating additional related, focused questions that allow for multiple avenues of exploration.

- W.8.8. Gather relevant information from multiple print and digital sources, using search terms effectively; assess the credibility and accuracy of each source; and quote or paraphrase the data and conclusions of others while avoiding plagiarism and following a standard format for citation.

- W.8.9. Draw evidence from literary or informational texts to support analysis, reflection, and research.

SPEAKING AND LISTENING STANDARDS

- SL.8.1. Engage effectively in a range of collaborative discussions (one-on-one, in groups, and teacher-led) with diverse partners on grade 8 topics, texts, and issues, building on others' ideas and expressing their own clearly.

- SL.8.1.A. Come to discussions prepared, having read or researched material under study; explicitly draw on that preparation by referring to evidence on the topic, text, or issue to probe and reflect on ideas under discussion.

- SL.8.1.B. Follow rules for collegial discussions and decision-making, track progress toward specific goals and deadlines, and define individual roles as needed.

- SL.8.1.C. Pose questions that connect the ideas of several speakers and respond to others' questions and comments with relevant evidence, observations, and ideas.

- SL.8.1.D. Acknowledge new information expressed by others, and, when warranted, qualify or justify their own views in light of the evidence presented.

- SL.8.2. Analyze the purpose of information presented in diverse media and formats (for example, visually, quantitatively, orally) and evaluate the motives (for example, social, commercial, political) behind its presentation.

- SL.8.4. Present claims and findings, emphasizing salient points in a focused, coherent manner with relevant evidence, sound valid reasoning, and well-chosen details; use appropriate eye contact, adequate volume, and clear pronunciation.

FRAMEWORK FOR 21ST CENTURY LEARNING

Interdisciplinary themes (financial, economic, & business literacy; environmental literacy); Learning and Innovation Skills; Information, Media & Technology Skills; Life and Career Skills

Table 4.14. Key Vocabulary for Lesson 5

Key Vocabulary	Definition
battery	a device that produces an electric current by harnessing chemical reactions that take place within the device
battery anode	the negative electrode of a battery from which electrons are released into an external circuit
battery cathode	the positive terminal of a battery
circuit	a closed path through which an electric current flows
electrical current	the flow of electric charge, often carried by electrons moving in a wire
electrical energy	a type of energy caused by the movement of electrons
electrolyte	a substance that becomes an ion when dissolved in a solvent such as water
ion	an atom or molecule in which the total number of electrons does not equal the total number of protons, resulting in the particle having a positive or negative electrical charge
oxidation	the loss of electrons from a molecule, atom, or ion that results in a more positive charge than the original particle had
photovoltaic cell	an electrical device that converts the energy of light directly into electricity; a device whose electrical characteristics, including voltage and current, vary when exposed to light; the building blocks of solar panels
photovoltaics	a method of converting solar energy into electricity using materials that create voltage or electric current when exposed to light
reduction	the gain of electrons in a molecule, atom, or ion that results in a more negative charge than the original particle had
solar panels	a photovoltaic module or group of photovoltaic cells electrically connected
solar power	energy from the sun that is converted into thermal (heat) or electrical energy
voltage	a way to express the difference in charge between two points in a circuit

TEACHER BACKGROUND INFORMATION

This lesson marks a shift in focus from organically based fuel sources to a focus on electrical energy. Students will begin by gaining a basic understanding of how solar power relates to electrical energy. The lesson will begin with introducing vehicles powered directly by solar power. After discussing the shortcomings of this design, students will gain an understanding of the role of batteries as electrical storage units and the operation of electric cars.

Solar Energy

Solar energy is the world's largest energy source. In fact, fossil fuels can be thought of as simply a way that solar energy is stored, since the plants and animals that are the source of fossil fuels utilized the energy of the sun to grow. According to the Energy Information Administration, if 4% of the world's desert areas were covered with photovoltaics, the resulting energy could supply all of the world's electricity needs. The challenges of solar energy are the widely varying intensities of solar radiation reaching Earth in different locations and fluctuations due to time and weather. This means that any successful large-scale use of solar energy requires a storage mechanism.

Students may be familiar with solar panels on homes or businesses or with small-scale solar cells used to power batteries in solar calculators and watches. Solar cars harness the sun's energy using similar technologies that convert the sun's rays into electricity; therefore, solar cars are essentially electric cars that use solar power as a source of electricity. Some solar cars direct that electricity directly to an electric motor that is used to operate the car. These directly solar-powered cars are not marketed by any major auto manufacturer due to the limitations involved with powering a car this way. Some car manufacturers have, however, introduced solar hybrid concept cars in which components, such as headlights, audio systems, and interior lights, are solar powered, and, as of 2022, several car manufacturers had begun incorporating solar panels into the roofs of cars to help charge the battery. Several solar car competitions across the world showcase the capacity of completely solar-powered cars. Among the best known are the long distance World Solar Challenge, a 1,872 mile race across Australia, and the Toyota American Solar Challenge, a 2,400 mile race from Dallas, Texas to Alberta, Canada.

The development of marketable passenger cars powered solely by solar energy faces several challenges: First, the solar cells necessary to create solar panels can be costly, and a car that can travel at the expected speeds of passenger cars (60 mph plus) for adequate distances can use thousands of solar cells. Achieving speeds of around 60 mph requires a solar car to be very lightweight and aerodynamic; as of

2022, most of the prototype solar cars that achieve this speed are single passenger, have three wheels, and a flat profile. Additionally, it is important to note that a car covered with solar panels creates a passenger cabin that heats up quickly and to high temperatures. Driving at night or on rainy days presents obvious problems for solar cars, and a battery to store energy becomes necessary for practicality, although a succession of dark or rainy days could mean that there is no energy to store in the battery.

In spite of these impracticalities, research and development efforts to discover effective ways to incorporate solar power into daily use vehicles continues. The advantages of solar power include that the energy source is free, solar cars are quiet, and solar energy produces no harmful emissions.

Photovoltaic Cells

A basic understanding of photovoltaics is helpful for a study of solar power. Sunlight is composed of particles of solar energy called photons. Photovoltaics is the direct conversion of light into electricity. This conversion occurs at the atomic level through the photoelectric effect that occurs when a photon makes contact with an electron on a metal surface and causes it to be emitted as photoelectrons. The free electrons can be captured to create an electrical current.

Photovoltaic (PV) cells or solar cells are made of semiconductor materials (materials with electrical conductivity between that of metals such as copper and insulators such as glass). Silicon is a common semiconductor used in PV cells. PV cells are made up of at least two semiconductor layers; one layer has a positive charge and one layer has a negative charge. When enough photons are absorbed by the PV cell, electrons are freed from the negatively charged side. These electrons move to the positive side, creating a voltage differential (like the negative and positive terminals in a battery). When the layers are connected to an external load (like a motor or light), electricity flows. Individual cells are between one and ten centimeters in width and produce only one or two watts of electricity, which is insufficient for most uses. To increase power output, cells are connected to form modules or panels. More than 95% of all PV panels (also called solar panels) are made from crystalline silicon, the second most abundant element on Earth. For more information on how solar cells work, see www.acs.org/content/acs/en/education/resources/highschool/chemmatters/past-issues/archive-2013-2014/how-a-solar-cell-works.html.

Electric Cars

This lesson will introduce electric cars. Since solar-powered cars are limited by the amount of sunlight available, one way to expand the use of solar energy is to store it in batteries that can be used to operate electric cars.

Electric cars were used in the U.S. as long ago as the 1880s and were popular in the late 19th and early 20th centuries. In 1900, in fact, about 38% of the cars in the U.S. were powered by electricity. However, advances in internal combustion engines and mass production of gasoline led to the increased use of gasoline-powered cars and a decline in the use of electric cars. Interest in electric vehicles peaked briefly in the 1970s and 1980s with those decades' energy crises; however, electric cars did not reach a wide market. Since about 2008, however, there has been renewed interest in electric vehicles. This focus can be attributed to rising oil prices, the need to reduce greenhouse gas emissions, and technological advances in batteries. The Nissan Leaf is an all-electric car with a range of about 149 miles (as of 2022). Tesla Motors also produces an all-electric car. Electric cars such as the Leaf must be recharged, either at a charging station or using a household outlet. This electricity typically comes from the electrical grid, which often means that the electricity is from fossil fuel sources (coal and natural gas). The video about Leilani Münter in Lesson 1 illustrated an alternative for powering an electric car, since Münter uses energy from solar panels on her roof to charge her Tesla. This may present a more practical alternative for powering vehicles using solar power.

The batteries used to store solar power are lead-acid batteries. These contain sulfuric acid and tend to be expensive and cumbersome because of the large size of the batteries required to store solar energy. The issue of storing solar power is one of the challenges to widespread use of solar power as an alternate energy source.

Batteries in electric vehicles (EVs) are different than the batteries found in gasoline-powered cars (known as SLI batteries because they power starting, lighting, and ignition). As of 2022, most EVs used lithium-ion batteries. For current information on batteries used in EVs, see https://afdc.energy.gov/vehicles/electric_batteries.html.

Hybrid vehicles are those that use two or more power sources to power a vehicle. Hybrid EVs combine an internal combustion engine and electric motors. EVs are often parallel hybrid vehicles where the electric motor and internal combustion engine can power the vehicle either individually or together. An alternative to this is a series hybrid vehicle, which functions as an EV while there is sufficient energy in the battery, with the engine acting as a generator to maintain battery power.

COMMON MISCONCEPTIONS

Students will have various types of prior knowledge about the concepts introduced in this lesson. Table 4.15 describes a common misconception students may have concerning these concepts. Because of the breadth of students' experiences, it is not possible to anticipate every misconception that students may bring as they approach this lesson. Incorrect or inaccurate prior understanding of concepts can influence student learning in the future, however, so it is important to be alert to misconceptions such as those presented in the table.

Table 4.15. Common Misconception About the Concepts in Lesson 5

Topic	Student Misconception	Explanation
Solar energy	Solar panels or photovoltaic (PV) cells are necessary to use solar energy for human purposes.	Passive solar energy can be harnessed for human use. For example, buildings can be designed to absorb and store the sun's heat by situating windows to maximize sun exposure and strategically choosing building materials.

PREPARATION FOR LESSON 5

Review the teacher background information provided, assemble the materials for the lesson, make copies of the student handouts, and preview the videos recommended in the Learning Components section below.

In this lesson, student teams will be challenged to devise a PV cell simulation using the students in the class and a set of materials. Students' solutions will likely involve some students acting as electrons and some as photons. The U.S. Department of Energy provides two simple PV cell simulations available at www.energy.gov/ sites/default/files/2014/06/f16/solar_cellsimulation.pdf and www.howtosmile.org/ resource/smile-000-000-003-686 that you should review in order to be prepared to provide students with guidance.

LEARNING COMPONENTS
Introductory Activity/Engagement

Connection to the Challenge: Begin each day of this lesson by directing students' attention to the module challenge, the Speed of Green Challenge. Remind students that they will work in teams to create plans for ways to minimize the environmental impact of powering a race car. Hold a brief class discussion each day of how students' learning in the previous days' lessons contributed to their ability to complete the challenge. You may wish to create a class list of key ideas on chart paper.

Science and Social Studies Classes: Ask students if they think a car can be powered by solar power (energy from the sun). Introduce students to the Bridgestone World Solar Challenge, a biennial solar-powered car race in Australia by showing a video such as "Bridgestone World Solar Challenge 2013 – DAY 5 FINISH LINE" at www. youtube.com/watch?v=DdJIS66UMw0.

Tell students that this event is a 3000 km race (1,864 miles) through Australia. Ask students what innovations the video featured that the winning team used (for example, concentrating lenses, aerodynamics).

Have students brainstorm a list of challenges associated with powering cars with solar energy, creating a class list on chart paper.

Tell students that they will investigate solar power in this lesson. Ask them if the other energy sources they have investigated used solar power. Introduce the concept that when we use fossil fuels (gasoline and natural gas) and biomass fuels, we are essentially releasing solar power that has been stored. Ask students to explain how and why this is.

Mathematics Connection: Ask students for their ideas about how far Earth is from the sun in miles, creating a class list of students' ideas. After eight to ten students have made estimates, have students calculate an average from these estimates. Next, tell students that the actual distance from Earth to the sun is about 93 million miles. Ask students if they had difficulty making their calculations with the large number of zeros in their guesses. Introduce the concept of scientific notation as a way to express numbers that are very large or very small and are therefore inconvenient to write in decimal notation.

ELA Connection: Choose a poem about the sun to share with the class (for example, *Summer Sun* by Robert Louis Stevenson, *The Sun – just Touched the Morning* by Emily Dickinson, *The Sun Rising* by John Donne). Tell students that the sun has fascinated human beings since the earliest recorded history. It has been the subject of songs, poems, scientific investigations, and even religious worship. In this lesson, students will create examples of figurative language using the sun and will use these as an entry point for creating an original piece of literature about the sun.

Activity/Exploration

Science Class: Students will investigate solar power, photovoltaic cells, and batteries via the following activities:

- PV Cell Simulation Challenge

- Solar Circuits Activity

- Life Cycle Analysis

Introduce PV cells by showing students an image of solar panels (attached at the end of this lesson) and ask students to identify the objects shown (solar, or PV, panels). Tell students that solar panels are made up of small individual solar cells called photovoltaic cells, or PV cells. These individual cells can produce only a small amount of electricity so they are connected together into panels.

Introduce the concept that sunlight is composed of photons, or particles of solar energy. A PV cell absorbs photons to generate electricity. Ask students if they recall what electricity is (moving electrons). Ask students to share their ideas about how PV cells can generate electricity.

Tell students that the panels (and cells) are made in layers, like a sandwich. One side is specially treated to make it attract electrons. This is called the p-layer. The other side is called the n-layer because it has a negative charge because it has more electrons. Explain to students that photons of light are absorbed by this n-layer. When enough photons are absorbed, electrons are freed, and they move to the p-layer. The space in between the layers is known as the p-n junction and this is the space where the electrons move. When these layers are connected to a light bulb or another external device, electrons flow to create electricity.

PV Cell Simulation Challenge

Tell students that they will be challenged to work in teams to devise a physical simulation of how PV cells work. Teams will use the EDP to devise the simulation. Tell students that the materials for the simulation are the students in the class, the materials you have assembled, and any other materials that are on hand in the classroom. Students should each complete an Engineer It! handout for the challenge (attached at the end of the Lesson 1 handout).

Students will need to begin by researching how PV cells operate. The following resources are a good place to start:

- Videos showing and describing PV cells such as the "How Photovoltaic Cells Work" video at www.youtube.com/watch?v=x2zjdtxrisc.

- NOVA "Solar Power" video at https://video.thinktv.org/video/nova-solar-power

- NASA "How do Photovoltaics Work?" website *at* https://science.nasa.gov/science-news/science-at-nasa/2002/solarcells

After students have devised their simulations, have each group present its simulation to the class.

Solar Circuits Activity

Next, students will apply their understanding of PV cells to create circuits using PV cells. Student teams will investigate the effect of varying amounts of light and panel angles on the flow of electricity. Introduce the idea that there is a difference between passive solar energy and active solar energy. A passive solar collector does not use mechanical devices, but simply captures energy from the sun for immediate use. Examples of passive solar collectors are windows, greenhouses, and solariums. These operate through convection, a process in which heat is transferred in liquids and gases. Active solar devices use mechanical means to collect and store solar energy and convert it to electric power and heat. These systems use a solar collector such as a PV cell. Solar panels are examples of active solar energy.

This activity will work best on a sunny day in a location with access to direct sunlight; it should be conducted outdoors if possible. Distribute an Engineer It! handout (attached at the end of Lesson 1) to each student; students will record their progress with the design process on the handouts. Distribute a Solar Circuits student handout to each student and a set of materials to each team of students. Have students follow the procedures on the handout.

Life Cycle Analysis – Solar Energy

At this point, students should have a basic understanding of how PV cells are used to generate electricity. Ask students if there are any other ways that solar power could be used to power cars other than putting solar panels on the car. Remind them about Leilani Münter, who runs her car on solar power (an electric car that she charges from her home using solar panels on her house). Electricity is a secondary energy source (it isn't renewable or non-renewable since it's an energy carrier – it gets its energy from a primary source like coal, natural gas, or wind). An electric car can get its power from solar energy. This energy has to be stored in the car somehow – ask students to offer their ideas on how the energy from the sun can be stored in an electric car (batteries).

Introduce the concept of electric cars. Point out that these cars do not have an internal combustion engine, but rather run from a battery. Students may know that gasoline-powered vehicles have batteries – point out to them that the battery in a gas-powered car is used to start the car and for accessories like the lights and radio while in an electrical vehicle (EV) the battery supplies the power to make the car move. To explain how electric cars work, show a video such as "How Electric Cars Work" found at www.youtube.com/watch?v=2LsSPFlCUu0.

Using the Life Cycle Analysis handouts (attached to Lesson 4), have teams work together to create a Life Cycle Analysis for solar energy to power a vehicle.

Social Studies Class: Students will investigate careers related to solar energy in the A Job in the Sun activity.

A Job in the Sun

Student teams will investigate various jobs associated with solar energy. Assign each team one of the following careers:

1. Photovoltaic cell manufacturing technician

2. Electrical engineer

3. Solar installer

4. Solar research technician

5. Solar sales

Teams should investigate their assigned career and each student should create a STEM Research Notebook entry that includes the following information:

- Job title

- Average salary

- Where this job is available (states or region)

- Education or certification requirements

- Job responsibilities

- Resources for more information about this job

- Things that the student finds interesting about this job

Direct students to the Bureau of Labor Statistics Occupational Outlook website at www.bls.gov/ooh/arts-and-design/home.htm for basic information about jobs.

Mathematics Connection: Continue the discussion about scientific notation, emphasizing that scientists and mathematicians often calculate very large or very small numbers like the distance from the Earth to the sun. Have students practice writing their guesses about the distance from the sun to the Earth in scientific notation. Ask students to offer ideas on how to add and subtract numbers in scientific notation. Demonstrate how to convert the numbers to the same power of ten for this purpose. Ask students to offer their ideas on how to multiply and divide numbers in scientific notation and demonstrate the procedure for both these operations. Next, have students recalculate the average of the class guesses about distance to the sun with the numbers in scientific notation.

Provide students opportunities to practice writing numbers in scientific notation and expressing quantities in scientific notation as numbers.

ELA Connection: Review basic types of figurative language with students, including metaphor, simile, personification, hyperbole, and symbolism. Have the class provide examples of each type of figurative language and record the examples on a class chart. Have students write a sentence about the sun using each type of figurative language. Pair students to peer review one another's work and provide feedback on their sentences. Ask peer reviewers to place a star next to the sentence that interests them the most.

Explanation

Science Class: Have each student complete an Energy Source STEM Research Notebook Entry for solar energy using the student handout from Lesson 2. Remind students that solar-powered cars utilize both solar panels and batteries.

Social Studies Class: Have each team give a brief (5 minutes or less) presentation about the career in solar energy they researched, including information such as job responsibilities, relationship to the solar energy industry, and training and education required.

Mathematics Connection: You may wish to explain to students how to use scientific or graphing calculators to make calculations with numbers in scientific notation. The procedure for this will vary according to the type of calculators students use.

ELA Connection: After students have completed their peer reviews of the sentences they created using figurative language, have each student create a piece of literature that incorporates figurative language (students may wish to use the example their peer reviewers starred). You may wish to give your students a choice among various types of text (for example, poetry, short story, song, advertisement).

Elaboration/Application of Knowledge

Science Class: Hold a discussion about electric cars to introduce the role of batteries in electric cars. First, ask students when they think electric cars started being made. Emphasize to students that early in the history of the U.S. automobile, there were more electric cars than gasoline-powered cars. Show a video about the history of electric cars such as "A Brief History of the Electric Car" found at www.youtube.com/watch?v=SVLLpRP4o1A.

Tell students that batteries are particularly important in electric cars. Show a video that provides an overview of how batteries work such as "Batteries and How They Work" found at www.youtube.com/watch?v=CX8415ZZHVg. Next, distribute the "How Do Batteries Work?" student handout to each student and review the handout as a class, identifying the parts of a battery, the basic chemical reactions involved, and the path the electrons take.

Students will have the opportunity to create their own batteries in the optional Lemon Power activity.

Lemon Power Activity (optional)

Tell students that they will use the principles from this handout to create a battery. Distribute a Lemon Power student handout to each student and a set of materials to each pair of students. Have students use the procedure provided on the handout to create a battery. As an option, after completing the activity, student teams can experiment with other types of fruit and vegetables (for instance, apples, oranges, potatoes).

Social Studies Class: Have students investigate the history of solar power in the U.S., including the role of government support in the development of solar technologies and the role of technological innovations in solar energy beginning in the 18th and 19th century.

Mathematics Connection: N.A.

ELA Connection: Have students share the piece of literature they created with the class.

Evaluation/Assessment

Students may be assessed on the following performance tasks and other measures listed.

Performance Tasks

- PV Cell Simulation challenge
- Engineer It! – PV Cell Simulation challenge
- Energy Careers handout
- A Job in the Sun presentation (see Appendix A for presentation rubric)
- Solar Circuits handout
- Engineer It! – Solar Circuits handout
- Lemon Power handout (optional)
- Energy Source STEM Research Notebook entry – solar energy
- Life Cycle Analysis – solar energy

Other Measures

- Teacher observations
- STEM Research Notebook entries
- Collaboration (see Appendix A for rubric)

INTERNET RESOURCES

"A Brief History of the Electric Car" video

- *www.youtube.com/watch?v=SVLLpRP4o1A*

American Chemical Society "How a Solar Cell Works"

- *www.acs.org/content/acs/en/education/resources/highschool/chemmatters/past-issues/archive-2013-2014/how-a-solar-cell-works.html*

"Batteries and How They Work" video

- *www.youtube.com/watch?v=CX84l5ZZHVg*

Batteries in EVs

- *https://afdc.energy.gov/vehicles/electric_batteries.html*

"Bridgestone World Solar Challenge 2013 – DAY 5 FINISH LINE" video

- *www.youtube.com/watch?v=DdJIS66UMw0*

Bureau of Labor Statistics Occupational Outlook

- *www.bls.gov/ooh/arts-and-design/home.htm*

"How Photovoltaic Cells work" video

- *www.youtube.com/watch?v=x2zjdtxrisc*

"How Electric Cars Work" video

- *www.youtube.com/watch?v=2LsSPFlCUu0*

NOVA "Solar Power"

- *https://video.thinktv.org/video/nova-solar-power*

NASA "How do Photovoltaics Work?"

- *https://science.nasa.gov/science-news/science-at-nasa/2002/solarcells*

American Chemical Society "How a Solar Cell Works"

- *www.acs.org/content/acs/en/education/resources/highschool/chemmatters/past-issues/archive-2013-2014/how-a-solar-cell-works.html*

PV Cell Simulations

- *www.energy.gov/sites/default/files/2014/06/f16/solar_cellsimulation.pdf*
- *www.howtosmile.org/resource/smile-000-000-003-686*

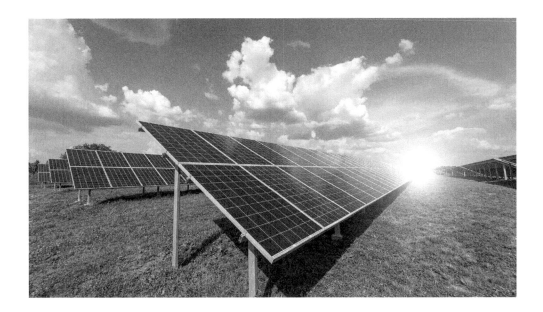

Solar Circuits Student Handout

Name: _____

In this activity you will investigate a simple circuit using a solar cell to operate a motor.

Materials

PV cell
Direct current motor
Propeller
2 wires with alligator clips
1 piece of black construction paper
Engineer It! handout (1 per student)

Your goal is to use the materials provided to make your propeller spin as fast as possible. Use the engineering design process (EDP) to put what you know about solar power and electricity to work.

Be sure to use the EDP and fill out your Engineer It! handout

After you have completed your design and created your circuit, do the following:

Cover portions of the solar cell with your black paper and record what happens:

25% covered: _____

50% covered: _____

75% covered: _____

100% covered: _____

What else, other than covering the solar panel, can you do to make the motor run more slowly or stop running?

_____

_____

How Do Batteries Work? Student Handout

SIMPLE ELECTRIC CIRCUIT

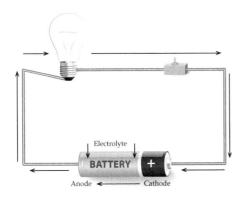

Electrolytes are substances that dissolve to become ions (charged particles). Many salts and acids are electrolytes

Ions are atoms in which the total number of protons does not equal the total number of electrons, giving the atom a positive or negative electrical charge.

Oxidation means that an element loses electrons (becomes a positively charged ion)

Reduction means that an element gains electrons (becomes a negatively charged ion)

Oxidation and Reduction always happen together!

The chemical reactions that occur to make electrons flow in a battery are called oxidation-reduction reactions (redox for short) – these reactions create ions.

Copper-Zinc Batteries:

Copper and Zinc are two elements that are often used in batteries.
When a piece of zinc (Zn) is placed in a salt solution, it loses an electron: $Zn = Zn^{2+} + 2\ e^-$
When copper (Cu) is in the same solution, it loses an electron too: $Cu = Cu^{2+} + 2\ e^-$
BUT zinc has a stronger tendency to lose electrons than copper, so copper will then pick up the electrons from the zinc: $Cu^{2+} + 2\ e^- = Cu$

Anode $\longleftarrow$ Cathode

So, in a battery, **zinc is the anode** since it tends to give up electrons. **Copper is the cathode** since it is picking up zinc's free electrons.

Lemon Power Student Handout
(Page 1 of 3)

In this activity, you will make your own copper – zinc battery and use it to power a clock/timer.

Materials

3 lemons
4 copper wires with alligator clips
4 galvanized (zinc coated) nails
4 pieces of copper wire (about 2″ each)
Digital clock or timer (normally powered by a 1.5 V watch-type battery)
1 knife
Paper towels
Safety goggles
Optional: Voltmeter or Multimeter

Procedure

1. Put on safety goggles.

2. Apply pressure to one lemon by rolling it across the table with your palm (to loosen the pulp).

3. Push the nail into the lemon. What do you think the coating on the nail is?

4. Pick a spot close to the nail and push the copper wire about halfway into the lemon.

5. Attach one alligator clip to the nail. Is this the anode or the cathode?

6. Attach one alligator clip to the copper wire. Is this the anode or the cathode?

7. Connect the ends of the wires to the voltmeter and record the reading (if it is negative, reverse the connections).

8. Look at the battery in the clock and determine how many volts of energy the clock requires to operate. Does your lemon battery provide enough?

9. Add a second lemon. Repeat steps 1–5 above. Attach the free end of the wire connected to the nail in lemon #1 to the copper wire in lemon #2.

10. Connect the ends of the wires to the voltmeter and record what the reading is (if it is negative, reverse the connections).

11. If the voltage reading on the voltmeter is still not equal to the clock battery voltage, add another lemon to your circuit and repeat the voltmeter reading.

NATIONAL SCIENCE TEACHING ASSOCIATION

Lemon Power Student Handout
(Page 2 of 3)

12. Now look at the battery holder in the clock. There are two contacts – one is positive and one is negative. The center contact is negative and the side contact is positive.

13. Connect the wires to the contacts in the clock.

14. Did the clock come on? If not, why do you think it is not operating?

Lemon Power Student Handout

(Page 3 of 3)

Data Sheet

Name: _____

Record your voltmeter readings here:

Number of Lemons			
Voltmeter Reading			

1. What acts as the anode in your battery?

_____

_____

2. What acts as the cathode in your battery?

_____

_____

3. What do you think is happening inside the lemon?

_____

_____

4. What do you think would happen if you added more lemons?

_____

_____

5. Do you think that any other metals would work? Why or why not?

_____

_____

Lesson Plan 6:
Capturing the Wind

This lesson will continue the discussion of electric vehicles (EVs) with the understanding that wind, while a valuable energy resource, is an impractical resource for directly powering vehicles. An overview of how wind provides power to electric-generating plants will be provided, and students will consider the advantages and disadvantages of wind as a direct and indirect source of power for vehicles. Students will understand the role of wind power within their regional context and will participate in a design challenge to create a device that uses wind power to generate energy and will use their understanding of wind energy to create an LCA for wind energy to power a race car.

ESSENTIAL QUESTIONS

- What is wind energy?

- What are the advantages and disadvantages of using wind energy as an energy source for cars?

- How can a vehicle be powered using wind energy?

- How does a wind turbine work?

ESTABLISHED GOALS AND OBJECTIVES

At the conclusion of this lesson, students will be able to do the following:

- Explain that wind energy is most practical as an energy source for vehicles when it is used as the energy source to charge a battery for an EV

- Identify geographical areas that utilize wind as an energy resource

- Describe the basic function of a wind turbine

- Apply a basic understanding of wind turbine components and functions to create their own wind turbines

- Demonstrate an understanding that the structure of wind turbine blades has implications for a wind turbine's performance

- Apply the EDP to solve a problem

- Analyze the implications of using wind energy as a power source for vehicles

TIME REQUIRED

2 days (approximately 45 minutes each day; see Table 3.8, p. 44)

MATERIALS

Required Materials for Lesson 6

- STEM Research Notebooks
- computer with internet access for viewing videos

Additional Materials for Capturing the Wind activity (1 for each group of 3–4 students)

- pinwheel pattern
- 1 piece of 8½″ × 11″ cardstock
- scissors
- thumbtack
- electric motor (see Lesson 5 materials)
- 2 alligator clip wires
- piece of clay or cork
- fan (1 for the class)
- voltmeter (1 for the class)
- Styrofoam plate
- small aluminum foil pan
- 6 craft sticks (regular size)
- 6 craft sticks (large size)
- 4 index cards (3″ × 5″)
- 6 plastic drinking straws
- 1 cork
- 5 rubber bands
- 1 roll masking tape

Additional Materials for Life Cycle Analysis of Wind Energy (for each team of 3–4 students)

- 1 set of markers
- scissors
- tape or glue

- 1 piece of 22″ × 28″ poster board (optional, see Preparation for Lesson 3, p. 125)

- 6 pieces of colored paper (optional, see Preparation for Lesson 3, p. 125)

SAFETY NOTES

1. Students should use caution when handling scissors and other pointed objects, as the sharp points and blades can cut or puncture skin.

2. Students should use caution when handling thumbtacks, as sharp ends can cut or puncture skin.

3. Caution students when cutting aluminum that sharp edges can cut or puncture skin.

4. Have students wear safety goggles during the Capturing the Wind activity.

5. Caution students of the risk of shock when using electricity in activities, even when voltage is low.

CONTENT STANDARDS AND KEY VOCABULARY

Table 4.16 lists the content standards from the *NGSS*, *CCSS*, and the Framework for 21st Century Learning that this lesson addresses, and Table 4.17 presents the key vocabulary. Vocabulary terms are provided for both teacher and student use. Teachers may choose to introduce some or all of the terms to students.

Table 4.16. Content Standards Addressed in STEM Road Map Module Lesson 6

NEXT GENERATION SCIENCE STANDARDS
PERFORMANCE OBJECTIVES
• MS-PS1–2. Analyze and interpret data on the properties of substances before and after the substances interact to determine if a chemical reaction has occurred.
• MS-PS1–3. Gather and make sense of information to describe that synthetic materials come from natural resources and impact society.
• MS-PS2–2. Plan an investigation to provide evidence that the change in an object's motion depends on the sum of the forces on the object and the mass of the object.
• MS-PS3–2. Develop a model to describe that when the arrangement of objects interacting at a distance changes, different amounts of potential energy are stored in the system.

Continued

Table 4.16. (*continued*)

- MS-PS3–5. Construct, use, and present arguments to support the claim that when the kinetic energy of an object changes, energy is transferred to or from the object.

- MS-ETS1–1. Define the criteria and constraints of a design problem with sufficient precision to ensure a successful conclusion, taking into account relevant scientific principles and potential impacts on people and the natural environment that may limit possible solutions.

- MS-ETS1–2. Evaluate competing design solutions using a systematic process to determine how well they meet the criteria and constraints of the problem.

- MS-ETS1–3. Analyze data from tests to determine similarities and differences among several design solutions to identify the best characteristics of each that can be combined into a new solution to better meet the criteria for success.

- MS-ETS1–4 Develop a model to generate data for iterative testing and modification of a proposed object, tool, or process such that an optimal design can be achieved.

SCIENCE AND ENGINEERING PRACTICES
Developing and Using Models

- Develop and use a model to describe phenomena.

Obtaining, Evaluating, and Communicating Information

- Gather, read, and synthesize information from multiple appropriate sources and assess the credibility, accuracy, and possible bias of each publication and methods used, and describe how they are supported or not supported by evidence.

Analyzing and Interpreting Data

- Analyze and interpret data to determine similarities and differences in findings.

Constructing Explanations and Designing Solutions

- Undertake a design project, engaging in the design cycle, to construct and/or implement a solution that meets specific design criteria and constraints.

- Apply scientific ideas or principles to design an object, tool, process, or system.

Planning and Carrying Out Investigations

- Plan an investigation individually and collaboratively, and in the design: identify independent and dependent variables and controls, what tools are needed to do the gathering, how measurements will be recorded, and how many data are needed to support a claim.

- Conduct an investigation and evaluate the experimental design to produce data to serve as the basis for evidence that can meet the goals of the investigation.

Engaging in Argument from Evidence

- Construct and present oral and written arguments supported by empirical evidence and scientific reasoning to support or refute an explanation or a model for a phenomenon or a solution to a problem.

DISCIPLINARY CORE IDEAS

PS3.A: *Definitions of Energy*

- Temperature is not a measure of energy; the relationship between the temperature and the total energy of a system depends on the types, states, and amounts of matter present.

- Motion energy is properly called kinetic energy; it is proportional to the mass of the moving object and grows with the square of its speed.

- A system of objects may also contain stored (potential) energy, depending on their relative positions.

PS3.B: *Conservation of Energy and Energy Transfer*

- When the motion energy of an object changes, there is inevitably some other change in energy at the same time.

- The amount of energy transfer needed to change the temperature of a matter sample by a given amount depends on the nature of the matter, the size of the sample, and the environment.

- Energy is spontaneously transferred out of hotter regions or objects and into colder ones.

PS3.C: *Relationship Between Energy and Forces*

- When two objects interact, each one exerts a force on the other that can cause energy to be transferred to or from the object.

ESS3.A: *Natural Resources*

- Humans depend on Earth's land, ocean, atmosphere, and biosphere for many different resources. Minerals, fresh water, and biosphere resources are limited, and many are not renewable or replaceable over human lifetimes. These resources are distributed unevenly around the planet as a result of past geologic processes.

ESS3.C: *Human Impacts on Earth Systems*

- Typically as human populations and per-capita consumption of natural resources increase, so do the negative impacts on Earth unless the activities and technologies involved are engineered otherwise.

ETS1.A: *Defining and Delimiting Engineering Problems*

- The more precisely a design task's criteria and constraints can be defined, the more likely it is that the designed solution will be successful. Specification of constraints includes consideration of scientific principles and other relevant knowledge that is likely to limit possible solutions.

Continued

Table 4.16. (*continued*)

ETS1.B: *Developing Possible Solutions*

- A solution needs to be tested, and then modified on the basis of the test results in order to improve it.

ETS1.C: *Optimizing the Design Solution*

- Although one design may not perform the best across all tests, identifying the characteristics of the design that performed the best in each test can provide useful information for the redesign process – that is, some of the characteristics may be incorporated into the new design.

- The iterative process of testing the most promising solutions and modifying what is proposed on the basis of the test results leads to greater refinement and ultimately to an optimal solution.

CROSS-CUTTING CONCEPTS

Scale, Proportion, and Quantity

- Time, space, and energy phenomena can be observed at various scales using models to study systems that are too large or too small.

Systems and System Models

- Models can be used to represent systems and their interactions—such as inputs, processes and outputs—and energy and matter flows within systems.

Energy and Matter

- The transfer of energy can be tracked as energy flows through a designed or natural system.

- Energy may take different forms (e.g. energy in fields, thermal energy, energy of motion).

Cause and Effect

- Cause and effect relationships may be used to predict phenomena in natural or designed systems.

Stability and Change

- Explanations of stability and change in natural or designed systems can be constructed by examining the changes over time and forces at different scales.

Structure and Function

- Structures can be designed to serve particular functions by taking into account properties of different materials, and how materials can be shaped and used

COMMON CORE STATE STANDARDS FOR MATHEMATICS

MATHEMATICAL PRACTICES

- MP 1. Make sense of problems and persevere in solving them.

- MP 2. Reason abstractly and quantitatively.

NATIONAL SCIENCE TEACHING ASSOCIATION

- MP 3. Construct viable arguments and critique the reasoning of others.

- MP 4. Model with mathematics.

- MP 5. Use appropriate tools strategically.

COMMON CORE STATE STANDARDS FOR ENGLISH LANGUAGE ARTS
READING STANDARDS

- RL.8.1. Cite the textual evidence that most strongly supports an analysis of what the text says explicitly as well as inferences drawn from the text.

WRITING STANDARDS

- W.8.3. Write narratives to develop real or imagined experiences or events using effective technique, relevant descriptive details, and well-structured event sequences.

- W.8.3.A. Engage and orient the reader by establishing a context and point of view and introducing a narrator and/or characters; organize an event sequence that unfolds naturally and logically.

- W.8.3.D. Use precise words and phrases, relevant descriptive details, and sensory language to capture the action and convey experiences and events.

- W.8.7. Conduct short research projects to answer a question (including a self-generated question), drawing on several sources and generating additional related, focused questions that allow for multiple avenues of exploration.

- W.8.8. Gather relevant information from multiple print and digital sources, using search terms effectively; assess the credibility and accuracy of each source; and quote or paraphrase the data and conclusions of others while avoiding plagiarism and following a standard format for citation.

- W.8.9. Draw evidence from literary or informational texts to support analysis, reflection, and research.

SPEAKING AND LISTENING STANDARDS

- SL.8.1. Engage effectively in a range of collaborative discussions (one-on-one, in groups, and teacher-led) with diverse partners on grade 8 topics, texts, and issues, building on others' ideas and expressing their own clearly.

- SL.8.1.A. Come to discussions prepared, having read or researched material under study; explicitly draw on that preparation by referring to evidence on the topic, text, or issue to probe and reflect on ideas under discussion.

- SL.8.1.B. Follow rules for collegial discussions and decision-making, track progress toward specific goals and deadlines, and define individual roles as needed.

- SL.8.1.C. Pose questions that connect the ideas of several speakers and respond to others' questions and comments with relevant evidence, observations, and ideas.

Continued

Table 4.16. (*continued*)

> - SL.8.1.D. Acknowledge new information expressed by others, and, when warranted, qualify or justify their own views in light of the evidence presented.
>
> - SL.8.2. Analyze the purpose of information presented in diverse media and formats (for example, visually, quantitatively, orally) and evaluate the motives (for example, social, commercial, political) behind its presentation.
>
> - SL.8.4. Present claims and findings, emphasizing salient points in a focused, coherent manner with relevant evidence, sound valid reasoning, and well-chosen details; use appropriate eye contact, adequate volume, and clear pronunciation.
>
> *FRAMEWORK FOR 21ST CENTURY LEARNING*
>
> Interdisciplinary themes (financial, economic, & business literacy; environmental literacy); Learning and Innovation Skills; Information, Media & Technology Skills; Life and Career Skills

Table 4.17. Key Vocabulary in Lesson 6

Key Vocabulary	Definition
kinetic energy	the energy of motion
turbine	a device that extracts energy from the flow of a liquid or air and uses it to turn rotate mechanical parts

TEACHER BACKGROUND INFORMATION
Wind Energy

Energy from wind is recognized as one of the cleanest ways to generate electricity. It is also the fastest-growing electricity source in the world. Some European nations utilize wind power more widely than the U.S.; however, wind capacity is growing in the U.S. due to technological innovations that are decreasing the cost of wind energy.

Wind is caused by air flowing from areas of high pressure to areas of low pressure. Because of Earth's rotation this air flow is deflected, and wind flows around areas of high and low pressure. Where areas of high and low pressure are close together (coastal areas for instance), there are stronger winds. Students should understand that wind is caused by the uneven heating of Earth's surface. Sunlight warms some areas more than others. Warm air is less dense than cold air, so it rises, leaving an area of low air pressure behind which the cooler, higher-pressure air replaces, resulting in wind. The Wind Resource Maps from the National Renewable Energy Laboratory (NREL) available at www.nrel.gov/gis/wind.html gives an overview of wind strength across the U.S.

A wind turbine's blades collect the wind's kinetic energy, transferring this energy to a drive shaft that turns an electric generator. The U.S. Office of Energy Efficiency & Renewable Energy provides an overview of the how wind turbines work and types of turbines at www.energy.gov/eere/wind/how-do-wind-turbines-work. Note that the focus of this lesson is on individually generated wind energy, not wind energy generated in wind farms as a public utility.

See the following websites for more information about wind energy:

- www.nrel.gov/research/re-wind.html

- www.eia.gov/renewable/

- www.midwestwindenergycenter.org/

COMMON MISCONCEPTIONS

Students will have various types of prior knowledge about the concepts introduced in this lesson. Table 4.18 outlines some common misconceptions students may have concerning these concepts. Because of the breadth of students' experiences, it is not possible to anticipate every misconception that students may bring as they approach this lesson. Incorrect or inaccurate prior understanding of concepts can influence student learning in the future, however, so it is important to be alert to misconceptions such as those presented in the table.

Table 4.18. Common Misconceptions About the Concepts in Lesson 6

Topic	Student Misconception	Explanation
Wind energy	Wind is a random movement of air with no discernible cause or predictable pattern.	Wind is caused by differences in atmospheric pressure. When air moves from areas of high to low pressure, winds result. The direction of the wind is influenced by Earth's rotation.
	Wind energy is free.	Although the wind itself cannot be bought or sold and is freely available, the initial investment to build wind turbines is considerable.

PREPARATION FOR LESSON 6

Review the teacher background information provided, assemble the materials for the lesson, make copies of the student handouts, and preview the videos recommended in the Learning Components section below.

You should familiarize yourself with wind energy production in your region before this lesson (see Teacher Background Information, p. 198).

LEARNING COMPONENTS
Introductory Activity/Engagement

Connection to the Challenge: Begin each day of this lesson by directing students' attention to the module challenge, the Speed of Green Challenge. Remind students that they will work in teams to create plans for ways to minimize the environmental impact of powering a race car. Hold a brief class discussion each day of how students' learning in the previous days' lessons contributed to their ability to complete the challenge. You may wish to create a class list of key ideas on chart paper.

Science and Social Studies Classes: Remind students of Leilani Münter and her use of solar power to operate her car. Ask students if the car was powered directly by solar power. Remind students that electricity is a carrier for energy and that solar power is a primary source of energy while the energy it generates is stored in a battery; this energy is delivered to the car using electricity.

Ask students if they can think of another renewable source of energy for a vehicle. Remind students of their Blown Away design challenge from Lesson 1 (wind was the energy source). In this case the wind directly powered their vehicles. Ask students if they think this is a practical way to power a vehicle.

Show students a video of an EV that uses wind as an energy source such as "This Car is Powered by Wind" at https://www.youtube.com/watch?v=Hz3DN8APAaY. Ask students if the vehicles featured in the video are directly powered by wind (typically the wind energy is used to charge a battery in the EV).

Ask students if they can think of any other ways that wind power is used. Show students the picture of wind turbines at a wind farm (attached at the end of this lesson). Ask students for their ideas about how that wind power gets from these turbines into homes and businesses to power electrical devices. Explain that the blades are connected to a drive shaft that turns an electric generator. As the wind moves the blades it turns the driveshaft, which turns the electric generator and generates electricity.

Show students the video "Moving Windmills: The William Kamkwamba Story," based upon the book *The Boy Who Harnessed the Wind* (found at www.youtube.com/watch?v=arD374MFk4w). Ask students if they have seen farms with windmills and what those windmills might be used for on farms (for example, pumping water, generating electricity). Kamkwamba's windmill was a fairly simple type, but the basic technologies are essentially the same. As a class, review the U.S. Department of Energy explanation of wind turbine design and function found at www.energy.gov/eere/wind/how-do-wind-turbines-work.

Have students work in groups to brainstorm various ideas of how wind could be used to power a car.

Mathematics Connection: Show students the image of the wind farm attached at the end of this lesson. Ask them to estimate how long they think the blades are on the turbines, creating a list of students' estimates. As a class visit the National Wind Watch website at www.wind-watch.org/faq-size.php to find the actual length of wind turbine blades (wind turbine blades often exceed 100 feet in length).

Ask students if they think the length of the blades on a wind turbine matters and how they think this length is determined. Use this discussion to introduce the concept of ratios. Introduce the idea that tip speed ratio (TSR) is an important factor in designing a wind turbine. This quantity is calculated by the following equation: TSR = Tip Speed of Blade ÷ Wind Speed

The length of the blade determines the circumference of the circle in which the blades travel. This circumference is directly related to the speed the blade rotates (measured as tip speed). See www.windynation.com/cm/wind_tip-speed-ratio-how-calculate-and-apply-tsr-blade-selection.pdf for more information on TSR and how to calculate it.

ELA Connection: Introduce William Kamkwamba's book *The Boy Who Harnessed the Wind*. Use this book to launch a discussion of biographies and autobiographies. Ask students to distinguish between biographies and autobiographies and provide examples of biographical and autobiographical texts with which they are familiar.

Activity/Exploration

Science and Social Studies Classes: Students will consider wind power via the following activities:

- Where's the Wind? Activity (includes Life Cycle Analysis for wind energy)

- Capturing the Wind activity

Students should create an Energy Source STEM Research Notebook Entry after completing the activities (see handout in Lesson 2).

Where's the Wind? Activity

(Note: this activity could be completed in Social Studies as an alternative.)

Point out to students that in order to know if they could charge an electric vehicle with their own wind turbine that they first need to know if there is enough wind.

Ask students to share their ideas about what wind is. Show a video about wind formation such as "Why Does the Wind Blow?" found at www.youtube.com/watch?v=xCLwbqmacck for an overview of how wind is formed.

After watching the video, ask students what parts of the country they think are the windiest based on what they know about wind.

Distribute a Where's the Wind handout to each student and have student teams work together to do the following:

1. Research what sort of wind resources there are in their area.

2. Investigate what the cost is to build an individual wind turbine.

3. Identify the environmental impacts associated with wind energy.

4. Create an LCA for an EV with a battery charged using a wind turbine.

The following websites will be useful for state-based information about wind:

- https://windexchange.energy.gov/states
- https://www.nrel.gov/gis/wind.html

Capturing the Wind Activity

This activity has two parts. In the first, students will create a pinwheel wind turbine using a pattern for blades and determine the amount of power it generates. Next, they will use the engineering design process to create new blades designed to maximize power output.

Distribute a Capturing the Wind student handout to each student for students to use for the first part of the activity. Students will complete the second part of the activity using the Engineer It! handouts (attached at the end of Lesson 1) to track their design process.

Mathematics Connection: Have students work in groups to determine a formula to determine the tip speed of a wind turbine blade. Remind students that speed is calculated as distance/time, and that wind turbine blades move in a circle (students will need to know the relationship between radius and circumference of a circle and that circumference = $2\pi r$). Encourage students to refer to the image of the wind farm and to sketch a picture of a wind turbine.

You may wish to give students sample data. For example, a wind turbine with blades that are 135 feet long makes three rotations per second. Ask students how they will calculate the tip speed of the blades. Students should conclude that the tip speed (V) is calculated as $V = 2\pi r \div$ time for one rotation.

After students have arrived at the formula for tip speed, have them practice calculating the tip speed ratio with various blade lengths and wind speeds using the formula TSR = Tip Speed of Blade $\div$ Wind Speed. Emphasize to students that they must use the same units throughout their calculations (i.e., if wind speed is in miles per hour, then a speed that is expressed in meters per second must be converted to miles per hour).

ELA Connection: Using William Kamkwamba as an example of a young inventor, have students research and create biographies of young inventors or innovators. These biographies can be created in a variety of media of your and/or your students' choice (for example, as posters, mini-documentary videos, PowerPoint presentations). Examples of inventors students might choose to research include:

- Anton van Leeuwenhoek (made impactful changes to microscopy at age 16)

- Louis Braille (developed the Braille system of reading and writing at age 15)

- George Westinghouse (obtained a patent for a steam engine at age 19)

- George Nissen (created the trampoline at age 16)

- Robert Heft (proposed the 50 star flag to congress at age 17)

- Rebecca Shroeder (invented the Glo-Sheet at age 10)

- Raymond Wang (invented a system to improve air quality on airplanes at age 17)

- Eesha Khare (invented a 30-second phone charger at age 18)

- Bishop Curry V (invented a device to help prevent hot car deaths at age 10)

Alternatively, you may choose to introduce a literature connection such as *Brainstorm! The Stories of Twenty American Kid Inventors* by Tom Tucker (ISBN-13: 978–0374409289) or *The Kid Who Invented the Popsicle: And Other Surprising Stories about Inventions* (ISBN-13: 978–0141302041).

Explanation

Science Class: Have each student team share its wind turbine design from the Capturing the Wind activity with the class. Students should explain the features of their designs and why they made the design choices they did and how their turbines performed. As a class, compare and contrast designs and create a list of design features from the best-performing and worst-performing turbines.

Have students create Energy Source STEM Research Notebook entries for wind using the handout in Lesson 2.

Social Studies Class: Have each team present their findings about one of the four areas they researched in the Where's the Wind? activity. Hold a class discussion about each point, having students share discrepant findings or adding additional information to teams' findings.

Mathematics Connection: Explain to students that a ratio is an expression that tells how two quantities compare (i.e., it compares the size of one thing to the size of another). Some ratios are expressed as "$x : y$" or "x to y," or they can be expressed as a quotient. When the quantities being compared have the same units, then the resulting ratio has no units. If the units are different, the ratio that results is often called a rate, as in miles per hour. Discuss how TSR is expressed, asking students whether ratios or quotients are typically used and why they think this is.

Ask students if they think that the TSR matters – i.e., is a wind turbine more efficient if the TSR is larger? Ask students to analyze the TSR formula to indicate what a TSR greater than 1 means (the blades are spinning faster than the wind) and what a TSR less than 1 means (the blades are spinning slower than the wind). Introduce the concept of ratios to students and emphasize that the TSR is a ratio of blade speed to wind speed; this affects how much energy a wind turbine can produce.

Historical windmills, such as those used to pump water or grind grain, had TSRs of around 1. In contrast, wind turbines today have TSRs around 5; however, higher TSRs are not necessarily better. If the blades spin too slowly, the wind passes between blades and is not captured to turn the rotor and create electricity. On the other hand, if the blades spin too fast, the blades act like a solid surface to the wind and it is not captured by the blades. There is a formula for TSR for maximum power output: $TSR_{maximum} = 4\pi \div n$ (where n= the number of blades on the turbine).

ELA Connection: Students should understand the similarities and differences in autobiographies and biographies. You may wish to have them create a Venn diagram to express these similarities and differences. You should emphasize the primary characteristics of each genre. Autobiographies have the following characteristics:

- Written in first person voice.

- Are accounts of the author's life or events in their life.

- The main character is the author.

- The reader learns about the author's values, goals, feelings, and thoughts.

Biographies have the following characteristics:

- Written in third person voice.

- Are descriptions of a person's life or events in their life.

- Written by someone who is familiar with the details of the subject's life.

- Describes how the subject affected others.

- May contain clues about how the author feels about the subject.

You may also wish to introduce the distinction between subjective (based on opinion, not fact) and objective (based on provable facts) information.

Elaboration/Application of Knowledge

Science and Social Studies Classes and Mathematics Connection: Have students use the turbines they created in the Capturing the Wind? activity to calculate their actual TSR and the maximum TSR for the number of blades they used on their pinwheel

wind turbines. Ask students to determine how they might alter their blades to achieve maximum TSR.

Using the information about wind resources from teams' Where's the Wind? research and the design features of the best-performing turbines in the Capturing the Wind activity, work as a class to propose an optimum location in your local area for a wind turbine, and to propose a design for a turbine, including the optimum TSR and materials they might use for a turbine.

ELA Connection: Have students continue to work on their biographies or the optional literature connections suggested in the Explanation section. If students created biographies, plan to have students share their biographies with the class.

Evaluation/Assessment

Students may be assessed on the following performance tasks and other measures listed.

Performance Tasks

- Where's the Wind? handout

- Life Cycle Analysis – wind

- Capturing the Wind handout

- Engineer It! handout - Capturing the Wind

- Energy Source STEM Research Notebook Entry – Wind

Other Measures

- Teacher observations

- Collaboration (see Appendix A for rubric)

INTERNET RESOURCES

"Moving Windmills: The William Kamkwamba Story" video

- *www.youtube.com/watch?v=arD374MFk4w*

National Wind Watch

- *www.wind-watch.org/faq-size.php*

Tip Speed Ratio

- *www.windynation.com/cm/wind_tip-speed-ratio-how-calculate-and-apply-tsr-blade-selection.pdf*

"This Car is Powered by Wind" video

- *www.youtube.com/watch?v=Hz3DN8APAaY*

U.S. Office of Energy overview of wind turbines

- *www.energy.gov/eere/wind/how-do-wind-turbines-work*

Why Does the Wind Blow?" video

- *www.youtube.com/watch?v=rCLwhqmacck*

Wind Resource Map, NREL

- *www.nrel.gov/gis/wind.html*

Wind energy resources

- *www.nrel.gov/research/re-wind.html*

- *www.eia.gov/renewable/*

- *www.midwestwindenergycenter.org*

Wind information by state

- *www.nrel.gov/gis/wind.html*

- *https://windexchange.energy.gov/states*

Where's the Wind? Student Handout

Name: _____

Can you power a race car with the wind? You and your team are going to collect some information that will help you determine how practical it is to power an electric vehicle (EV) with a wind turbine. Use this handout to organize your findings.

How available are wind resources in your state?

What features of the geography in your city might be useful for wind energy? What might be a problem?

Where did you find this information?

How much would it cost to build a wind turbine of your own?

Where did you find this information?

What are the environmental impacts of building a wind turbine?

Using what you found out, complete a Life Cycle Analysis handout for using individually generated wind energy to power a car.

Complete an Energy Source STEM Research Notebook Entry for wind energy.

NATIONAL SCIENCE TEACHING ASSOCIATION

Pinwheel Pattern Student Handout

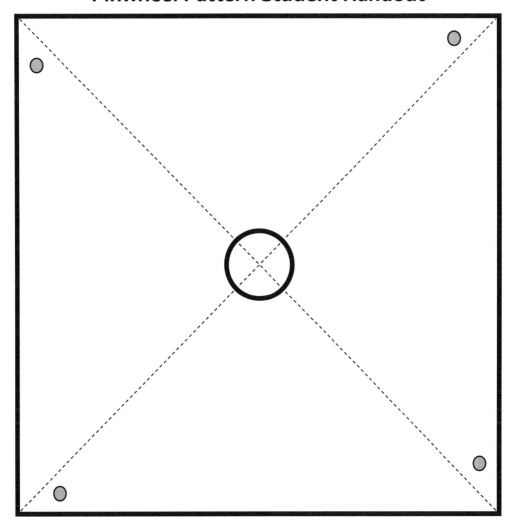

1. Cut out pattern on solid lines.

2. Cut dotted lines just to the edge of the circle in the middle (try not to cut into the center circle).

3. Use a pencil to punch holes in the dots on the four corners.

4. Make the small circles meet the center circle.

5. Follow the directions on the Capturing the Wind handout.

Capturing the Wind Student Handout
(Page 1 of 2)

Name: _____

There are two parts to this activity. In the first part, you and your team will follow instructions to create a wind turbine and determine how much power it generates. In the second part, you and your team will try to improve on the blade design.

Part I:

Materials
Cardstock
Thumbtack
Electric motor
Alligator clip wires
Piece of clay or cork
1 Capturing the Wind data sheet per person
Fan (1 for the class)
Voltmeter (1 for the class)

Procedure

1. Use the pinwheel pattern to create your pinwheel.

2. Put the shaft of the motor through the center of the pinwheel.

3. Put the clay or cork on the end of the shaft to keep the pinwheel in place.

4. Place your turbine in front of the fan to make sure that it will spin.

5. Attach the alligator clips to the motor and the voltmeter and record the amount of energy your turbine produces on your data sheet.

Part II:

Materials	Procedure
All materials from Part 1	1. Use the engineering design process* to create new blades for your turbine.
Styrofoam plate	
Small foil pan	2. Test it with the fan and the voltmeter. Record your findings on your data sheet
6 craft sticks (regular size)	
6 craft sticks (large size)	3. Improve on your design or try a new design.
4 index cards (3″ × 5″)	4. Repeat steps 1–3.
6 plastic drinking straws	* Be sure to fill out your Engineer It! handout.
cork	
5 rubber bands	
Masking tape	

Capturing the Wind Student Handout
(Page 2 of 2)
Data Sheet

Name: _____

Blade Type				
	Pinwheel pattern			
Blade Characteristics (material, size, etc.)	Cardstock, 4 inch diameter, from pattern			
Energy Output (volts)				

1. What material worked best? _____

2. What materials didn't work well? _____

3. Did the diameter of the turbine affect the amount of energy it produced? If so, how?

   _____

4. What happens when you change the angles of the blades on your turbine?

   _____

Lesson Plan 7:
The EV Mini Prix

Students will consider design factors associated with vehicles' energy requirements, including aerodynamics, body weight, and friction. Student teams will use these concepts, along with their understanding of electric vehicles and the EDP, to create their own EVs to compete in a race.

ESSENTIAL QUESTIONS

- How can we create an EV with a given set of materials?

- What is friction and how does it affect car performance?

- What is aerodynamic drag and how does it affect car performance?

- What effect do weight of materials have on car performance?

ESTABLISHED GOALS AND OBJECTIVES

At the conclusion of this lesson, students will be able to do the following:

- Demonstrate a conceptual understanding of friction

- Demonstrate a conceptual understanding of aerodynamic drag as a special type of friction

- Understand that weight of materials affects car performance

- Use their understanding of friction, aerodynamics, materials, and batteries to create their own EV

- Use the EDP to solve a problem

TIME REQUIRED

3 days (approximately 45 minutes each day; see Tables 3.9–3.10, p. 45)

MATERIALS

Required Materials for Lesson 7

- STEM Research Notebooks

- computer with internet access for viewing videos

Additional Materials for EV Mini Prix (for each group of 3–4 students unless otherwise indicated):

- 2 water bottles (500 mL) with caps

- 1 piece of balsa wood (about 4″ × 6″)

- 4 wooden disks with hole in the middle

- 4 CDs

- 4 plastic drinking straws (non-bendable)

- 4 wooden skewers

- 10 pennies

- 5 rubber bands (6 mm width)

- 1 rubber band (1 mm width)

- 1 12V direct current motor

- 2 9V batteries

- 9V battery connectors

- 2 alligator clip wires

- 1 roll masking tape

- 1 hot glue gun and 2 glue sticks

- stopwatch (1 per class)

- race area about 40 feet long (1 per class)

SAFETY NOTES

1. Students should use caution when handling scissors and other pointed objects, as the sharp points and blades can cut or puncture skin.

2. Caution students when cutting plastic or other rigid materials that sharp edges can cut or puncture skin.

3. Remind students that personal protective equipment (safety glasses or goggles, aprons, and gloves) must be worn during the setup, hands-on, and takedown segments of the EV Mini Prix activity.

4. Caution students that hot glue and hot glue guns can burn skin; demonstrate to students how to safely use hot glue and supervise students' use of hot glue guns closely.

5. Caution students of the risk of shock when using electricity in activities, even when voltage is low.

CONTENT STANDARDS AND KEY VOCABULARY

Table 4.19 lists the content standards from the *NGSS*, *CCSS*, and the Framework for 21st Century Learning that this lesson addresses, and Table 4.20 presents the key vocabulary. Vocabulary terms are provided for both teacher and student use. Teachers may choose to introduce some or all of the terms to students.

Table 4.19. Content Standards Addressed in STEM Road Map Module Lesson 7

NEXT GENERATION SCIENCE STANDARDS
PERFORMANCE OBJECTIVES

- MS-PS1–2. Analyze and interpret data on the properties of substances before and after the substances interact to determine if a chemical reaction has occurred.

- MS-PS1–3. Gather and make sense of information to describe that synthetic materials come from natural resources and impact society.

- MS-PS2–2. Plan an investigation to provide evidence that the change in an object's motion depends on the sum of the forces on the object and the mass of the object.

- MS-PS3–2. Develop a model to describe that when the arrangement of objects interacting at a distance changes, different amounts of potential energy are stored in the system.

- MS-PS3–5. Construct, use, and present arguments to support the claim that when the kinetic energy of an object changes, energy is transferred to or from the object.

- MS-ETS1–1. Define the criteria and constraints of a design problem with sufficient precision to ensure a successful conclusion, taking into account relevant scientific principles and potential impacts on people and the natural environment that may limit possible solutions.

- MS-ETS1–2. Evaluate competing design solutions using a systematic process to determine how well they meet the criteria and constraints of the problem.

- MS-ETS1–3. Analyze data from tests to determine similarities and differences among several design solutions to identify the best characteristics of each that can be combined into a new solution to better meet the criteria for success.

- MS-ETS1–4 Develop a model to generate data for iterative testing and modification of a proposed object, tool, or process such that an optimal design can be achieved.

SCIENCE AND ENGINEERING PRACTICES

Developing and Using Models

- Develop and use a model to describe phenomena.

Obtaining, Evaluating, and Communicating Information

- Gather, read, and synthesize information from multiple appropriate sources and assess the credibility, accuracy, and possible bias of each publication and methods used, and describe how they are supported or not supported by evidence.

Analyzing and Interpreting Data

- Analyze and interpret data to determine similarities and differences in findings.

Constructing Explanations and Designing Solutions

- Undertake a design project, engaging in the design cycle, to construct and/or implement a solution that meets specific design criteria and constraints.

- Apply scientific ideas or principles to design an object, tool, process, or system.

Planning and Carrying Out Investigations

- Plan an investigation individually and collaboratively, and in the design: identify independent and dependent variables and controls, what tools are needed to do the gathering, how measurements will be recorded, and how many data are needed to support a claim.

- Conduct an investigation and evaluate the experimental design to produce data to serve as the basis for evidence that can meet the goals of the investigation.

Engaging in Argument from Evidence

- Construct and present oral and written arguments supported by empirical evidence and scientific reasoning to support or refute an explanation or a model for a phenomenon or a solution to a problem.

DISCIPLINARY CORE IDEAS

PS1.A: *Structure and Properties of Matter*

- Substances are made from different types of atoms, which combine with one another in various ways. Atoms form molecules that range in size from two to thousands of atoms.

- Each pure substance has characteristic physical and chemical properties (for any bulk quantity under given conditions) that can be used to identify it.

- Gases and liquids are made of molecules or inert atoms that are moving about relative to each other.

- The changes of state that occur with variations in temperature or pressure can be described and predicted using these models of matter.

PS1.B: *Chemical Reactions*

- Substances react chemically in characteristic ways. In a chemical process, the atoms that make up the original substances are regrouped into different molecules, and these new substances have different properties from those of the reactants.

PS3.A: *Definitions of Energy*

- Temperature is not a measure of energy; the relationship between the temperature and the total energy of a system depends on the types, states, and amounts of matter present.

Continued

Table 4.19. (*continued*)

- Motion energy is properly called kinetic energy; it is proportional to the mass of the moving object and grows with the square of its speed.

- A system of objects may also contain stored (potential) energy, depending on their relative positions.

PS3.B: *Conservation of Energy and Energy Transfer*

- When the motion energy of an object changes, there is inevitably some other change in energy at the same time.

- The amount of energy transfer needed to change the temperature of a matter sample by a given amount depends on the nature of the matter, the size of the sample, and the environment.

- Energy is spontaneously transferred out of hotter regions or objects and into colder ones.

PS3.C: *Relationship Between Energy and Forces*
- When two objects interact, each one exerts a force on the other that can cause energy to be transferred to or from the object.

ESS3.A: *Natural Resources*

- Humans depend on Earth's land, ocean, atmosphere, and biosphere for many different resources. Minerals, fresh water, and biosphere resources are limited, and many are not renewable or replaceable over human lifetimes. These resources are distributed unevenly around the planet as a result of past geologic processes.

ESS3.C: *Human Impacts on Earth Systems*

- Typically as human populations and per-capita consumption of natural resources increase, so do the negative impacts on Earth unless the activities and technologies involved are engineered otherwise.

ETS1.A: *Defining and Delimiting Engineering Problems*

- The more precisely a design task's criteria and constraints can be defined, the more likely it is that the designed solution will be successful. Specification of constraints includes consideration of scientific principles and other relevant knowledge that is likely to limit possible solutions.

ETS1.B: *Developing Possible Solutions*

- A solution needs to be tested, and then modified on the basis of the test results in order to improve it.

ETS1.C: *Optimizing the Design Solution*

- Although one design may not perform the best across all tests, identifying the characteristics of the design that performed the best in each test can provide useful information for the redesign process – that is, some of the characteristics may be incorporated into the new design.

• The iterative process of testing the most promising solutions and modifying what is proposed on the basis of the test results leads to greater refinement and ultimately to an optimal solution.

CROSS-CUTTING CONCEPTS
Patterns
• Macroscopic patterns are related to the nature of microscopic and atomic-level structure.

Scale, Proportion, and Quantity
• Time, space, and energy phenomena can be observed at various scales using models to study systems that are too large or too small.

Systems and System Models
• Models can be used to represent systems and their interactions—such as inputs, processes and outputs—and energy and matter flows within systems.

Energy and Matter
• The transfer of energy can be tracked as energy flows through a designed or natural system.

• Energy may take different forms (e.g. energy in fields, thermal energy, energy of motion).

Cause and Effect
• Cause and effect relationships may be used to predict phenomena in natural or designed systems.

Structure and Function
• Structures can be designed to serve particular functions by taking into account properties of different materials, and how materials can be shaped and used

COMMON CORE STATE STANDARDS FOR MATHEMATICS
MATHEMATICAL PRACTICES
• MP 1. Make sense of problems and persevere in solving them.

• MP 2. Reason abstractly and quantitatively.

• MP 3. Construct viable arguments and critique the reasoning of others.

• MP 4. Model with mathematics.

• MP 5. Use appropriate tools strategically.

MATHEMATICAL CONTENT
• 8.F.B.4. Construct a function to model a linear relationship between two quantities. Determine the rate of change and initial value of the function from a description of a relationship or from two (x, y) values, including reading these from a table or from a graph. Interpret the rate of change and initial value of a linear function in terms of the situation it models, and in terms of its graph or a table of values.

Continued

Table 4.19. *(continued)*

- 8.F.B.5. Describe qualitatively the functional relationship between two quantities by analyzing a graph (for example, where the function is increasing or decreasing, linear or nonlinear). Sketch a graph that exhibits the qualitative features of a function that has been described verbally.

COMMON CORE STATE STANDARDS FOR ENGLISH LANGUAGE ARTS
SPEAKING AND LISTENING STANDARDS

- SL.8.1. Engage effectively in a range of collaborative discussions (one-on-one, in groups, and teacher-led) with diverse partners on grade 8 topics, texts, and issues, building on others' ideas and expressing their own clearly.

- SL.8.1.A. Come to discussions prepared, having read or researched material under study; explicitly draw on that preparation by referring to evidence on the topic, text, or issue to probe and reflect on ideas under discussion.

- SL.8.1.B. Follow rules for collegial discussions and decision-making, track progress toward specific goals and deadlines, and define individual roles as needed.

- SL.8.1.C. Pose questions that connect the ideas of several speakers and respond to others' questions and comments with relevant evidence, observations, and ideas.

- SL.8.1.D. Acknowledge new information expressed by others, and, when warranted, qualify or justify their own views in light of the evidence presented.

- SL.8.2. Analyze the purpose of information presented in diverse media and formats (for example, visually, quantitatively, orally) and evaluate the motives (for example, social, commercial, political) behind its presentation.

- SL.8.4. Present claims and findings, emphasizing salient points in a focused, coherent manner with relevant evidence, sound valid reasoning, and well-chosen details; use appropriate eye contact, adequate volume, and clear pronunciation.

FRAMEWORK FOR 21ST CENTURY LEARNING

Interdisciplinary themes (financial, economic, & business literacy; environmental literacy); Learning and Innovation Skills; Information, Media & Technology Skills; Life and Career Skills

Table 4.20. Key Vocabulary in Lesson 7

Key Vocabulary	Definition
aerodynamic drag	the resistance caused by air to an object traveling through it – also called air resistance or wind resistance
axle	a bar on which a wheel turns
chassis	the frame upon which the main parts of an automobile are built
downforce	a downward vertical force produced by air flowing around an object

Key Vocabulary	Definition
forces	pushes or pulls on an object
friction	the resistance that one surface or object encounters when moving over another
power	the energy used in a certain amount of time when work is being done
work	using a force to move something

TEACHER BACKGROUND INFORMATION

In this lesson, students will consider factors that affect car performance and fuel efficiency, including friction, aerodynamic drag, and materials. Students will apply these concepts and their understanding of electric cars to design and build a small EV.

Structural Components of Vehicles

Students should understand some basic terminology associated with vehicle design so that they can discuss and make decisions about EV design features. In particular, students should recognize that a chassis is the frame upon which a vehicle is built and that an axle is a bar on which a wheel turns. The axle typically connects two wheels on opposite sides of the car. Axle design will be particularly important for student designs since it must be designed in such a way that the axle can be secured to the vehicle yet allow the wheels to spin freely. For information on the physics of race cars, see *The Physics of Racing Series* by Brian Beckman at http://ceb.ac.in/knowledge-center/E-BOOKS/Physics%20Of%20Racing%20Series%20-%20Brian%20Beckman.pdf.

Friction

Friction is caused by atoms and molecules sliding over each other. A rough surface produces more friction than a smooth surface, but no matter how smooth a surface appears, it is still "rough" at the atomic level. Friction causes kinetic energy to be converted to thermal energy and therefore some amount of heat is always generated through friction.

There are several types of friction, that fall into two major categories:

1. Static friction is friction between two items that are not moving (adhesion or electrical friction/static electricity).

2. Kinetic friction is friction between two moving objects (this encompasses rolling friction, sliding friction, and fluid friction).

Friction does not depend on the amount of contact surface area of the two bodies or on the relative speed of the two bodies in contact. The major consideration for friction

is the type of surface. Tire traction is a type of friction that is important in car design. Race car engineers, in particular, seek to balance the friction needed to keep the car on the track with the need for speed.

Aerodynamic drag

Aerodynamic drag is a type of friction (fluid friction) that affects vehicle performance. Also known as "wind resistance," drag is the resisting force that an object encounters as it moves through air. This force is proportional to an object's speed and its shape.

While race cars are designed to have streamlined profiles to reduce wind resistance, the "wings" on a race car are designed to generate air resistance that works with gravity to create a downward force known as the downforce. This force helps the car to remain stable and keeps the car from slipping off the racetrack. Race car designers need to balance the need to reduce wind resistance with the need for grip. More information on aerodynamic drag and race cars is available from www.indycar.com/News/2014/05/5-9-Working-with-aerodynamic-drag-on-Indy-road-course.

Race cars have a number of features designed with considerations for aerodynamics. For example:

- Front wings that are designed to provide downforce.

- Wheel design: the biggest source of drag in a race car's profile are its wheels (they account for about 60% of drag), so endplates on the front wings help to direct air around the wheels

- Rear wings that can be adjusted for maximum performance on a given track.

Since aerodynamics are so important for race cars, the cars are tested in wind tunnels to allow race teams to experiment with different designs and wing angles since even a small reduction in drag coefficient can give them a significant track advantage.

Materials

Materials in car design affect friction, aerodynamic drag, and the weight of the vehicle. Body materials for race cars are chosen with weight and safety considerations in mind. Carbon fibers, aluminum, and reinforcing materials such as Zylon are all materials used in race cars because of their strength and light weight. Students should make the connection that the weight of body materials affects car performance (speed) and safety.

The design challenge included in this lesson, The EV Mini Prix, is intended to be an open-ended design challenge in which students use the EDP to design and build a vehicle. An option for this challenge is to accelerate the design process by scaffolding student work with additional information about propulsion systems. With the set

of materials provided, students will be able to create two basic propulsion systems (based upon what material they attach to the motor). The following video "How to Build an Electric Car" gives an example of a car with a wind-powered propulsion system: www.youtube.com/watch?v=UnxNe_XjlWg. Alternatively, students can use a rubber band to turn the car's axle. A sample design is provided here: https://mini science.com/kits/car-elec/.

COMMON MISCONCEPTIONS

Students will have various types of prior knowledge about the concepts introduced in this lesson. Table 4.21 outlines some common misconceptions students may have concerning these concepts. Because of the breadth of students' experiences, it is not possible to anticipate every misconception that students may bring as they approach this lesson. Incorrect or inaccurate prior understanding of concepts can influence student learning in the future, however, so it is important to be alert to misconceptions such as those presented in the table. In addition, the U.S. Environmental Protection Agency discusses common misconceptions about EVs at www.epa.gov/greenvehicles/electric-vehicle-myths.

Table 4.21. Common Misconceptions About the Concepts in Lesson 7

Topic	Student Misconception	Explanation
Electric vehicles (EVs)	EVs always run without any use of fossil fuel.	EVs' batteries must be charged using a source of electricity; often the electricity used to charge the batteries is from coal or natural gas.
	You can travel only short distances in an EV without having to stop to charge the battery.	As of 2022, most electric vehicles had a range of 200–300 miles.
	The need to manufacture batteries for EVs makes driving them worse for the environment than driving gasoline-powered cars.	Even when accounting for battery manufacturing, EVs emit fewer greenhouse gases over their lifespan than do gasoline-powered cars (www.epa.gov/greenvehicles/electric-vehicle-myths#Myth5).

PREPARATION FOR LESSON 7

Review the teacher background information provided, assemble the materials for the lesson, make copies of the student handouts, and preview the videos recommended in the Learning Components section below.

Identify an area for students to race their vehicles. The designated race area may be either indoors or outdoors and should be about 40 feet long, flat, have a

relatively smooth surface, and have a marked finish line (chalk line for outdoors, masking tape for indoors).

LEARNING COMPONENTS

Introductory Activity/Engagement

Connection to the Challenge: Begin each day of this lesson by directing students' attention to the module challenge, the Speed of Green Challenge. Remind students that they will work in teams to create plans for ways to minimize the environmental impact of powering a race car. Hold a brief class discussion each day of how students' learning in the previous days' lessons contributed to their ability to complete the challenge. You may wish to create a class list of key ideas on chart paper.

Science or Social Studies Class: Ask students if they think that there are any race cars that are electric vehicles (EVs). Tell students that there is a Formula E racing organization in which vehicles are EVs. Show a video about Formula E such as "Formula E – the future of motorsport?" at www.youtube.com/watch?v=ULSnB6Zsf50. Ask students to share their ideas about the benefits and disadvantages to EV race cars, creating a class list.

Point out to students that many design and safety features in today's passenger vehicles came from race cars (rear view mirrors, seat belts, infant safety seat technology, lightweight body materials, etc.). Developing technologies for new energy sources is now a focus for racing. Next, show students a video about Purdue University's EV Grand Prix, a program in which university students design and race EV go-karts (for example, "Boiler Bytes: Inaugural EV Grand Prix" at www.youtube.com/watch?v=8n_J7zYw3bo. Ask students what design features they noticed in the go-karts and how these are similar or different than design features in their family cars. Create a list of the features students notice.

Social Studies Class and ELA Connections: Have students read an article about Ralph Nader, an early activist for auto safety (for example, the November 26, 2015 article in the *New York Times* commemorating the 50th anniversary of Nader's book *Unsafe at Any Speed* – www.nytimes.com/2015/11/27/automobiles/50-years-ago-unsafe-at-any-speed-shook-the-auto-world.html?_r=0).

Hold a class discussion about what factors in Nader's life might have led to him become so passionately interested in auto safety.

Mathematics Connection: N.A.

Activity/Exploration

Science Class: In this lesson, students will participate in the EV Mini Prix, working in teams to build an electric vehicle. Before beginning the challenge, have the class work together to compile a list of design considerations that might affect their vehicles' performance in a race. Use the race car photo (attached at the end of this lesson plan) as a visual aid to students as they brainstorm. Guide students to include the following in the list:

- Aerodynamic drag: Race cars are designed to have streamlined profiles to reduce wind resistance. In addition, the "wings" on a race car are designed to generate air resistance to create downward force known as the downforce. This force keeps the car from slipping off the racetrack. Race car designers need to balance the need to reduce wind resistance with the need for grip. Body shapes that allow air to flow smoothly over the vehicle are the most aerodynamic.

- Weight: The weight of body materials affects vehicle performance and fuel efficiency. Ask students if they know what materials the chassis of race cars such as Indy Cars are made from (carbon fiber and aluminum – both lightweight materials).

- Friction: Tires must grip the track enough so the car doesn't slide, but too much grip will slow down the car and affect fuel efficiency. At the atomic level, friction is caused by atoms and molecules sliding over each other. A rough surface produces more friction than a smooth surface.

- Power: A vehicle needs to have sufficient power to overcome the various forces acting on it (aerodynamic drag, friction, etc.). Power is the amount of work that a force does over time. This is sometimes measured in horsepower (hp). Race cars that travel at 200 mph usually have at least 650 hp. Of the available horsepower in this case, about 350 hp goes into overcoming air resistance (from *The Physics of Racing Series* by Brian Beckman).

Distribute the EV Grand Prix student handout (attached at the end of this lesson plan) and an Engineer It! handout (attached at the end of Lesson 1) to each student. As a class, review the instructions and design constraints. Provide each team of students with a set of materials. Be sure to tell students how much time they have to complete their design (note that they must complete one round of testing and redesign during this time).

Social Studies Class and ELA Connection: Have students work in groups to research Ralph Nader and create a biography in the format of their choice (for example, poster, PowerPoint, song, skit). You may wish to have each group member research a different part of Nader's history (childhood, education, career, contributions to auto safety, etc.) and then synthesize this information to create a cohesive biography.

Mathematics Connection: Have students collect data about the various car designs in the EV Mini Prix. Have students create tables in which they can record data on variables

such as weight, width, and length for each team's car. Students should include a space in the table to record data about each car's performance.

Explanation

Science Class: Student teams should continue with the building, testing, and improving process for their EV Mini Prix vehicles.

Social Studies Class and ELA Connection: Student teams should continue work on their biographies and prepare to present their biographies to the class.

Mathematics Connection: Review the various types of graphs available for representing data (for example, line graphs, pie charts, bar charts, pictographs). As a class, discuss what type of graph is most appropriate for representing data about the EV Mini Prix vehicles.

Elaboration/Application of Knowledge

Science Class: Have each team run their EV car on the track you prepared. Each team should be given three trials. Time each trial and record each team's best time. Discuss the design features of the best-performing vehicles and create a list of these features. Ask students for their ideas about how these features might affect the amount of fuel a car uses.

Social Studies Class and ELA Connection: Have each team present their biography of Ralph Nader. An optional extension is to build on students' understanding of Ralph Nader and auto safety by investigating the impact of the 1966 National Traffic and Motor Vehicle Safety Act and identify auto safety innovations that stemmed from race car design (for instance, rear view mirrors). The original text of this legislation can be accessed at http://uscode.house.gov/statutes/pl/89/563.pdf.

Mathematics Connection: Have students prepare graphs using the data they collected for each variable identified and the cars' times on the course. Students should then use these graphs to identify trends and make predictions about design features that enhanced vehicle performance.

Evaluation/Assessment

Students may be assessed on the following performance tasks and other measures listed.

Performance Tasks

- EV Mini Prix vehicle design and performance (see Appendix A for prototype design rubric)

- Engineer It! handout – EV Mini Prix

Other Measures

- Teacher observations

- Collaboration (see Appendix A for rubric)

INTERNET RESOURCES

1966 National Traffic and Motor Vehicle Safety Act

- *http://uscode.house.gov/statutes/pl/89/563.pdf*

Aerodynamic drag and race cars

- *www.indycar.com/News/2014/05/5-9-Working-with-aerodynamic-drag-on-Indy-road-course*

"Boiler Bytes: Inaugural EV Grand Prix" video

- *www.youtube.com/watch?v=8n_J7zYw3bo*

Electric car with rubber band propulsion – sample

- *https://miniscience.com/kits/car-elec*

"Formula E – the future of motorsport?" video

- *www.youtube.com/watch?v=ULSnB6Zsf50*

"How to Build an Electric Car" using wind power video

- *www.youtube.com/watch?v=UnxNe_XjlWg*

Ralph Nader information

- *www.nytimes.com/2015/11/27/automobiles/50-years-ago-unsafe-at-any-speed-shook-the-auto-world.html?_r=0*

The Physics of Racing Series by Brian Beckman

- *http://ceb.ac.in/knowledge-center/E-BOOKS/Physics%20Of%20Racing%20Series%20-%20Brian%20Beckman.pdf*

U.S. Environmental Protection Agency, common misconceptions about EVs

- *www.epa.gov/greenvehicles/electric-vehicle-myths*

EV Mini Prix Student Handout
(Page 1 of 2)

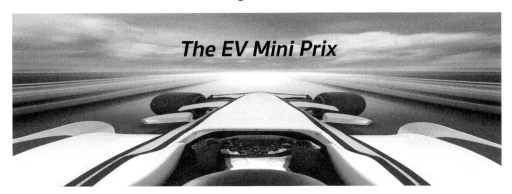

The EV Mini Prix

You and your team will use the engineering design process to create an electric vehicle to compete in a race, the *EV Mini Prix.*

The following are the rules you should follow to qualify for the race:

1. Use only the materials provided. Keep in mind that you do not need to use all the materials.

2. Use the engineering design process. Each team member must have a completed Engineer It! handout to submit at the end of the challenge.

3. Your vehicle must use the provided motor for its power source.

4. Your vehicle must be able to travel the entire course (40 feet) in a straight line.

5. You may not use human means (pushing, blowing, etc.) to start your car's movement.

6. You must have at least one test run and redesign/revision done before the race begins. Your teacher will tell you how much time you have.

7. All members of the team must participate in the design and building process.

EV Mini Prix Student Handout
(Page 2 of 2)

Materials:

2 water bottles (500 mL) with caps

1 piece of balsa wood (about 4″ × 6″)

4 wooden disks with hole in the middle

4 CDs

4 plastic drinking straws (non-bendable)

4 wooden skewers

10 pennies

5 rubber bands (6 mm width)

1 rubber band (1 mm width)

1 12V direct current motor

2 9V batteries

9V battery connectors

2 alligator clip wires

1 roll of masking tape

1 hot glue gun and 2 glue sticks

1 Engineer It! handout per team member

Lesson Plan 8:
The Speed of Green Challenge

Students will apply their understanding of energy sources in transportation by working in teams to create plans for race teams to fuel their vehicles with the least possible environmental impact. As part of this process, students will use what they have learned about various energy sources throughout the module to choose an energy source for their race team's car. Each team will consider its car's materials, source of materials (transportation distance and associated impacts), and other design features in their plan. Teams will each create a LCA that demonstrates their plan and create an argument for its efficiency and low environmental impact. Teams will each create a prototype of an innovation that plays a role in their life cycle analysis, and will create a video presentation with the goal of garnering funding for their race team.

ESSENTIAL QUESTIONS

- How can we power a race car with minimal environmental impact in an efficient and cost-effective manner?

- How can we sell our ideas to a group of investors?

ESTABLISHED GOALS AND OBJECTIVES

At the conclusion of this lesson, students will be able to do the following:

- Demonstrate their understanding of the EDP and use it to create a solution to the module challenge

- Apply their understanding of various non-renewable and renewable energy sources to identify an energy source that they believe has minimal environmental impact

- Justify their choice of energy source

- Demonstrate their understanding of technologies or products associated with their energy source by creating a prototype or model

- Use persuasive language in a presentation that demonstrates their learning during the module

TIME REQUIRED

4 days (approximately 45 minutes each day; see Table 3.10, p. 45)

MATERIALS

Required Materials for Lesson 8

- STEM Research Notebooks

- computer with internet access for viewing videos

- various art supplies for student presentations (depends on students' choice of presentation media)

- video camera or device to record team presentations (if you choose to record presentations)

Additional Materials for The Speed of Green Challenge

- safety glasses (1 per student)

- disposable non-latex gloves (1 per student)

Because each team will be devising its own prototype or model, you should plan to have on hand a variety of supplies, including the types of supplies used design challenges and activities in previous lessons. You may also wish to allow students to bring supplies from home. Supplies you may wish to provide include (these examples are supplies used in previous lessons):

- cardstock

- black construction paper

- scissors

- thumbtacks

- electric motors

- mini PV cells

- small propeller to attach to motor

- 1 piece of black construction paper

- alligator clip wires

- clay or cork

- non-latex balloons

- Styrofoam plates

- small aluminum foil pans

- craft sticks (regular size)

- craft sticks (large size)

- index cards (3″ × 5″)

- plastic drinking straws

- rubber bands

- wooden skewers

- rolls of masking tape

SAFETY NOTES

1. Students should use caution when handling scissors and other pointed objects, as the sharp points and blades can cut or puncture skin.

2. Have students wear safety goggles during any activity in which a fan may blow objects toward them.

3. Caution students of the risk of shock when using electricity in activities, even when voltage is low.

CONTENT STANDARDS AND KEY VOCABULARY

Table 4.22 lists the content standards from the *NGSS*, *CCSS*, and the Framework for 21st Century Learning that this lesson addresses, and Table 4.23 presents the key vocabulary. Vocabulary terms are provided for both teacher and student use. Teachers may choose to introduce some or all of the terms to students.

Table 4.22. Content Standards Addressed in STEM Road Map Module Lesson 8

NEXT GENERATION SCIENCE STANDARDS
PERFORMANCE OBJECTIVES

- MS-PS1–2. Analyze and interpret data on the properties of substances before and after the substances interact to determine if a chemical reaction has occurred.

- MS-PS1–3. Gather and make sense of information to describe that synthetic materials come from natural resources and impact society.

- MS-PS2–2. Plan an investigation to provide evidence that the change in an object's motion depends on the sum of the forces on the object and the mass of the object.

- MS-PS3–2. Develop a model to describe that when the arrangement of objects interacting at a distance changes, different amounts of potential energy are stored in the system.

Continued

Table 4.22. (*continued*)

- MS-PS3–5. Construct, use, and present arguments to support the claim that when the kinetic energy of an object changes, energy is transferred to or from the object.

- MS-ETS1–1. Define the criteria and constraints of a design problem with sufficient precision to ensure a successful conclusion, taking into account relevant scientific principles and potential impacts on people and the natural environment that may limit possible solutions.

- MS-ETS1–2. Evaluate competing design solutions using a systematic process to determine how well they meet the criteria and constraints of the problem.

- MS-ETS1–3. Analyze data from tests to determine similarities and differences among several design solutions to identify the best characteristics of each that can be combined into a new solution to better meet the criteria for success.

- MS-ETS1–4 Develop a model to generate data for iterative testing and modification of a proposed object, tool, or process such that an optimal design can be achieved.

SCIENCE AND ENGINEERING PRACTICES
Developing and Using Models
- Develop and use a model to describe phenomena.

Obtaining, Evaluating, and Communicating Information
- Gather, read, and synthesize information from multiple appropriate sources and assess the credibility, accuracy, and possible bias of each publication and methods used, and describe how they are supported or not supported by evidence.

Analyzing and Interpreting Data
- Analyze and interpret data to determine similarities and differences in findings.

Constructing Explanations and Designing Solutions
- Undertake a design project, engaging in the design cycle, to construct and/or implement a solution that meets specific design criteria and constraints.

- Apply scientific ideas or principles to design an object, tool, process, or system.

Planning and Carrying Out Investigations
- Plan an investigation individually and collaboratively, and in the design: identify independent and dependent variables and controls, what tools are needed to do the gathering, how measurements will be recorded, and how many data are needed to support a claim.

- Conduct an investigation and evaluate the experimental design to produce data to serve as the basis for evidence that can meet the goals of the investigation.

Engaging in Argument from Evidence
- Construct and present oral and written arguments supported by empirical evidence and scientific reasoning to support or refute an explanation or a model for a phenomenon or a solution to a problem.

DISCIPLINARY CORE IDEAS

PS3.A: *Definitions of Energy*

- Temperature is not a measure of energy; the relationship between the temperature and the total energy of a system depends on the types, states, and amounts of matter present.

- Motion energy is properly called kinetic energy; it is proportional to the mass of the moving object and grows with the square of its speed.

- A system of objects may also contain stored (potential) energy, depending on their relative positions.

PS3.B: *Conservation of Energy and Energy Transfer*

- When the motion energy of an object changes, there is inevitably some other change in energy at the same time.

- The amount of energy transfer needed to change the temperature of a matter sample by a given amount depends on the nature of the matter, the size of the sample, and the environment.

- Energy is spontaneously transferred out of hotter regions or objects and into colder ones.

PS3.C: *Relationship Between Energy and Forces*

- When two objects interact, each one exerts a force on the other that can cause energy to be transferred to or from the object.

ESS3.A: *Natural Resources*

- Humans depend on Earth's land, ocean, atmosphere, and biosphere for many different resources. Minerals, fresh water, and biosphere resources are limited, and many are not renewable or replaceable over human lifetimes. These resources are distributed unevenly around the planet as a result of past geologic processes.

ESS3.C: *Human Impacts on Earth Systems*

- Typically as human populations and per-capita consumption of natural resources increase, so do the negative impacts on Earth unless the activities and technologies involved are engineered otherwise.

ETS1.A: *Defining and Delimiting Engineering Problems*

- The more precisely a design task's criteria and constraints can be defined, the more likely it is that the designed solution will be successful. Specification of constraints includes consideration of scientific principles and other relevant knowledge that is likely to limit possible solutions.

ETS1.B: *Developing Possible Solutions*

- A solution needs to be tested, and then modified on the basis of the test results in order to improve it.

Continued

Table 4.22. (*continued*)

ETS1.C: *Optimizing the Design Solution*

- Although one design may not perform the best across all tests, identifying the characteristics of the design that performed the best in each test can provide useful information for the redesign process – that is, some of the characteristics may be incorporated into the new design.

- The iterative process of testing the most promising solutions and modifying what is proposed on the basis of the test results leads to greater refinement and ultimately to an optimal solution.

CROSS-CUTTING CONCEPTS
Scale, Proportion, and Quantity

- Time, space, and energy phenomena can be observed at various scales using models to study systems that are too large or too small.

Systems and System Models

- Models can be used to represent systems and their interactions—such as inputs, processes and outputs—and energy and matter flows within systems.

Energy and Matter

- The transfer of energy can be tracked as energy flows through a designed or natural system.

- Energy may take different forms (e.g. energy in fields, thermal energy, energy of motion).

Cause and Effect

- Cause and effect relationships may be used to predict phenomena in natural or designed systems.

Stability and Change

- Explanations of stability and change in natural or designed systems can be constructed by examining the changes over time and forces at different scales.

Structure and Function

- Structures can be designed to serve particular functions by taking into account properties of different materials, and how materials can be shaped and used

COMMON CORE STATE STANDARDS FOR MATHEMATICS
MATHEMATICAL PRACTICES

- MP 1. Make sense of problems and persevere in solving them.
- MP 2. Reason abstractly and quantitatively.
- MP 3. Construct viable arguments and critique the reasoning of others.
- MP 4. Model with mathematics.
- MP 5. Use appropriate tools strategically.

MATHEMATICAL CONTENT

- 8.F.B.4. Construct a function to model a linear relationship between two quantities. Determine the rate of change and initial value of the function from a description of a relationship or from two (x, y) values, including reading these from a table or from a graph. Interpret the rate of change and initial value of a linear function in terms of the situation it models, and in terms of its graph or a table of values.

- 8.F.B.5. Describe qualitatively the functional relationship between two quantities by analyzing a graph (for example, where the function is increasing or decreasing, linear or nonlinear). Sketch a graph that exhibits the qualitative features of a function that has been described verbally.

COMMON CORE STATE STANDARDS FOR ENGLISH LANGUAGE ARTS
READING STANDARDS

- RL.8.1. Cite the textual evidence that most strongly supports an analysis of what the text says explicitly as well as inferences drawn from the text.

- RL.8.9. Analyze a case in which two or more texts provide conflicting information on the same topic and identify where the texts disagree on matters of fact or interpretation.

WRITING STANDARDS

- W.8.1. Write arguments to support claims with clear reasons and relevant evidence.

- W.8.1.A. Introduce claim(s), acknowledge and distinguish the claim(s) from alternate or opposing claims, and organize the reasons and evidence logically.

- W.8.1.B. Support claim(s) with logical reasoning and relevant evidence, using accurate, credible sources and demonstrating an understanding of the topic or text.

- W.8.1.C. Use words, phrases, and clauses to create cohesion and clarify the relationships among claim(s), counterclaims, reasons, and evidence.

- W.8.1.E. Provide a concluding statement or section that follows from and supports the argument presented.

- W.8.2. Write informative/explanatory texts to examine a topic and convey ideas, concepts, and information through the selection, organization, and analysis of relevant content.

- W.8.2.A. Introduce a topic clearly, previewing what is to follow; organize ideas, concepts, and information into broader categories; include formatting (for example, headings), graphics (for example, charts, tables), and multimedia when useful to aiding comprehension.

- W.8.2.B. Develop the topic with relevant, well-chosen facts, definitions, concrete details, quotations, or other information and examples.

- W.8.2.C. Use appropriate and varied transitions to create cohesion and clarify the relationships among ideas and concepts.

Continued

Table 4.22. (*continued*)

- W.8.2.D. Use precise language and domain-specific vocabulary to inform about or explain the topic.

- W.8.7. Conduct short research projects to answer a question (including a self-generated question), drawing on several sources and generating additional related, focused questions that allow for multiple avenues of exploration.

- W.8.8. Gather relevant information from multiple print and digital sources, using search terms effectively; assess the credibility and accuracy of each source; and quote or paraphrase the data and conclusions of others while avoiding plagiarism and following a standard format for citation.

- W.8.9. Draw evidence from literary or informational texts to support analysis, reflection, and research.

SPEAKING AND LISTENING STANDARDS

- SL.8.1. Engage effectively in a range of collaborative discussions (one-on-one, in groups, and teacher-led) with diverse partners on grade 8 topics, texts, and issues, building on others' ideas and expressing their own clearly.

- SL.8.1.A. Come to discussions prepared, having read or researched material under study; explicitly draw on that preparation by referring to evidence on the topic, text, or issue to probe and reflect on ideas under discussion.

- SL.8.1.B. Follow rules for collegial discussions and decision-making, track progress toward specific goals and deadlines, and define individual roles as needed.

- SL.8.1.C. Pose questions that connect the ideas of several speakers and respond to others' questions and comments with relevant evidence, observations, and ideas.

- SL.8.1.D. Acknowledge new information expressed by others, and, when warranted, qualify or justify their own views in light of the evidence presented.

- SL.8.2. Analyze the purpose of information presented in diverse media and formats (for example, visually, quantitatively, orally) and evaluate the motives (for example, social, commercial, political) behind its presentation.

- SL.8.4. Present claims and findings, emphasizing salient points in a focused, coherent manner with relevant evidence, sound valid reasoning, and well-chosen details; use appropriate eye contact, adequate volume, and clear pronunciation.

FRAMEWORK FOR 21ST CENTURY LEARNING

Interdisciplinary themes (financial, economic, & business literacy; environmental literacy); Learning and Innovation Skills; Information, Media & Technology Skills; Life and Career Skills

Table 4.23. Key Vocabulary for Lesson 8

Key Vocabulary	Definition
model	a representation of an object used to demonstrate important aspects of the original object; may be larger or smaller than the original object
prototype	a functional version of a product, often on a small scale, used for performance evaluation and product improvement

TEACHER BACKGROUND INFORMATION

In this lesson, students will address the module challenge, the Speed of Green Challenge, by working in teams to create plans for their race teams to power their cars with minimal environmental impact. Students will learn that they will be pitching their ideas to (fictional) investors in a setting similar to the *Shark Tank* television show. Since the challenge synthesizes student learning from all content areas, it is presented as an integrated activity for science and social studies classes and mathematics and ELA connections. Students should work in teams of three to four each for the challenge.

Students will complete the following tasks during the design challenge:

1. Decide on an energy source for their vehicle and create an LCA.

2. Identify at least two design features for their car that contribute to low environmental impact.

3. Research one innovation associated with their plan.

4. Design and build a model or prototype of this innovation.

5. Create a presentation to "sell" their plan to investors.

Students should understand that a prototype is a small-scale, functional version of a product, while a model may or may not be functional and is intended to represent important aspects of an object's or product's design. For example, the electric cars students built in the last lesson could be considered prototypes for a full-scale vehicle. If, alternatively, they had focused only on body materials and created a non-working car to showcase body design, it would be considered a model. In either case, the prototypes or models student teams create should reflect their research of a topic or concept and their understanding of design and function. This may be a basic

exterior model accompanied by a diagram explaining function. Some examples of possible projects are listed below:

- A plan to convert farm biogas into electricity. Students could create a model of an anaerobic digester, the tank in which manure is digested to create methane. A *Popular Science* article "Chinese Cow Manure Generates Electricity In Largest-Ever Methane Capture System" provides an example of such an endeavor (see www.popsci.com/technology/article/2010-11/chinese-cow-manure-generates-electricity-largest-ever-methane-capture-system). Alternatively, students may wish to include a model of a generator that converts methane to electricity.

- A plan to produce their ethanol using a source that is more easily fermentable than corn. Examples of fermentation tank designs can be accessed by conducting an internet search using search terms such as "fermentation tank design."

- A plan to use solar energy as a source for their cars. Teams may, for example, create a moveable mounting bracket for solar panels that can direct the panel toward the sun.

- A plan to use fossil fuels for a vehicle designed to be very lightweight to improve fuel efficiency. Teams may, for example, research and create a model of the microscopic structure of a material such as carbon nanofiber.

Keep in mind that these are only suggestions intended to guide students to think more broadly about their projects and there are many possible approaches to the challenge.

Teams' presentations can be made live or video recorded. One option for the final competition is to invite industry professionals (from motorsports or the energy industry) to act as fictional investors and question students about their designs. Each team needs a minimum investment of $500,000 to field a race team. The investors can then offer the students a fictional investment based upon their presentation. Each investor will have $1,000,000 to invest and can invest any amount up to $500,000 in a team or they can choose to pass. Alternatively, the class can act as the investors, with non-team members asking questions of the team members. Each class member can decide on an "investment" amount that they write down anonymously. These amounts can then be totaled for each team to determine which team garnered the most investment.

COMMON MISCONCEPTIONS

Since in this lesson students are synthesizing their learning from previous lessons to address the module challenge, no new misconceptions are introduced. It will, however, be helpful to review the misconceptions introduced in Lessons 1–7 and be alert to ongoing misconceptions such as those presented.

PREPARATION FOR LESSON 8

Review the teacher background information provided, assemble the materials for the lesson, duplicate student handouts, and preview videos included within the Learning Components. Because students will be devising their own models or prototypes it is not possible to provide a precise list of materials required. Instead, you should provide the types of materials used in previous lessons' design challenges and activities. You may also encourage students to bring supplies from home if you wish. Ensure that you have access to video-recording equipment if you choose to video record teams' presentations. If you decide to invite outside guests as fictional investors, confirm the time and location with volunteers and provide them with a copy of the Speed of Green Student Packet and paper for taking notes. Be sure to explicitly state your expectations of these visitors by clarifying what sort of questions they should ask, how much time they will have to ask questions, guidelines for making their fictional investments, and what type of feedback you would like the investors to give teams on their presentations and plans. You may wish to have all teams make their presentations before asking your fictional investors to make their final investment decisions.

LEARNING COMPONENTS
Introductory Activity/Engagement

Connection to the Challenge: As students begin work on their final challenge, it is important that they remain focused on the driving question for the module: How can a motorsports race team power its car with minimal environmental impact? As students work on their challenge solutions, remind them that their previous work (especially the Energy Source STEM Research Notebook entries) will be a key source of information.

Science and Social Studies Classes and Mathematics and ELA Connections: Tell students that in this lesson they will take on their final challenge – creating a plan to power a race car with minimal environmental impact. The twist is that they will need to pitch their ideas to "investors." Ask students if they are familiar with the *Shark Tank* television show, where entrepreneurs present their ideas to investors. You may wish to provide students with examples of successful Shark Tank pitches. You can identify these with a Google search using terms such as "successful Shark Tank pitches."

In this challenge, the "investors" are interested in race teams that field cars with low environmental impact. Tell students that their teams will ask investors for $500,000 for their race team, but they will have to be able to answer questions about their design and ideas from the investors.

Ask students if they think that $500,000 is enough to support a race team for a season. In 2013, fielding an Indy Car cost around $1 million. An option for the

lesson is to have students read the article "How Much Does it Cost to Field a Car in the Indy 500?" at www.usatoday.com/story/sports/motor/indycar/2013/05/13/indianapolis-500-cost-izod-indycar/2156011/.

Activity/Exploration

Science and Social Studies Classes and Mathematics and ELA Connections: Because this final challenge incorporates students' learning from all subject areas in the module, this section will be presented as an integrated project. The tasks associated with the challenge can be completed within different classes if you wish.

The Speed of Green Challenge

Distribute the Speed of Green Challenge Student Packet (attached at the end of this lesson). Review the contents of the student handout with the class, focusing on the contents of the portfolio students will submit:

1. Team Member Agreement

2. Team Energy Plan handout

3. Design Features handout

4. Innovation Research handout

5. Engineer It! handout for prototype or model (attached at the end of Lesson 1 lesson plan)

6. Sell It handout

Explanation

Science and Social Studies Classes and Mathematics and ELA Connections: Explain the differences between a model and a prototype (see Teacher Background section, p. 237, for more information). Explain to students that their work throughout the module, collected in their STEM Research Notebooks, is their main resource for this challenge.

Elaboration/Application of Knowledge

Science and Social Studies Classes and Mathematics and ELA Connections: Tell students that each investor has $1,000,000 to invest. Investors can invest any amount up to $500,000 in a team or they can choose to pass, but each team needs a minimum investment of $500,000 in order to be able to field its race team. Have student teams each present their videos to the investors and answer questions. After all the presentations have been made, have each investor write on a piece of paper how much he or she is willing to invest in each team. After the investments have been made, total the investments for each team and create a chart listing the investments for each team.

As an optional extension for the module, have students reflect on how they could use their learning from this module in real-life decision-making. For example, you may wish to have students create a journal entry in which they reflect on how their learning might influence their decisions in buying a car in the future. Alternatively, you may wish to have students investigate and write about the source(s) of energy for their homes, identifying the primary source (for example, coal, wind, natural gas), how this primary energy source is converted into a secondary energy source, the geographical route from the primary source to their homes, and the environmental impacts of this energy source.

Evaluation/Assessment

Students may be assessed on the following performance tasks and other measures listed.

Performance Tasks

- Speed of Green Student Packet handouts

- Engineer It! Handouts – Speed of Green

- Prototype or model (see Appendix A for prototype design rubric)

- Speed of Green team presentation (see Appendix A for presentation rubric)

Other Measures

- Teacher observations

- Collaboration (see Appendix A for rubric)

INTERNET RESOURCES

"Chinese Cow Manure Generates Electricity In Largest-Ever Methane Capture System"

- *www.popsci.com/technology/article/2010-11/chinese-cow-manure-generates-electricity-largest-ever-methane-capture-system*

"How Much Does it Cost to Field a Car in the Indy 500?"

- *www.usatoday.com/story/sports/motor/indycar/2013/05/13/indianapolis-500-cost-izod-indycar/2156011/*

The Speed of Green Challenge
Student Packet

How can a motorsports race team minimize its car's environmental impact?

This is the question that you and your race team will answer in this challenge. You will design a plan to power a race car in a way that you believe minimizes its environmental impact. Your team will pitch that plan to a fictional group of investors with the aim of getting the minimum of $500,000 that is required to field your race team.

You will have five major tasks to complete during this challenge:

- ✓ Decide on an energy source for your vehicle and create a life cycle analysis in presentation format.

- ✓ Identify at least two design features for your car that contributes to low environmental impact. Create presentation materials for your car that focus on these features.

- ✓ Research one innovation associated with your plan.

- ✓ Design and build a model or prototype of this innovation.

- ✓ Create a presentation to "sell" your plan to investors.

Your individual work will be assembled in a portfolio, and your teamwork will be assessed based upon your final presentation and your teacher's assessment of how your team collaborated.

First, you must decide on a name for your race team.

Next, you should read over the team member expectations page and sign the agreement. This will be the first page in your portfolio.

Team Member Expectations
The Speed of Green Challenge

As a member of the _____ race team, I understand that the following is expected:

I will be responsible for my own work as part of the team. This means that:

- ✓ I will be prepared to work with my team.

- ✓ I will communicate with my team members and complete the tasks agreed upon.

- ✓ I will actively participate in my team's work.

- ✓ I will complete my tasks on time.

- ✓ I will use feedback from other team members to improve my work.

I will be responsible for helping the team work well together. This means that:

- ✓ I will help my team solve problems.

- ✓ I will clearly express my ideas, ask questions of other team members, and respond to their questions thoughtfully.

- ✓ I will give useful feedback to others.

- ✓ I will help other team members when they need it.

I will behave in a professional and respectful manner with my team. This means that:

- ✓ I will be polite and respectful to other team members.

- ✓ I will respect others' ideas and perspectives.

I understand that meeting these expectations will help my team to be successful in the Speed of Green Challenge.

Signature: _____ Date: _____

Printed Name: _____

Team Energy Plan Student Handout

Name: _____   Team Name: _____

Using your Energy Source STEM Research Notebook entries, discuss with your team what would be the best source of energy for your race car (note: you will not build the race car or power source).

Rules:

1. If you choose to use an EV, you must be able to charge your battery using energy that you generate on site (for instance, if you choose wind power, you must provide your own wind turbine).

2. If you choose to use fuel (ethanol, biogas, or fossil fuels) you need not produce the fuel on site, but you must know where the fuel is produced and describe how it will be delivered to your site and stored.

3. Your team must create a detailed life cycle analysis of your energy source. Remember, your argument to the "investors" will rely on this, so be as detailed as possible!

4. Your team must create a visual presentation version of your life cycle analysis (on poster board, by a PowerPoint presentation, etc.)

5. Each team member must include a copy of this Team Energy Plan Handout in his or her individual portfolio.

****

Each team member should complete the following:

1. My team chose the following energy source for our race car:

   _____

2. Sketch out the life cycle analysis for this energy source on the back of this page.

3. Benefits to using this energy source:

   _____

   _____

4. Disadvantages to using this energy source:

   _____

   _____

Design Features Handout

Name: _____   Team Name: _____

- Decide on at least two specific design features that will help to minimize your car's environmental impact.

- Think about the impact of the weight of materials, aerodynamic drag, and friction on fuel efficiency. Do some research to support your ideas – remember, you will need to argue for your design features in your presentation to investors.

- Create presentation materials about your design features to present to the investors.

- Each member of the team should include a copy of this handout in his or her individual portfolio.

    1. My team chose the following two design features to include:

        a. _____

        b. _____

    2. We chose these features because (list advantages of each):

        _____

        _____

        _____

        _____

    3. Sketch your design features on the back of this paper.

    4. How will your team present these design features (pictures, PowerPoint, brochure, etc.)?

        _____

        _____

Innovation Models Student Handout
(Page 1 of 2)

Name: _____   **Team Name:** _____

Your team will build a prototype or model of one innovation that contributes to your plan. This can be an original idea or an improvement on an existing idea.

Think about your energy source. What is necessary to create that energy? What technology is used? What about your design features? Could you model one of those? Can you improve on one of the designs you made this semester (for instance, your electric car)?

Your task is to research something associated with your energy source, find out how it works, and create a prototype or model that represents how it fits into your plan. Be sure to keep track of your sources of information during your research!

Model or Prototype Rules:

1. Complete the Innovation Model Handout first (this will help your team decide on what technology they will model or prototype). Every team member must complete a handout.

2. Your team must use the EDP to decide on and build your model or prototype.

3. Each team member must complete an Engineer It! handout.

4. Your model must be built using materials available in the classroom.

5. All team members must participate in the planning and building process.

6. If you build a model that shows just the exterior of the device, include a graphic or picture that indicates how it works.

NATIONAL SCIENCE TEACHING ASSOCIATION

Innovation Models Student Handout

(Page 2 of 2)

Name: _____   Team Name: _____

> 1. Brainstorm ideas with your team. Based on what you know about your energy source, what are some technologies or products that are necessary or could be helpful?

> 2. Do some research. Is there something in the process that you think you could improve upon? What technologies or products might be used for this improvement?

> 3. Discuss with your team what you will build. List your decision here, and include a list of materials you will need and who will provide those.

Sell It!
Presentation Guide

Your last task as a team is to prepare a presentation that incorporates all the work you've done in the Speed of Green Challenge so far.

Here are the rules for your team's presentation:

1. It must include an explanation of your energy choice for your car and the life cycle analysis of that energy source.

2. It must include information about your design innovations, including visual depictions.

3. It must include your model or prototype along with a complete explanation of it.

4. It must include an argument about why the "investors" should give you funding for your plan.

5. Your presentation should be at least 5 minutes long, but no longer than 7 minutes.

6. Your presentation must be video recorded.

7. All team members must participate in the presentation.

8. Your team must be prepared to answer questions about the information included in your presentation.

Remember, you are selling your idea so you must make a compelling argument to "investors" while keeping their interest in your presentation. Think about what makes a presentation interesting to watch while conveying information and be creative!

REFERENCES

Skone, T. J., Littlefield, J., Marriott, J., Cooney, G. Jamieson, M., Hakian, J., & Schively, G. (2014). *Life cycle analysis of natural gas extraction and power generation.* Report DOE/NETL-2014/1646 prepared for U.S. Department of Energy National Energy Technology Laboratory.

Whyatt, G. A. (2010). *Issues affecting adoption of natural gas fuel in light-and heavy-duty vehicles.* Report PNNL-19745 prepared for U.S. Department of Energy.** This reaction will produce carbon dioxide and the bags will expand – they could even pop! If the bag becomes too inflated, release some of the gas and note this in your observations.

TRANSFORMING LEARNING WITH THE SPEED OF GREEN AND THE *STEM ROAD MAP CURRICULUM SERIES*

Carla C. Johnson

This chapter serves as a conclusion to The Speed of Green integrated STEM curriculum module, but it is just the beginning of the transformation of your classroom that is possible through use of the *STEM Road Map Curriculum Series.* In this book, many key resources have been provided to make learning meaningful for your students through integration of science, technology, engineering, and mathematics, as well as social studies and English language arts, into powerful problem- and project-based instruction. First, The Speed of Green curriculum is grounded in the latest theory of learning for students in grade 8 specifically. Second, as your students work through this module, they engage in using the engineering design process (EDP) and build prototypes like engineers and STEM professionals in the real world. Third, students acquire important knowledge and skills grounded in national academic standards in mathematics, English language arts, science, and 21st century skills that will enable their learning to be deeper, retained longer, and applied throughout, illustrating the critical connections within and across disciplines. Finally, authentic formative assessments, including strategies for differentiation and addressing misconceptions, are embedded within the curriculum activities.

The Speed of Green curriculum in the Sustainable Systems STEM Road Map theme can be used in single-content classrooms (for example, science) where there is only one teacher or expanded to include multiple teachers and content areas across classrooms. Through the exploration of The Speed of Green lesson plans, students engage in a real-world STEM problem on the first day of instruction and gather necessary knowledge and skills along the way in the context of solving the problem.

DOI: 10.4324/9781003362357-7

The other topics in the *STEM Road Map Curriculum Series* are designed in a similar manner, and NSTA Press and Routledge have published additional volumes in this series for this and other grade levels and have plans to publish more.

For an up-to-date list of volumes in the series, please visit www.routledge.com/ STEM-Road-Map-Curriculum-Series/book-series/SRM (for titles co-published by Routledge and NSTA Press), or www.nsta.org/book-series/stem-road-map-curriculum (for titles published by NSTA Press).

If you are interested in professional development opportunities focused on the STEM Road Map specifically or integrated STEM or STEM programs and schools over-all, contact the lead editor of this project, Dr. Carla C. Johnson, Professor of Science Education at NC State University. Someone from the team will be in touch to design a program that will meet your individual, school, or district needs.

APPENDIX A

RUBRICS

Energy Source STEM Research Notebook Entry Rubric

Criteria	Points Possible	Points Earned
The energy source is identified.	5	
The description of the production of the energy source is thorough, and energy inputs and environmental impacts are marked.	5	
The pros and cons of the energy source are identified.	5	
Technologies necessary to use this energy source are identified.	5	
The entry is grammatically correct and neat.	5	
TOTAL	**25**	

Comments:

COLLABORATION RUBRIC
(Page 1 of 2)

Student Name: _____   Team Name: _____

	Below Standard (0–1)	Approaching Standard (2–3)	Meets or Exceeds Standard (4–5)	Student Score
Individual Performance **Individual accountability**	• Student is unprepared. • Student does not communicate with team members and does not manage tasks as agreed upon by the team. • Student does not complete or participate in project tasks. • Student does not complete tasks on time. • Student does not use feedback from others to improve work.	• Student is usually prepared. • Student sometimes communicates with team members and manages tasks as agreed upon by the team, but not consistently. • Student completes or participates in some project tasks but needs to be reminded. • Student completes most tasks on time. • Student sometime uses feedback from others to improve work.	• Student is consistently prepared. • Student consistently communicates with team members and manage tasks as agreed upon by the team. Student discusses and reflects on ideas with the team. • Student completes or participates in project tasks without being reminded. • Student completes tasks on time. • Student uses feedback from others to improve work.	

COLLABORATION RUBRIC
(Page 2 of 2)

Individual Performance	Below Standard (0–3)	Approaching Standard (4–7)	Meets or Exceeds Standard (8–10)	Student Score
Team participation	• Student does not help the team solve problems; may interfere with team work. • Student does not express ideas clearly, pose relevant questions, or participate in group discussions. • Student does not give useful feedback to other team members. • Student does not volunteer to help others when needed.	• Student cooperates with the team but may not actively help solve problems. • Student sometimes expresses ideas, poses relevant questions, and elaborates in response to questions, and participates in group discussions. • Student provides some feedback to team members. • Student sometimes volunteers to help others.	• Student helps the team solve problems and manage conflicts. • Student makes discussions effective by clearly expressing ideas, posing questions, and responding thoughtfully to team members' questions and perspectives. • Student gives useful feedback to others so they can improve their work. • Student volunteers to help others if needed.	
Professionalism & respect for team members	• Student is impolite or disrespectful to other team members. • Student does not acknowledge or respect others' ideas and perspectives.	• Student is usually polite and respectful to other team members. • Student usually acknowledges and respects others' ideas and perspectives.	• Student is consistently polite and respectful to other team members. • Student consistently acknowledges and respects others' ideas and perspectives.	
TOTAL SCORE				
COMMENTS				

PROTOTYPE/MODEL DESIGN RUBRIC

Team Name: _____

Team Performance Area	Below Standard (0–1)	Approaching Standard (2–3)	Meets or Exceeds Standard (4–5)	Team Score
Creativity and innovation	• Design reflects little creativity with use of materials, lack of understanding of project purpose, and no innovative design features. • Design is impractical. • Design has several elements that do not fit.	• Design reflects some creativity with use of materials, a basic understanding of project purpose, and limited innovative design features. • Design is limited in practicality and function. • Design has some interesting elements, but may be excessive or inappropriate.	• Design reflects creative use of materials, a sound understanding of project purpose, and distinct innovative design features. • Design is practical. • Design is well-crafted, includes interesting elements that are appropriate for the purpose.	
Conceptual understanding	• Design incorporates no or few features that reflect conceptual understanding of the science concepts in the unit.	• Design incorporates some features that reflect a limited conceptual understanding of science concepts.	• Design incorporates several features that reflect a sound conceptual understanding of science concepts.	
Designed within specified requirements	• Design violates challenge rules and/or specifications, design is not finished.	• Design meets most challenge rules and/or specifications, design is finished on time.	• Design meets all challenge rules and/or specifications, design is finished on time.	
TOTAL SCORE				
COMMENTS				

PRESENTATION RUBRIC
(Page 1 of 2)

Team Name: _____

Presentation Topic: _____

Team Performance Area	Below Standard (0–1)	Approaching Standard (2–3)	Meets or Exceeds Standard (4–5)	Team Score
Sources of information	• Team does not include references to information sources.	• Team includes some references to sources of information.	• Team includes multiples sources for research • Team includes complete references.	
Ideas and organization	• Team does not have a main idea or organizational strategy. • Presentation does not include an introduction and/or conclusion. • Presentation is confusing and uninformative. • Team uses presentation time poorly.	• Team has a main idea or organizational strategy, but it is not clear or coherent. • Presentation includes either an introduction or conclusion, but not both. • Presentation is somewhat coherent, but not well organized, and is somewhat informative. • Presentation may be somewhat too long or too short.	• Team has a clear main idea and organizational strategy. • Presentation includes both an introduction and conclusion. • Presentation is coherent, well organized, and informative. • Team uses presentation time well and presentation is neither too short nor too long.	
Presentation style	• Only one or two team members participate in the presentation. • Presenters are difficult to understand. • Presentation is not creative and not interesting to watch. • Presenters use language inappropriate for audience (uses slang, poor grammar, frequent filler words such as "uh," "um").	• Some, but not all, team members participate in the presentation. • Most presenters are understandable, but volume may be too low or some presenters may mumble. • Presentation has some creativity. • Presenters use some language inappropriate for audience (slang, poor grammar, some use of filler words such as "uh," "um").	• All team members participate in the presentation. • Presenters are easy to understand. • Presentation displays creativity and is interesting to watch. • Presenters use appropriate language for audience (no slang, correct grammar, infrequent use of filler words such as "uh," "um").	

NATIONAL SCIENCE TEACHING ASSOCIATION

PRESENTATION RUBRIC
(Page 2 of 2)

Team Name: _____   **Presentation Topic:** _____

Team Performance Area	Below Standard (0–1)	Approaching Standard (2–3)	Meets or Exceeds Standard (4–5)	Team Score
Visual aids	• Team does not use any visual aids to presentation.	• Team uses some visual aids to presentation, but they may be poorly executed or distract from the presentation.	• Team uses well-produced visual aids or media that clarify and enhance presentation.	
Response to audience questions	• Team fails to respond to questions from audience or responds inappropriately.	• Team responds appropriately to audience questions but responses may be brief, incomplete, or unclear.	• Team responds clearly and in detail to audience questions and seeks clarification of questions.	
TOTAL SCORE				
COMMENTS				

APPENDIX B
CONTENT STANDARDS ADDRESSED
IN THIS MODULE

NEXT GENERATION SCIENCE STANDARDS

Table B1 (p. 262) lists the science and engineering practices, disciplinary core ideas, and cross-cutting concepts this module addresses. The supported performance expectations are as follows:

- MS-PS1–2. Analyze and interpret data on the properties of substances before and after the substances interact to determine if a chemical reaction has occurred.

- MS-PS1–3. Gather and make sense of information to describe that synthetic materials come from natural resources and impact society.

- MS-PS2–2. Plan an investigation to provide evidence that the change in an object's motion depends on the sum of the forces on the object and the mass of the object.

- MS-PS3–2. Develop a model to describe that when the arrangement of objects interacting at a distance changes, different amounts of potential energy are stored in the system.

- MS-PS3–5. Construct, use, and present arguments to support the claim that when the kinetic energy of an object changes, energy is transferred to or from the object.

- MS-ETS1–1. Define the criteria and constraints of a design problem with sufficient precision to ensure a successful conclusion, taking into account relevant scientific principles and potential impacts on people and the natural environment that may limit possible solutions.

- MS-ETS1–2. Evaluate competing design solutions using a systematic process to determine how well they meet the criteria and constraints of the problem.

- MS-ETS1–3. Analyze data from tests to determine similarities and differences among several design solutions to identify the best characteristics of each that can be combined into a new solution to better meet the criteria for success.

Table B.1 Next Generation Science Standards (NGSS)

Science and Engineering Practices
DEVELOPING AND USING MODELS • Develop and use a model to describe phenomena. OBTAINING, EVALUATING, AND COMMUNICATING INFORMATION • Gather, read, and synthesize information from multiple appropriate sources and assess the credibility, accuracy, and possible bias of each publication and methods used, and describe how they are supported or not supported by evidence. ANALYZING AND INTERPRETING DATA • Analyze and interpret data to determine similarities and differences in findings. CONSTRUCTING EXPLANATIONS AND DESIGNING SOLUTIONS • Undertake a design project, engaging in the design cycle, to construct and/or implement a solution that meets specific design criteria and constraints. • Apply scientific ideas or principles to design an object, tool, process or system. PLANNING AND CARRYING OUT INVESTIGATIONS • Plan an investigation individually and collaboratively, and in the design: identify independent and dependent variables and controls, what tools are needed to do the gathering, how measurements will be recorded, and how many data are needed to support a claim. • Conduct an investigation and evaluate the experimental design to produce data to serve as the basis for evidence that can meet the goals of the investigation. ENGAGING IN ARGUMENT FROM EVIDENCE • Construct and present oral and written arguments supported by empirical evidence and scientific reasoning to support or refute an explanation or a model for a phenomenon or a solution to a problem.
Disciplinary Core Ideas
PS1.A: STRUCTURE AND PROPERTIES OF MATTER • Substances are made from different types of atoms, which combine with one another in various ways. Atoms form molecules that range in size from two to thousands of atoms. • Each pure substance has characteristic physical and chemical properties (for any bulk quantity under given conditions) that can be used to identify it. • Gases and liquids are made of molecules or inert atoms that are moving about relative to each other. • The changes of state that occur with variations in temperature or pressure can be described and predicted using these models of matter. PS1.B: CHEMICAL REACTIONS • Substances react chemically in characteristic ways. In a chemical process, the atoms that make up the original substances are regrouped into different molecules, and these new substances have different properties from those of the reactants. PS3.A: DEFINITIONS OF ENERGY • Temperature is not a measure of energy; the relationship between the temperature and the total energy of a system depends on the types, states, and amounts of matter present. • Motion energy is properly called kinetic energy; it is proportional to the mass of the moving object and grows with the square of its speed. • A system of objects may also contain stored (potential) energy, depending on their relative positions.

NATIONAL SCIENCE TEACHING ASSOCIATION

Disciplinary Core Ideas

PS3.B: CONSERVATION OF ENERGY AND ENERGY TRANSFER
- When the motion energy of an object changes, there is inevitably some other change in energy at the same time.
- The amount of energy transfer needed to change the temperature of a matter sample by a given amount depends on the nature of the matter, the size of the sample, and the environment.
- Energy is spontaneously transferred out of hotter regions or objects and into colder ones.

PS3.C: RELATIONSHIP BETWEEN ENERGY AND FORCES
- When two objects interact, each one exerts a force on the other that can cause energy to be transferred to or from the object.

ESS3.A: NATURAL RESOURCES
- Humans depend on Earth's land, ocean, atmosphere, and biosphere for many different resources. Minerals, fresh water, and biosphere resources are limited, and many are not renewable or replaceable over human lifetimes. These resources are distributed unevenly around the planet as a result of past geologic processes.

ESS3.C: HUMAN IMPACTS ON EARTH SYSTEMS
- Typically as human populations and per-capita consumption of natural resources increase, so do the negative impacts on Earth unless the activities and technologies involved are engineered otherwise.

ETS1.A: DEFINING AND DELIMITING ENGINEERING PROBLEMS
- The more precisely a design task's criteria and constraints can be defined, the more likely it is that the designed solution will be successful. Specification of constraints includes consideration of scientific principles and other relevant knowledge that is likely to limit possible solutions.

ETS1.B: DEVELOPING POSSIBLE SOLUTIONS
- A solution needs to be tested, and then modified on the basis of the test results in order to improve it.

ETS1.C: OPTIMIZING THE DESIGN SOLUTION
- Although one design may not perform the best across all tests, identifying the characteristics of the design that performed the best in each test can provide useful information for the redesign process – that is, some of the characteristics may be incorporated into the new design.
- The iterative process of testing the most promising solutions and modifying what is proposed on the basis of the test results leads to greater refinement and ultimately to an optimal solution.

Cross-cutting Concepts

PATTERNS
- Macroscopic patterns are related to the nature of microscopic and atomic-level structure.

SCALE, PROPORTION, AND QUANTITY
- Time, space, and energy phenomena can be observed at various scales using models to study systems that are too large or too small.

SYSTEMS AND SYSTEM MODELS
- Models can be used to represent systems and their interactions—such as inputs, processes and outputs—and energy and matter flows within systems.

ENERGY AND MATTER
- The transfer of energy can be tracked as energy flows through a designed or natural system.
- Energy may take different forms (e.g. energy in fields, thermal energy, energy of motion).

Continued

Table B.1 (*continued*)

Cross-cutting Concepts
CAUSE AND EFFECT • Cause and effect relationships may be used to predict phenomena in natural or designed systems. STABILITY AND CHANGE • Explanations of stability and change in natural or designed systems can be constructed by examining the changes over time and forces at different scales. STRUCTURE AND FUNCTION • Structures can be designed to serve particular functions by taking into account properties of different materials, and how materials can be shaped and used.

Source: NGSS Lead States. (2013). *Next Generation Science Standards: For states, by states.* National Academies Press. *www.nextgenscience.org/next-generation-science-standards.*

Table B.2 Common Core Mathematics and English/Language Arts (ELA) Standards

Common Core State Mathematics Standards	Common Core State English Language Arts (ELA)
MATHEMATICAL PRACTICES • MP1. Make sense of problems and persevere in solving them. • MP2. Reason abstractly and quantitatively. • MP3. Construct viable arguments and critique the reasoning of others. • MP4. Model with mathematics. • MP5. Use appropriate tools strategically. MATHEMATICAL CONTENT • 8.F.B.4. Construct a function to model a linear relationship between two quantities. Determine the rate of change and initial value of the function from a description of a relationship or from two (x, y) values, including reading these from a table or from a graph. Interpret the rate of change and initial value of a linear function in terms of the situation it models, and in terms of its graph or a table of values. • 8.F.B.5. Describe qualitatively the functional relationship between two quantities by analyzing a graph (for example, where the function is increasing or decreasing, linear or nonlinear). Sketch a graph that exhibits the qualitative features of a function that has been described verbally.	READING STANDARDS • RL.8.1. Cite the textual evidence that most strongly supports an analysis of what the text says explicitly as well as inferences drawn from the text. • RL.8.9. Analyze a case in which two or more texts provide conflicting information on the same topic and identify where the texts disagree on matters of fact or interpretation. WRITING STANDARDS • W.8.1. Write arguments to support claims with clear reasons and relevant evidence. • W.8.1.A. Introduce claim(s), acknowledge and distinguish the claim(s) from alternate or opposing claims, and organize the reasons and evidence logically. • W.8.1.B. Support claim(s) with logical reasoning and relevant evidence, using accurate, credible sources and demonstrating an understanding of the topic or text. • W.8.1.C. Use words, phrases, and clauses to create cohesion and clarify the relationships among claim(s), counterclaims, reasons, and evidence. • W.8.1.E. Provide a concluding statement or section that follows from and supports the argument presented.

Common Core State Mathematics Standards	Common Core State English Language Arts (ELA)
	• W.8.2. Write informative/explanatory texts to examine a topic and convey ideas, concepts, and information through the selection, organization, and analysis of relevant content. • W.8.2.A. Introduce a topic clearly, previewing what is to follow; organize ideas, concepts, and information into broader categories; include formatting (for example, headings), graphics (for example, charts, tables), and multimedia when useful to aiding comprehension. • W.8.2.B. Develop the topic with relevant, well-chosen facts, definitions, concrete details, quotations, or other information and examples. • W.8.2.C. Use appropriate and varied transitions to create cohesion and clarify the relationships among ideas and concepts. • W.8.2.D. Use precise language and domain-specific vocabulary to inform about or explain the topic. • W.8.3. Write narratives to develop real or imagined experiences or events using effective technique, relevant descriptive details, and well-structured event sequences. • W.8.3.A. Engage and orient the reader by establishing a context and point of view and introducing a narrator and/or characters; organize an event sequence that unfolds naturally and logically. • W.8.3.D. Use precise words and phrases, relevant descriptive details, and sensory language to capture the action and convey experiences and events. • W.8.7. Conduct short research projects to answer a question (including a self-generated question), drawing on several sources and generating additional related, focused questions that allow for multiple avenues of exploration. • W.8.8. Gather relevant information from multiple print and digital sources, using search terms effectively; assess the credibility and accuracy of each source; and quote or paraphrase the data and conclusions of others while avoiding plagiarism and following a standard format for citation. • W.8.9. Draw evidence from literary or informational texts to support analysis, reflection, and research.

Continued

Table B.2 (*continued*)

Common Core State Mathematics Standards	Common Core State English Language Arts (ELA)
	SPEAKING AND LISTENING STANDARDS • SL.8.1 Engage effectively in a range of collaborative discussions (one-on-one, in groups, and teacher-led) with diverse partners on grade 8 topics, texts, and issues, building on others' ideas and expressing their own clearly. • SL.8.1.A. Come to discussions prepared, having read or researched material under study; explicitly draw on that preparation by referring to evidence on the topic, text, or issue to probe and reflect on ideas under discussion. • SL.8.1.B. Follow rules for collegial discussions and decision-making, track progress toward specific goals and deadlines, and define individual roles as needed. • SL.8.1.C. Pose questions that connect the ideas of several speakers and respond to others' questions and comments with relevant evidence, observations, and ideas. • SL.8.1.D. Acknowledge new information expressed by others, and, when warranted, qualify or justify their own views in light of the evidence presented. • SL.8.2. Analyze the purpose of information presented in diverse media and formats (for example, visually, quantitatively, orally) and evaluate the motives (for example, social, commercial, political) behind its presentation. • SL.8.4. Present claims and findings, emphasizing salient points in a focused, coherent manner with relevant evidence, sound valid reasoning, and well-chosen details; use appropriate eye contact, adequate volume, and clear pronunciation.

Source: National Governors Association Center for Best Practices and Council of Chief State School Officers (NGAC and CCSSO). (2010). *Common core state standards.* NGAC and CCSSO.

Table B.3 21st Century Skills Addressed in STEM Road Map Module (www.p21.org)

21st Century Skills	Learning Skills & Technology Tools	Teaching Strategies	Evidence of Success
Interdisciplinary themes	• Global Awareness • Economic, Business, and Entrepreneurial Literacy • Health Literacy • Environmental Literacy	• Draw connections between academic content and career pathways by facilitating student research about careers in solar power. • Facilitate student research about renewable energy sources used globally. • Facilitate student use of the engineering design process (EDP) to create electric vehicles (EVs) and a plan for a race team that minimizes economic impact. • Facilitate students' development of life cycle analyses (LCAs) for various fuel sources for vehicles, emphasizing economic efficiency and environmental impacts.	• Students demonstrate an understanding that there are a variety of jobs in energy fields. • Students demonstrate an understanding of the EDP and use it successfully to create EVs and plans for a race team with minimal environmental impact. • Students are able to develop and present materials that highlight the benefits of their race team plan.
Learning and innovation skills	• Creativity and Innovation • Critical Thinking and Problem Solving • Communication and Collaboration	• Introduce the EDP as a problem-solving framework. • Facilitate critical thinking and problem-solving skills through the design and building of an EV and the creation of a plan to power a race car in a way that minimizes environmental impact.	• Students demonstrate an understanding of the EDP through teamwork to design EVs and prototypes or models of energy innovations and through the creation of a plan to power a race car in a way that minimizes environmental impact. • Students demonstrate creativity and innovation, critical thinking and problem solving, communication, and collaboration as they design EVs and prototypes or models of energy innovations and create plans for powering a race car.

Continued

The Speed of Green, Grade 8

Table B.3 (*continued*)

21st Century Skills	Learning Skills & Technology Tools	Teaching Strategies	Evidence of Success
Information, media and technology skills	• Information Literacy • Media Literacy • Information Communication and Technology Literacy	• Engage students in guided practice and scaffolding strategies through the use of developmentally appropriate books, videos, and websites to advance their knowledge. • Facilitate students' use technology to conduct research on energy sources. • Provide students with resources to create a presentations of their final projects.	• Student presentations include information from internet research and/or multimedia presentation techniques. • References are acknowledged and cited where appropriate.
Life and career skills	• Flexibility and Adaptability • Initiative and Self-Direction • Social and Cross-Cultural Skills • Productivity and Accountability • Leadership and Responsibility	• Facilitate student collaborative group work to foster life and career skills. • Use the EDP to teach flexibility (through redesign), time management, and goal management. • Provide guidelines and practice opportunities for student presentations, emphasizing professionalism and inclusion of all team members.	• Throughout this module, students collaborate to conduct research, complete design projects, and create a plan for a race team. • Student presentations are appropriate for an audience including peers, industry professionals, and teachers as evidenced by students' use of appropriate language. • Students are able to respond to questions regarding their challenge solution and prototype or model design.

Source: Partnership for 21st Century Learning. (2015). Framework for 21st Century Learning. *www.p21.org/our-work/p21-framework.*

Table B.4 English Language Development Standards Addressed in STEM Road Map Module

English Language Development Standards: Grades 6–8 (WIDA, 2012)
ELD Standard 1: Social and Instructional Language
English language learners communicate for Social and Instructional purposes within the school setting.
ELD Standard 2: The Language of Language Arts
English language learners communicate information, ideas and concepts necessary for academic success in the content area of Language Arts.
ELD Standard 3: The Language of Mathematics
English language learners communicate information, ideas and concepts necessary for academic success in the content area of Mathematics.
ELD Standard 4: The Language of Science
English language learners communicate information, ideas and concepts necessary for academic success in the content area of Science.
ELD Standard 5: The Language of Social Studies
English language learners communicate information, ideas and concepts necessary for academic success in the content area of Social Studies.

Source: WIDA. (2012). 2012 amplification of the English language development standards: Kindergarten–grade 12. *www.wida.us/standards/eld.aspx.*

INDEX

Page numbers in **bold** refer to tables, those in *italics* refer to figures.

NATIONAL SCIENCE TEACHING ASSOCIATION

T

teacher background information: lesson 1 54–7; lesson 2 85–8; lesson 3 123–4; lesson 4 150–3; lesson 5 174–6; lesson 6 198–9; lesson 7 219–21; lesson 8 237–8

Team Energy Plan handout 244

team members expectations 243

tiered assignments and scaffolding 33

Tucker, T. 203

21st Century Learning framework **53**, **84**, **122**, **149**, **172**, **198**, **218**, **236**

V

vocabulary, key **53–4**, **84–5**, **123**, **150**, **172**, **173**, **198**, **218–19**, **237**

W

websites *see* internet resources

We've Bean Using Energy: activity 60–2; handout 67–70

Where's the Wind?: activity 201–2; handout 208

wind energy 198–9; Capturing the Wind (lesson 6) 191–211

writing standards **52–3**, **83**, **121–2**, **148–9**, **171–2**, **197**, **235–6**

Z

Zimmerman, B. J. 16

For Product Safety Concerns and Information please contact our EU
representative GPSR@taylorandfrancis.com Taylor & Francis Verlag GmbH,
Kaufingerstraße 24, 80331 München, Germany

Batch number: 08159318

Printed by Printforce, the Netherlands